The Empowered Paralegal
Cause of Action Handbook

CAROLINA ACADEMIC PRESS

————————

THE EMPOWERED PARALEGAL SERIES
Robert E. Mongue

The Empowered Paralegal: Effective, Efficient and Professional

The Empowered Paralegal: Working with the Elder Client

The Empowered Paralegal Professionalism Anthology

The Empowered Paralegal
Cause of Action Handbook

Robert E. Mongue

ASSOCIATE PROFESSOR
DEPARTMENT OF LEGAL STUDIES
THE UNIVERSITY OF MISSISSIPPI

CAROLINA ACADEMIC PRESS

Durham, North Carolina

Library Resource Center
Renton Technical College
3000 N.E. 4th Street
Renton, WA 98056

Library of Congress Cataloging-in-Publication Data

Library of Congress Cataloging-in-Publication Data

Mongue, Robert E.
  The empowered paralegal cause of action handbook / Robert E. Mongue.
    pages cm
  Includes bibliographical references and index.
  ISBN 978-1-59460-933-6 (alk. paper)
  1. Causes of actions--United States. 2. Legal assistants--United States--
Handbooks, manuals, etc. I. Title.

KF8863.M66 2013
346.7302'1

2013021992

CAROLINA ACADEMIC PRESS
700 Kent Street
Durham, North Carolina 27701
Telephone (919) 489-7486
Fax (919) 493-5668
www.cap-press.com

Printed in the United States of America

Dedicated to

David D. Gregory
Professor of Law
University of Maine

"In the collective memory of his students, Professor Gregory will always be remembered for the Socratic genius that he employed so effectively in class; his keen wit, often accompanied by a knowing smile and twinkle in his eyes; his passion for ferreting out seemingly elusive legal principles; and his compassion and warth for those he instructed." 53 Me. L. Rev. 1 (2001).

It was from Professor Gregory that I gained my first real understanding of the role of causes of action.

Contents

Preface   xiii
Acknowledgments   xv

Part One · Understanding the Role of Causes of Action

Chapter One · Introduction   3
  The Legal Team   3
  Causes of Action, Facts, Evidence, and Proof   6
    Causes of Actions and Their Elements   6
      Facts   7
      Evidence   7
      Proof   8
  Stages of a Civil Proceeding   12
    Stage One: Before Litigation   13
    Stage Two: Pre-Trial   15
    Stage Three: Trial   16
  Our Hypothetical   16
  Conclusion   18

Chapter Two · Using the Elements of a Cause of Action
              before Litigation   19
  Using Cause of Action Analysis to Prepare for and Conduct
    a Client Interview   19
  Using Cause of Action Analysis to Prepare for and Conduct
    Pre-Filing Investigation and Legal Research   32
    Legal Research Planning   34
    Investigation Planning   39
  Conclusion   45

**Chapter Three · Using the Elements of a Cause of Action
in Pre-Trial Litigation**   47
Using Cause of Action Analysis in Drafting the Complaint
    and Other Pleadings   49
    The Complaint   49
    Responsive Pleadings—The Answer   51
    Responsive Pleadings—Rule 12(b)(6) Motion to Dismiss   52
    Responsive Pleadings—Defenses   53
Using Cause of Action Analysis to Prepare for and Conduct
    Discovery   54
Using Cause of Action Analysis to Prepare for and Conduct
    Alternative Dispute Resolution   59
Using Cause of Action Analysis in Motions for Summary Judgment   64
Conclusion   67

**Chapter Four · Using the Elements of a Cause of Action
in Preparing for Trial**   69
Trial Tactics   69
    Searching for Truth in All the Wrong Places   70
    Presentation Counts—The Best Dog & Pony Show Wins   71
        Demonstrative Aids and Exhibits   71
    Be Prepared   72
    Establish a Theme—Tell a Story   73
Litigation Notebooks   74
Trial Notebooks   79
Evidence Trees   80
    Exhibit Lists and Pages   87
    Witness Lists and Pages   91
Conclusion   93

Part Two · Common Causes of Action, Doctrines, Rules and Defenses

Chapter Five · Contracts   97
Contract Elements   98
    1. Offer   98
    2. Acceptance   100
    3. Intent/Mutual Assent   102
    4. Consideration   103
    5. Legality   105
    6. Capacity   106

Contract Causes of Action 108
   1. Breach of Contract 108
   2. Breach of Express Contract Warranties 109
   3. Breach of Implied Warranty of Merchantability 110
   4. Breach of Implied Warranty of Fitness for Particular Use 112
Contractual Remedies 114
   1. Damages 114
      1.1 Compensatory Damages 114
      1.2 Punitive Damages 116
      1.3 Consequential Damages 118
      1.4 Liquidated Damages 120
   2. Specific Performance 123
   3. Rescission 125
   4. Reformation 126
Equitable Causes of Action as Contract Alternatives 128
   1. Promissory Estoppel 128
   2. Equitable Estoppel 130
   3. Unjust Enrichment 132
   4. Quasi-Contractual Remedies: *Quantum meriut* and
      Quantum valebant 133
Defenses 135
   1. Duress 136
   2. Fraud 137
   3. Misrepresentation 137
   4. Undue Influence 138
   5. Unconscionability 139
   6. Mutual Mistake 141
   7. Waiver 143

Chapter Six · Negligence 145
Negligence Causes of Action 145
   1. Negligence 145
   2. Gross Negligence 147
   3. Negligence *per se* 147
   4. Negligent Infliction of Emotional Distress 148
Negligence Doctrines and Rules 149
   1. *Res ipsa loquitur* 149
   2. Public Duty Doctrine 150
   3. Good Samaritan Doctrine 151
   4. Emergency Rule 153

    5. Substantial Factor Rule   154
    6. Foreseeability Test for Proximate Cause   155
  Negligence Defenses   156
    1. Contributory Negligence   156
    2. Comparative Negligence   158
    3. Assumption of Risk   159
    4. Waiver (Written Assumption of Risk)   160
    5. Good Samaritan Immunity   162
    6. Sovereign Immunity   164

Chapter Seven · Strict Liability and Other Special Liability Actions   167
  Strict Liability   168
    1. Animal Owners Liability—Wildlife   168
    2. Animal Owners Liability—Domestic Animals   169
    3. Abnormally Dangerous Activities   170
    4. Strict Product Liability   171
  Other Special Liability Actions   173
    1. Product Liability—Negligence   173
    2. Product Liability—Breach of Warranty   174
    3. Premises Liability   177
    4. Premises Liability—Attractive Nuisance   178
    5. Vicarious Liability   179
    6. Motor Vehicle Vicarious Liability   181
  Doctrines and Rules   182
    1. Vicious Propensity Rule   182
    2. Frolic and Detour Rule   183
    3. Coming and Going Rule   184
    4. Dangerous Instrumentality Doctrine   186
  Defenses   188

Chapter Eight · Intentional Torts   189
  Intentional Tort Causes of Action   190
    1. Assault   190
    2. Battery   192
    3. Intentional Infliction of Emotional Distress   194
    4. Invasion of Privacy   196
      4.1 Invasion of Privacy—Unreasonable Intrusion   196
      4.2 Invasion of Privacy—Appropriation   198
      4.3 Invasion of Privacy—Public Disclosure of Private Facts   200

4.4 Invasion of Privacy—False Light in the Public Eye   203
5. Trespass   204
    5.1 Trespass to Land   204
    5.2 Trespass to Chattel   206
    5.3 Toxic Trespass   208
6. Conversion   209
7. Defamation   211
    7.1 Libel/Slander   211
    7.2 Slander of Title   213
    7.3 Commercial Disparagement   215
8. Nuisance   217
    8.1 Private Nuisance   217
    8.2 Public Nuisance   220
9. False Imprisonment   221
10. Sexual Harassment   223
11. Fraud and Misrepresentation   224
    11.1 Fraud   225
    11.2 Misrepresentation (Negligent Misrepresentation)   227
12. Malicious Prosecution/Abuse of Process   229
Doctrines and Rules   230
    1. Transferred Intent Doctrine   230
    2. Actual Malice Rule   232
    3. Defamation *per se*   235
    4. "Coming to Nuisance" Doctrine   237
Defenses   238
    1. Consent   238
    2. Self-Defense   240
    3. Defense of Others   241
    4. Defense of Property   242
    5. Privilege   243

Index   245

Preface

Even as it is just beginning a new case, a good legal team may envision it-self weeks, months, or years, in the future at the point where the judge in that case is instructing the jury. The team members envision themselves as confi-dent in the outcome of the case as the judge instructs the jury that they must apply the law to the evidence of facts produced at trial. Since the judge is in-structing the jury to apply the law which has provided the team with the frame-work on which the team has built its case from the beginning through each stage of the legal proceeding, the members of the legal team are confident they have produced evidence of each fact necessary to prove each element of the causes of action now being explained to the jury by the judge.

This relatively short scenario has much more substance and requires much more understanding than may first appear. That substance and understanding is the subject of Part One of this book. In Chapter One, some of the key con-cepts are introduced:

1. The legal team,
2. The difference between facts, evidence, and proof,
3. Causes of action and their elements,
4. The connection between the elements of causes of action, facts, evi-dence, and proof of those elements,
5. Stages of a civil proceeding.

In Chapter One we introduce a hypothetical fact pattern which will be used to demonstrate the utilization of those concepts at each stage of a legal proceeding, starting with preparation for a client interview and ending with the trial, to achieve the vision described above.

Each of the following chapters in Part One illustrates that utilization. In Chapter Two we focus on using cause of action analysis to prepare for and con-duct a client interview, investigate a client's case, conduct legal research, en-gage in settlement discussion, and draft the initial pleadings. Chapter Three then examines the role of cause of action analysis in preliminary motion practice, discovery and pre-trial motion practice. Chapter Four demonstrates the use of cause of action analysis to develop a trial strategy and a trial notebook designed to implement that strategy.

Part Two then delves into a variety of the more common civil litigation causes of action, defenses, and legal doctrines. They are arranged by topic, with a primary emphasis on substantive law areas that commonly entail civil litigation: negligence, strict liability and other special negligence issues, intentional torts, and contracts. Within each topic the various causes of action, defenses, and legal doctrine are treated separately. For most topics, a general definition is given followed by a listing of the elements commonly associated with that cause of action, defense, or doctrine. Finally, a synopsis of a case illustrating the application of the cause of action, defense, or doctrine is provided.

A word of caution is due here. The definitions, elements, and explanations contained in this volume are of a general "textbook" type. It is not unusual for a cause of action, defense, or legal doctrine to be interpreted or applied by individual state courts, or to have been modified by a state statute, in a way that may make significant differences in the utilization of those elements as illustrated in this book. The materials provided here will provide a good quick reference, so that the practitioner can gain a working understanding of a cause of action or quickly refresh their recollection of the general tenets of a legal doctrine. Each practitioner, however, should use this work as a starting, not an ending, point for a thorough understanding of the substantive law in that practitioner's jurisdiction.

Acknowledgments

A portfolio project is required in each course I teach. When I teach torts that project is a "Cause of Action Handbook." Each student must research each tort, doctrine, rule, and defense we cover, and compile a handbook consisting of a defining statement, a list of the elements, and a synopsis of a sample case for each of them. One student, Billie Lord York, did such a fine job it inspired me to write a handbook that included both an explanation of the role of causes of action in civil litigation and a more comprehensive version of the handbook. I recruited Billie to assist. She was soon joined by Tommie McGrew and then Laura Shields, two students who had demonstrated superior capabilities. Together they provided research and initial written materials for Part Two of this book and assisted with editing Part One. Tommie was particularly helpful in this regard. This project would not have been completed in its present form without their assistance.

Throughout the project, as has been the case in all my academic and literary endeavors, my wife, Denise, has been an unending source of support, encouragement, and editorial genius.

Part One

Understanding the Role of Causes of Action

Chapter One

Introduction

The focus of this book is an understanding of the nature of causes of action and their role in the legal process, leading to utilization of causes of action throughout the legal process in a way best designed to result in success. In this chapter we introduce some key concepts underlying the legal process itself as a foundation for that understanding.

The Legal Team

Those of you familiar with the philosophy of *The Empowered Paralegal* series are already familiar with its concept of the legal team, which varies in some important respects from the traditional concept. In this section we re-visit the legal team concept in the context of developing a case throughout the legal process.

A diagram of the traditional concept of the legal team looks much like a corporation or government organizational chart with a rigid hierarchy of commands, responsibilities and duties:

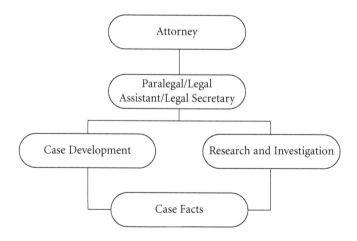

This traditional view of the legal team suffers from several flaws, the most prominent of which is that it fails to recognize any role for the client. Every law office gives some importance to the client in the sense they acknowledge that without the client there is no case and no fee. This type of recognition results in only a minor change to the chart:

However, recognizing this importance of the client to the law office is not the same as recognizing the client as part of the legal team; rather it keeps the client apart from the team and, to a great extent, from the very legal matter which brought the client to the attorney. The most effective legal team is one that includes the client in the process, informing her of the basics of the process and the causes of action on which the case (plaintiff's or defendant's) is based.

While a paralegal cannot give legal advice, it is usually the paralegal that has the most direct contact with the client and has the responsibility of keeping the client informed. *The Empowered Paralegal: Effective, Efficient, and Professional* focuses on communicating with a client in a way that ensures the client is not only given information, but understands and can utilize that information. It also provides methods for overcoming obstacles to a client's gaining the understanding necessary to be a useful member of the legal team. In this book, we will concentrate primarily on gaining an understanding of causes of action that can be conveyed by a paralegal to a client as well as utilized by a paralegal in his capacity as legal professional assisting the attorney.

For now, it is necessary only that we be aware that the client, the paralegal and the attorney are all members of the legal team. This conception of the role of each member in the legal team is better illustrated by the following diagram:

Case Development

Case Facts

Client

Paralegal

Attorney

This diagram begins to account for fundamental interrelationships and responsibilities:

- The interrelationship between the facts and development of those facts into a successful case based on the applicable law, i.e., the cause of action.
- The interrelationship between the client, the paralegal and the attorney.
- The joint responsibility and involvement of all members of the legal team for achieving a successful outcome, albeit each with a different role in that process.

As discussed in *The Empowered Paralegal: Effective, Efficient, and Professional,* these interrelationships and responsibilities are more complex than they have often been characterized. Recognizing these interrelationships assists the paralegal in management of each of the key components of her work: time, file, docket, but especially management of the client. In this book, we will not often make specific reference to the client's role in the legal process as part of the legal team. However, it is important as we discuss the legal process and the use of causes of action in that process that we keep the client's role in mind and attempt to gain an understanding that can be effectively communicated to the client.

Causes of Action, Facts, Evidence, and Proof

In the end the side that wins a lawsuit is the side that "proves" the elements of the cause of action or disproves[1] an element of the other side's cause of action. While proving an element of a cause of action requires providing the factfinder with admissible and understandable evidence for each of the facts meeting that element, facts, evidence and proof are not the same. Many clients do not understand the difference.[2] A well-informed client is the easiest to manage and most able to be an effective member of the legal team. You will often find it necessary to explain the differences between facts, evidence, and proof, and how each of them relates to the case.

Causes of Actions and Their Elements

This requires a rudimentary understanding of the legal underpinnings of the case itself: "causes of action" and "elements." Each case involves one or more "causes of action." For example, a case involving the sale of a defective product may have causes of action for breach of contract, breach of express warranty and breach of implied warranty. A case for defective construction of a home may have causes of action for breach of contract, breach of statutory requirements, negligence and legal doctrines such as unjust enrichment.

Each of these causes of action has its own "elements," that is, things that must be proved. The elements of a cause of action differ from the definition or description of that cause of action. For example, one might define the cause of action of negligence as, "the failure to exercise a reasonable amount of care in a situation that can cause harm to someone or something," but this is not sufficiently helpful in determining exactly what must be proven in order to establish the cause of action. For that we look to the cause of action's elements.

---

1. As a matter of law, the defense does not have to "disprove" an element. Normally, the party advancing a claim must meet the burden of proof, usually "preponderance of the evidence," meaning that the opposing party need only prevent the party advancing the claim from proving the element, rather than disproving the element. If the advancing party does not meet that burden, the opposing party need do nothing.

2. In some instances attorneys do not understand or, at least, do not clearly articulate the difference. I was recently involved in an appeal process in which the opposing attorney has stated, "There is no proof" of certain propositions that the factfinder found in favor of my client. The essence of his argument, however, is that there is insufficient evidence to constitute proof of those propositions. The lack of clarity lessened the effectiveness of his argument.

An action for negligence is generally considered to require establishing four elements:

(a) The defendant owed a duty to the plaintiff,
(b) The defendant breached that duty,
(c) The plaintiff was harmed, and
(d) There is a causal relationship between the defendant's breach and the plaintiff's harm.

The plaintiff will win her case if she establishes each of these elements to the satisfaction of the factfinder. Doing so requires that the legal team understand facts, evidence, and proof.

Facts

Facts of a case are the bits and pieces that comprise what happened—the event which brought the parties to court; the particularities of the automobile accident, the assault, the boundary dispute, the contract dispute and so on. For example, it may be a fact of an automobile accident case that the defendant went through an intersection when the traffic light in his direction was red. However, this "fact" may be contested by the parties. One party will say the light was red and the other party will say it was green. Which version of the event is believed by the factfinder will depend on what evidence is presented and how it is presented.

Evidence

Evidence is something that tends to show, confirm or verify a fact. It can be testimony such as the driver testifying he looked at the light before he entered the intersection. Not all evidence is equally convincing. Testimony from an uninvolved third party such as a school crossing guard that the light was red or green may be more convincing than the testimony of the driver of either car involved in the accident. A picture taken by a camera set up to track drivers' speed may be even more convincing.

From the lawyer's perspective, evidence is more important than actual facts. Cases must be evaluated and presented based on the evidence available for presentation rather than on the facts the attorney believes are true. We are more concerned about what can be proven than what occurred. We can assure our clients that we believe the doctor told them they would never be the same, but must make them understand that what matters is what the doctor says in his reports and on the witness stand. If the doctor's report states, "Patient is fully recovered," the *fact* the doctor said something else to the client at some point is likely to be outweighed by the *evidence* in the form of the doctor's report.[3]

Proof

Proof is simply whatever evidence is sufficient to convince a jury to accept a fact as true. Thus, a driver's testimony that the light was green when she went through the intersection is proof if it is credible enough for the jury to accept it as a true statement of the facts and is not proof if the jury does not accept it. Evidence becomes proof when it convinces a jury. Regardless of the intrinsic value of the evidence, it is not convincing unless the jury hears or sees it, understands it and is persuaded by it.

Thus, the goal of the plaintiff's legal team is to locate and present to the factfinder admissible evidence of each fact necessary to establish each element of the cause of action sufficient to convince the factfinder that the fact is more likely than not to exist,[4] i.e., the preponderance of the evidence. The goal of the defendant's legal team is to locate and present to the factfinder admissible evidence regarding each alleged fact sufficient to establish that one or more causes of action has not been established by the plaintiff.[5] This is illustrated in the following diagram, which I refer to as an "evidence tree." Both of these goals begin with a thorough understanding of the elements of the cause of action. An analysis of the facts as well as the evidence available to confirm each of the facts of the underlying event, when taken together, establish each of those elements.

In this sense, the legal team is not, as trials are popularly characterized, necessarily searching for "the truth." Rather it is searching for the best evidence and the best way to present evidence in order to convince a jury that the evi-

---

3. Scenarios such as this pose tactical problems for the attorney that clients will find difficult to understand. While there is still evidence of what the doctor told the client, i.e., the client's testimony, and that evidence may become proof if it is accepted by the factfinder, there is significant danger in having the client give that testimony on the witness stand. If she gives that testimony, opposing counsel will likely impeach her testimony by using the doctor's report or doctor's testimony, thus undermining her credibility. It may be possible to get the doctor to corroborate the conversation, but then she herself will be subject to impeachment based on her own report.

4. It is tempting to refer to such facts as "true facts" and to say that facts with which we disagree are "false" or "mistaken." Yet this cannot be the case. A fact is a real occurrence. If something is a "fact," then it is by definition true. If something stated to be a "fact" is false or mistaken, then it is not a fact at all.

5. These roles and goals are reversed when a defendant is depending on an affirmative defense which, like causes of action, must be analyzed in terms of its elements.

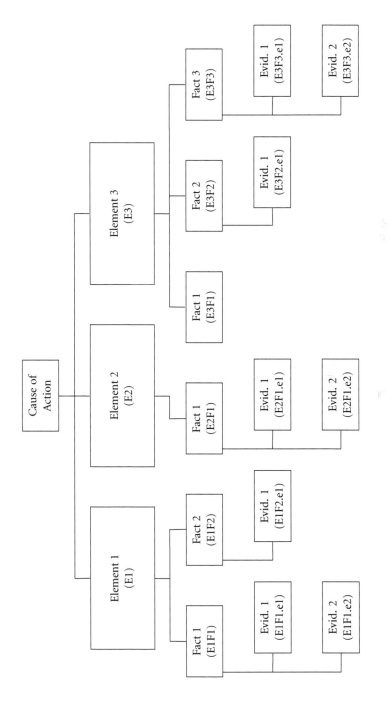

dence is sufficient to constitute proof of facts which establish the elements of the causes(s) of action or defense at issue in the legal action. Since the search for evidence begins when the case starts, this process must start when the case starts: during, or even before, the initial client interview. This will be the focus of Chapter Two—Before Litigation.

For the present we need only establish the basics. From the start of the case, the paralegal and attorney must:

- Know the elements of the case and what is needed both theoretically and practically to prove each one of them. (More on this when we discuss litigation and trial notebooks in Chapter Four—Trial.)
- Make the client part of the legal team by explaining the process to them in terms they can understand, including the relevant causes of action and defenses,
- Develop an investigation and discovery plan designed around the elements of the causes of action.
- Be aware of the problems with evidence.
  - No piece of evidence is "proof positive."
  - Any piece of evidence can be made to look other than it is.
  - Every piece of evidence is influenced by how it came into existence, how it has been handled and how it has been/is being perceived by the parties, witnesses, attorneys, judge and jury (each of whom bring their own pre-conceptions to the courtroom).
  - Often *how* evidence is presented is as important as *what* evidence is presented.

Looking back at the negligence cause of action we might posit a hypothetical motor vehicle accident in which our client contends that the defendant must pay for damages to her car that resulted from a collision that occurred when the defendant failed to stop at a stop sign.[6] In this situation our very basic analysis might look like this:

Element 1: Defendant owed a duty to plaintiff
> Fact: There was a stop sign in defendant's direction at
> the intersection at which the collision occurred.

---

6. This hypothetical forms the basis for extensive exposition of the formation and use of a trial notebook in *The Empowered Paralegal: Effective, Efficient, and Professional.* Only a brief sketch of it is given here. Another hypothetical based on a contract action is more fully fleshed out later in this chapter. The contract hypothetical will be used to illustrate the role of causes of action and the implementation of the litigation process based on that role throughout the litigation process, including the formation and use of a trial notebook.

Evidence: 1. Plaintiff's testimony that the stop sign was there.
2. Testimony of the investigating police officer that the stop sign was there.
3. Photograph of intersection with stop sign.

Element 2: Defendant breached his duty to plaintiff.
Fact: Defendant failed to stop for stop sign.
Evidence: 1. Plaintiff's testimony that defendant did not stop.
2. Testimony of eye-witness.

Element 3: Plaintiff was harmed.
Fact: Plaintiff suffered bruises and cuts.
Evidence: 1. Plaintiff's testimony.
2. EMT's testimony.
3. EMT's treatment record.
4. Photographs.

Element 4: Defendant's breach caused plaintiff's harm.
Fact: Plaintiff's bruises and cuts resulted from collision.
Evidence: 1. Plaintiff's testimony.
2. Testimony of plaintiff's wife that he did not have bruises or cuts ten minutes before when he left his house.

Based on this analysis we can safely conclude that facts exist which can establish the elements of the cause of action of negligence. Anyone who has taken a basic Introduction to Law course will recognize this as the application of the basic steps of legal reasoning: 1. Gather the facts, 2. Find the law, 3. Apply the law to the facts, and 4. Come to a conclusion and report. Here the legal reasoning process is applied as part of a process that also seeks to determine whether there is sufficient evidence to present to a factfinder that will allow that factfinder to conclude that the cause of action of negligence has been proven.

The underlying premise of this book is that the elements of a cause of action or defense must be the focus of the legal team throughout the entire legal process from the initial interview to post-judgment motions and appeals. In the next section, we will take a brief look at the basic stages of a civil proceeding and the role causes of action play in each stage.

Stages of a Civil Proceeding

Much of the joy and excitement of a litigation practice is the assurance that no two cases are exactly alike. They each spring forth from their own set of facts and their development is determined by the differences in clients, legal teams, evidence, opposing counsel, judges, and juries that make for almost infinite variations. However, each case develops and progresses with a certain regularity determined by the nature of the civil litigation proceeding and the structure provided by the rules of procedure governing that process. In this section we will introduce that nature and structure in the context of the effect they have on the role of causes of action in the process.

The path each case takes depends on the vagaries of that case. No case stops at every point along the route. The primary stops on the route might look like this:

Injury
   Client Interview
   Investigation
   Settlement Demand

Complaint
   Summons
   Service of Process
   Certificate of Service/ Return of Service
   Returned to Court with Original Summons

Answer—with or without counterclaims
   Admit or deny allegations
   Counterclaims

Plaintiff's response to Counterclaims
   Sometimes compulsory, sometimes permissive

Pre-Trial Motions
   Motion to Dismiss
   Motion to Strike
   Motion to Make More Definite and Certain
   Motion for Judgment on the Pleadings
   Motion to Compel Discovery
   Motion for Summary Judgment

Discovery
   Interrogatories

Depositions
Request for Production of Documents
Request for Admissions

Trial Preparation
Witnesses (both factual and expert)
Exhibits
Displays
Trial Notebook

Pre-Trial Conference

Jury Selection
Voir Dire
Challenge

Trial
Plaintiff's Case
Motion for a Directed Verdict
Defendant's Case
Closing Arguments
Jury Instructions
Verdict

Post-Trial Motions
Motion for Judgment Notwithstanding the Verdict
Motion for New Trial

Appeal

Few cases stop at all the stops and few actually make it all the way to the end. Many cases leave the route altogether due either to settlement of the claims or because they are eliminated through a Motion to Dismiss, Motion for Summary Judgment, or similar dispositive motion.

For purposes of this book, the civil litigation process is divided into stages. In each of these stages causes of action play an essential role, for it is around the causes of action that the activities associated with that stage must be organized and implemented.

Stage One: Before Litigation

The first stage begins with the event precipitating the cause of action or, more accurately, the event precipitating the process by which we determine whether or not a cause of action exists and whether to proceed to prosecute those causes of action with some viability. It ends when a decision is made to formally commence a lawsuit. Our concern with the causes of action that may arise from this event comes into being as soon as the legal professional is presented with the facts (or at least our client's rendition of the facts), usually at the initial client interview.

To see why this is the case, it may be helpful to start at the end of the case. As stated previously, ultimately a factfinder—often, but not always a jury— will be determining whether or not to render a verdict in favor of our client based upon the evidence presented to that factfinder sufficient to satisfy them that facts exist establishing each element of a cause of action. Each step in the process leading to this endpoint must focus on moving the process closer to a successful outcome at the endpoint.

When we are first presented with the facts they are an unorganized jumble of data. Whether or not they can lead to a successful outcome at the endpoint depends on whether or not they can be organized into a form that can be presented to a jury as a cause of action, i.e., whether there are facts that will establish each of the elements of a cause of action. Only those facts that either confirm or disaffirm the existence of an element of a cause of action are relevant to that process. Other facts are not legally relevant. They can and should be eliminated from consideration. On the other hand, we must make sure we gather all available legally relevant facts.

Of course, our clients do not know when they are relating the facts to us what is legally relevant and what is not, so we must guide them in the interview, asking questions intended to elicit *only* legally relevant facts (despite their intense desire to tell us about Aunt Hattie's recent problems with Uncle Ben) and *all available* legally relevant facts. We, on the other hand, have the capacity to ask those questions that must be asked, provided we recognize the causes of action that might have viability given the initial facts presented by the client.

As discussed more fully in Chapter Two, this process is cyclical rather than lineal. It continues throughout the litigation, but is of special concern in this initial stage as we investigate the client's case. Our investigation cannot be just a random collection of additional data. There is some data that has a high degree of probability of being relevant to an element of a viable cause of action and some data that will have an equally high degree of probability of having no relevance. Our investigation must focus on gathering data tending towards the former.

Once our investigation is complete we can determine whether or not facts exists which, if proven, will establish all the necessary elements of a cause of action or defense. This determination is essential for the commencement of a lawsuit because our initial pleading, a "complaint"[7] under the Federal Rules of Civil Procedure and state rules of procedure modeled on the federal rules, must state a claim for relief [8] or be subject to dismissal.[9] As indicated above, while the role and goal of the defense is reversed from that of the plaintiff, the cause of action analysis is the same as it files its responsive pleadings, usually an "answer" often accompanied by a "counterclaim."[10]

Stage Two: Pre-Trial

The second stage includes all the stops along the route from the initial pleadings through the beginning of trial. While some of these stops are only tangentially related to the underlying causes of action, the primary stops require cause of action analysis and implementation. For example, the determination of whether or not to file a Motion to Dismiss for Failure to State a Claim[11] depends on an analysis of whether the complaint or counterclaim sets forth facts that, if accepted as proven, would establish each of the elements of a cause of action. Similar analysis is needed for other motions as will be discussed in Chapter Three.

Most of what happens during this stage, however, is related to the use of the various discovery tools provided under the rules of procedure.[12] As with our initial investigation, discovery, regardless of the tools used, should focus on obtaining facts or evidence relating to facts, relevant to an element of a cause of action involved in the pending litigation. This is especially true given the propensity of judges to limit the use of discovery tools when issuing Case Management Orders. When each party is limited, e.g., to just 15 interrogatories, the legal team must use those interrogatories judiciously, focusing on facts and evidence that will confirm or negate the existence of an element of the cause of action.

---

7. Federal Rule of Civil Procedure 3, "A civil action is commenced by filing a complaint with the court."

8. Federal Rule of Civil Procedure 8: "A pleading that states a claim for relief must contain:

(2) a short and plain statement of the claim showing that the pleader is entitled to relief; ..."

9. Federal Rule of Civil Procedure 12(b): "Every defense to a claim for relief in any pleading must be asserted in the responsive pleading if one is required. But a party may assert the following defenses by motion:

(6) failure to state a claim upon which relief can be granted; ..."

10. Federal Rule of Civil Procedure 7.

11. Often referred to as a "12(b)(6) motion" after Rule of Civil Procedure 12(b)(6). *See* note 9, *supra.*

12. *See generally,* Federal Rules of Civil Procedure 26-37.

Stage Three: Trial

The entire trial revolves around the causes of action set forth in the pleadings. Again, this may be best illustrated by starting at the end. The jury, if it is the factfinder in the proceeding, will be instructed by the judge that it must determine whether or not a party has proven facts sufficient to establish each element of each cause of action. Thus each party must organize the entire trial around presentation of admissible, understandable, and convincing evidence of sufficient facts to establish each element of the causes of action being litigated. Not only will the presentation of evidence be organized around this principle(through the trial notebook as illustrated in Chapter Four—Trial), but opening statements, closing arguments, motions during trial, and most objections will rest upon the battle to establish or negate one or more elements of a cause of action.

Our Hypothetical

The intent of Part One of this book is not only to discuss causes of action and their role in the litigation process, but to illustrate their use and implementation in each step of the litigation process. This is best done by "walking through" the litigation process as applied to a particular set of facts. Outside of an actual proceeding, this is most often accomplished through use of a hypothetical scenario. The following hypothetical will be used throughout Part One for purposes of illustration. It is based upon a real case, but the facts have been changed, not out of concern for the parties, but simply to make the hypothetical "work" better for our purposes. The major portions of those facts are set forth here. The hypothetical may be supplemented from time to time in Part One in order to better illustrate a particular point.

RING BUYER v. STORE

Ring Buyer lives in a rural area of Mississippi with his wife and daughter. On the Friday after Thanksgiving, Ring Buyer's wife and daughter went shopping at a shopping center in a metropolitan area a significant distance from their home. Daughter, about thirteen years old, noticed Wife admiring a particular ring in a store window. This was not a jewelry store per se, but an "art store" or gallery that included metal-smith art such as rings and other jewelry.

When they returned home, Daughter took Ring Buyer aside and told him about Wife's admiration of the ring and urged him to buy it for Wife as a

Christmas/Anniversary present. Ring Buyer took the hint and called Store the very next day. Ring Buyer explained that he had not seen the ring, but was following up on his young daughter's admiration for the ring, so he was depending on the knowledge of the Store as to whether the ring was appropriate. He then explained the purpose of the ring, i.e., it would be both a Christmas and Anniversary gift which Wife would likely wear on a regular basis, not just for special occasions. The salesperson who answered the phone informed Ring Buyer the ring was not Wife's size, but there would be no difficulty having one custom made in time for Christmas—after all each ring was custom made by the artist anyway. Ring Buyer gave his credit card number and delivery address to the salesperson.

About two weeks later the ring arrived in the mail with the credit card receipt. Ring Buyer confirmed with the Daughter that it was a duplicate of the admired ring—three diamonds set in platinum. Ring Buyer wrapped the present and hid it away until Christmas.

On Christmas morning the ring did prove to be a great surprise for Wife, who was thrilled and immediately put the ring on. Later that day, Ring Buyer and Wife were sitting by the fire enjoying some wine while the children wandered off to play with their gifts. Wife held up her hand to admire her new ring and was horrified. One of the diamonds had fallen out. The rest of Christmas was spent futilely searching for the lost stone.

The next day Wife and Daughter headed back to the store and explained the problem. Store took the ring back and assured them the stone would be replaced. Once again, the ring arrived in the mail with three diamonds set in the platinum base. Wife took it to her insurance agent to insure, but the agent required an appraisal, so Wife took it to a local jeweler for appraisal. Unfortunately the jeweler was unwilling to perform an appraisal because, in his opinion, the settings were faulty and the ring could not be worn without risk of losing the diamonds.

This did not sit well with Ring Buyer, who returned the ring to Store and demanded a refund. Store declined, stating that the ring was custom made and did conform to Ring Buyer's specifications, i.e., it matched the one in the store window. It was a work of art, not jewelry to be worn every day. Ring Buyer responded that he had told the salesperson of the specific purpose for which the ring would be used. Ring Buyer wants our office to sue Store.

Conclusion

In this chapter we have introduced the legal team and some key basic concepts, including facts, evidence, proof, and causes of action including their elements. We have also sketched out the route of a civil lawsuit, highlighting some of the stops along that route in the context of the role causes of action play at those points in the process. The basic path of civil litigation was divided into stages, each of which will be discussed in detail in a separate chapter of Part One of this Handbook. Finally, we set forth a hypothetical scenario that will be used to illustrate the role of causes of action in each stage of the litigation process, with specific examples at each of the major stops along the litigation path. With all this in place, we begin our closer examination in Chapter Two.

Chapter Two

Using the Elements of a Cause of Action before Litigation

There are times in life that are enhanced by pure, unplanned spontaneity and serendipity. Few of these times occur within the practice of law, especially during the litigation process. With few exceptions, the results obtained through litigation are better when the legal professional has engaged in effective planning and preparation. This is true not only of the litigation process as a whole, but of each stage in that process. In this chapter we will discuss the role of causes of action in effective planning, preparation, and implementation in the pre-litigation stage: the client interview, investigation, and legal research that provides the facts and law on which the litigation will be based.

Using Cause of Action Analysis to Prepare for and Conduct a Client Interview

Effective planning and preparation for a trial begins with effective planning and preparation for the initial client interview.[1] Seldom will you meet with a client without some idea regarding either who the client is, what the topic of the meeting is, or both. Rarely does a client succeed in making an appointment on nothing more than the assertion that, "I just want to talk to an attorney." Generally you will have some idea of the topic of the interview—the client is considering a divorce, has been in a car accident, was just fired, wants to buy a

---

1. The benefits of effective planning and preparation for the initial client interview, as well as effective use of the client interview for client management, are discussed at length in *The Empowered Paralegal: Effective, Efficient, and Professional*. Here, the discussion will be limited to planning and preparation in terms of the role of causes of action in the litigation process.

house, is arguing with a neighbor over a boundary, etc. Much can be gained by anticipating what will be required to make the most out of the meeting.

The goal is to make the most out of the initial interview in the minimal amount of time, and to minimize the need for following up with the client to obtain additional information that could have been elicited at the initial interview. There are basic steps that can be taken to this end. Most offices have a general information form for all client meetings to obtain information necessary to open a file, establish billing, and other standard law office procedures. The paralegal and attorney must be prepared to dispel common misconceptions held by lay people about legal processes. For example, many clients will believe that there is no difference between facts, evidence and proof, a distinction discussed in Chapter One. Many people believe they have an "open and shut" case because there is an "eye witness," but they have no understanding of the vagrancies of eye witnesses and the effects of cross examination.

Such general preparation is indeed helpful, but preparation and planning for the initial interview should go well beyond generalities. The general information forms should be supplemented with information intake forms designed to elicit the information needed for specific topics. There should at least be an outline of the information likely to be needed from the client. Better yet would be a checklist developed for the interview or selected from a set of topic-specific standardized checklists kept on hand by the office. The person conducting the interview should quickly review the applicable law. In addition, the interviewer should:

- Consider what visual aids might be helpful. For example, a chart showing the standard path for civil litigation, or a list of documents needed to begin an estate administration;
- Anticipate documents it would be helpful for your client to sign such as healthcare information releases, forms appointing your office as agent for purposes of the IRS, and the like; and,
- Consider whether it will be helpful to have pre-set diagrams or charts available for the client to use in explaining his problem to you. For example, in a personal injury case it is often helpful to have a diagram of the human form available for the client to show the nature and extent of injuries.

All of this can be done based on minimal pre-interview information combined with basic legal reasoning and an understanding of causes of action. Consider the following example based on our hypothetical:

> *It is an unusually cold and snowy day in northern Mississippi. Many clients have called to cancel appointments, but one client called anxious*

to take advantage of an open appointment slot. He is a returning client calling about a new matter. All he has told the receptionist who scheduled the appointment is that he wants his attorney to do something about a store that sold him a ring he bought as a Christmas present for his wife. Your attorney is in court, but you will conduct the initial interview, provide the information to the attorney when she returns and she will call the client with advice on how to proceed.

After you and he settle in to the conference room with hot coffee, he explains his situation. When he is done your notes state:

On the Friday after Thanksgiving Ring Buyer's Wife and Daughter went shopping at a shopping center in a metropolitan area a significant distance from their home. Daughter, about thirteen years old, noticed Wife admiring a particular ring in a store window.

When they returned home, Daughter took Ring Buyer aside and told him about Wife's admiration of the ring and urged him to buy it for Wife as a Christmas/Anniversary present. Ring Buyer took the hint and called Store the very next day and made arrangements to buy the ring and have it shipped to his office.

About two weeks later the ring arrived in the mail. Ring Buyer confirmed with the Daughter that it was a duplicate of the admired ring— three diamonds set in platinum. Ring Buyer wrapped the present and hid it away until Christmas.

On Christmas morning the ring did prove to be a great surprise for Wife, who was thrilled and immediately put the ring on. Later that day, Ring Buyer and Wife were sitting by the fire enjoying some wine while the children wandered off to play with their gifts. Wife held up her hand to admire her new ring and was horrified. One of the diamonds had fallen out. The rest of Christmas was spent futilely searching for the lost stone.

The next day Wife and Daughter headed back to the store and explained the problem. Store took the ring back and assured them the stone would be replaced. Once again, the ring arrived in by mail with three diamonds set in the platinum base. Wife took it to her insurance agent to insure, but the agent required an appraisal, so Wife took it to a local jeweler for appraisal. Unfortunately the jeweler was unwilling to perform an appraisal because, in his opinion, the settings were faulty and the ring could not be worn without risk of losing the diamonds.

This did not sit well with Ring Buyer, who returned the ring to Store and demanded a refund. Store refused. Ring Buyer wants our office to sue Store.

You will no doubt have noticed that your notes are quite similar to the hypothetical set forth in Chapter One. But the information in your notes is not as complete as that in the hypothetical. If the client leaves at this point it will be necessary to contact him again to get additional information necessary to determine what advice the attorney should give him.

This will not be the call the client expects as he anticipates the attorney calling with advice based on the information obtained during the interview. What the attorney will need to give this advice, however, is sufficient information to make a preliminary determination as to whether evidence exists that she can use to establish facts supporting one or more causes of action and the likelihood that the Store's attorney will be able to produce evidence establishing facts showing that either an element of each cause of action *does not* exist or that all the elements of a defense *do* exist.

This information is best elicited from the client if we enter the interview prepared to ask the client questions designed to ascertain facts and evidence supporting those facts regarding elements of causes of action that arise from the client's situation. We can make reasonable assumptions regarding those causes of action based on the basic information provided in the initial phone call: *He wants his attorney to do something about a store that sold him a ring he bought as a Christmas present for his wife.* This is done by applying legal reasoning and basic legal concepts to this information in the context of known causes of action.

The information that this client is concerned with a purchase he made from a store invokes all of our knowledge of contract law. Ultimately, we may need to delve deeply into our state's version of the Uniform Commercial Code (UCC). But for now we can prepare for this interview by developing checklists based on likely causes of action, doctrines, and defenses. Most of the common contract causes of action, doctrines, and defenses can be found in Part Two of this *Handbook.*[2] We must begin, of course, with establishing whether or not a contract was created and, if so, what the terms of that contract were. We are further aware that, at least under the UCC, certain warranties may exist—an implied warranty of fitness for particular use and an implied warranty of merchantability. If a contract was not formed, equitable remedies (each of which has its own elements) such as unjust enrichment, *quantum meriut*, and equitable or promissory estoppel, may come into play.

We can form our interview checklists directly from the elements of each of the pertinent causes of action, doctrines, and defenses. Once the checklists are formed, we consider appropriate visual aids, anticipate the need for docu-

---

2. Page xiv, *infra.*

ments, and select previously prepared forms, instructions, diagrams, and charts, to maximize the potential of the interview.

For purposes of this illustration we will limit ourselves to an interview checklist based on the potential existence of a contract and potential application of the warranties of fitness for particular use and merchantability. Our checklist will not tell us the specific questions to ask. We depend on our critical thinking, analytical thinking, communication, and other skills for that. We also depend on being familiar with the meaning of terms used in the statement of elements for each cause of action. Part Two of this *Handbook* will also be helpful in this respect. However, the checklist will serve to ensure that we *do ask* questions that seek facts establishing each necessary element and evidence confirming or disaffirming those facts.

We can start with the elements of a contract, keeping in mind that some of those elements have elements. Under each element or sub-element we can leave space to indicate what facts we elicit from the interview that help establish that element, space to record possible evidence relevant to affirming or disaffirming those facts, and (anticipating the next section of this chapter a bit) possible sources for additional facts or evidence that might be obtained through investigation:

Contract Supplemental Interview Checklist

<u>Existence of a contract:</u>

Offer
1. The offeror must manifest a present contractual intent
   Facts:
   Evidence:
   Investigation:

2. The offer must be communicated to the offeree; and
   Facts:
   Evidence:
   Investigation:

3. The offer must be certain and definite in its terms.
   Facts:
   Evidence:
   Investigation:

Acceptance
1. Must be unequivocal and unqualified.
   Facts:

Evidence:
Investigation:

2. Must be exact manner and form of offer.
Facts:
Evidence:
Investigation:

Intent

1. Parties actually intend
Facts:
Evidence:
Investigation:

2. To enter into a contract
Facts:
Evidence:
Investigation:

3. For the same bargain
Facts:
Evidence:
Investigation:

4. At the same time.
Facts:
Evidence:
Investigation:

Consideration

1. Legal value
Facts:
Evidence:
Investigation:

2. Benefit conferred or
Facts:
Evidence:
Investigation:

3. Detriment incurred.
   a. Give up a legal right

   b. At the request of the other party
   c. In exchange for something of legal value
   Facts:
   Evidence:
   Investigation:

Legal Purpose
   Facts:
   Evidence:
   Investigation:

Capacity
1. Must be of legal age
    Facts:
    Evidence:
    Investigation:

2. Must have mental competence
    Cognitive test—ability to understand nature and consequences
    of transaction
    Volitional test—whether person had ability to act reasonably
    with respect to transaction
    Facts:
    Evidence:
    Investigation:

3. Other party's awareness of the person's mental condition
    (if competency is denied.)
    Facts:
    Evidence:
    Investigation:

A couple of points are worth making here. First, we are all aware that we do not normally have time to sit down and parse out a checklist of this nature during the course of standard day at the office. For this reason, I recommend developing forms that can be selected from a form bank that is best maintained as a computer file rather than a hard copy file, or simply working from the materials in Part Two of this *Handbook*. In a moment we'll take a look at a possible way to quickly obtain the elements for causes of action not covered in Part Two.

Second, checklists are intended as guidelines to be used in conjunction with critical and analytical thinking and other skills. They should not be used mindlessly. For example, the interviewer would not mechanically ask questions regarding elements about which there appears to be no doubt or likely controversy, such as the legality of a contract for the purchase and sale of a ring.[3]

Finally, the process we are beginning here is a cyclical, not a straight line process. We select causes of action based on the information we have. We use those causes of action to gather additional information. Based on the additional information we may add or eliminate causes of action. This, in turn, will influence the questions we ask and investigation we undertake and, perhaps, result in additional changes in causes of action. For example, in the last paragraph I suggested that we would not go into the interview expecting to ask extensive questions regarding the legality of purpose with regard to a transaction for the purchase and sale of a ring. However, it is not inconceivable that legality could be drawn into question during the interview, necessitating that we "drill down" on that issue, perhaps requiring that we establish the sub-elements of the legality element.

As with checklists, so with causes of action themselves. We do not select and convert them into checklists for interviews based simply on the topic, e.g., this is likely a contract action and contracts (at least under the UCC) include implied warranties, so I *must* include a checklist for questions about all implied warranties. Throughout the legal process causes of action play an essential role in legal reasoning, they do not substitute for legal reasoning.

The legal reasoning process calls upon us to (1) gather facts, (2) determine applicable law, (3) analyze (by breaking down into elements) and apply the law to the facts, and (4) come to a conclusion. While step three may require very specific and deep understanding of one or more of the elements of a cause of action, a general understanding of the elements can assist in step two. If, based on the facts we have at any point we see that an element clearly does not apply, we can eliminate that cause of action from consideration (until, as discussed above, we obtain information which would draw that cause of action

---

3. I have experienced many instances of attorneys who take this approach at depositions and even during examination of witnesses at trial, coming in with lists of questions from which they do not appear able to vary, regardless of the responses they receive. A classic example is this exchange:

Q: Please state and spell your name for the record.
A: Henry William Haven (H-A-V-E-N). I reside at 1100 Mulholland Drive, Los Angeles, California, where I've been for about 10 years.
Q: Please state your current residence.
A: Ah, ... 1100 Mulholland Drive, Los Angeles, California.
Q: And how long have you lived at that address....
(The exchange is real. The details have been changed.)

back in). In our present hypothetical, for example, in their basic form the elements of an implied warranty of merchantability under the UCC include that the seller is a merchant with respect to goods of the kind which is the subject matter of the transaction in dispute. If our initial information from Ring Buyer was, *"He wants his attorney to do something about a neighbor that sold him a ring he bought at a yard sale as a Christmas present for his wife,"* we would likely not include a checklist for that implied warranty. However, we ought to include, at least, a question confirming that the neighbor's yard sale was not such as to constitute the neighbor as a merchant. Again, we do not want any part of the legal process, including this form of legal reasoning, to become mindless. We keep ourselves open to re-interpretation of all data and re-analysis of all conclusions as we continue through the cyclical process.

As suggested above, preparation for an interview does not, indeed most often cannot, include extensive cause of action research. As a practical matter it makes no sense to conduct that kind of research until our interviews and investigation indicate that the research is needed and may be productive. Thus, I suggest using pre-developed checklists or the description of elements in Part Two of this *Handbook*.[4] There will, of course, be times when possible causes of action include causes not covered in Part Two or your interview form databank. In such cases, I suggest that you start at the end, that is, with jury instructions. While breach of the implied warranty of fitness for particular use *is* covered in Part Two, we will use it as an example because it pertains to our hypothetical.

Jury instructions are particularly useful for these purposes for a number of reasons. As discussed in Chapter One, the entire litigation process is geared towards presenting evidence to the factfinder that will assist the factfinder in determining whether or not a cause of action has been established. Using the language from the very instructions the jury will hear setting forth the elements of that cause of action has obvious advantages. In addition, using the jury instructions from *your* jurisdiction, avoids the difficulties inherent in using more general statements of the elements of a cause of action. However, jury

---

4. Keeping in mind the caveat stated in the preface: "A word of caution is due here. The definitions, elements, and explanations contained in this volume are of a general "textbook" type. It is not unusual for a cause of action, defense, or legal doctrine to be interpreted or applied by individual state courts, or to have been modified by a state statute, in a way that may make significant differences in the utilization of those elements as illustrated in this book. The materials provided here will provide a good quick reference, so that the practitioner can gain a working understanding of a cause of action or quickly refresh their recollection of the general tenets a legal doctrine. Each practitioner, however, should use this work as a starting, not an ending, point for a thorough understanding of the substantive law in that practitioner's jurisdiction." *Supra,* at 108–114.

instructions typically lack the explanatory and illustrative benefits of Part Two of this *Handbook*.

Here, for example, is the California jury instruction for Implied Warranty of Fitness for Particular Use:

> 1232. Implied Warranty of Fitness for a Particular Purpose—
> Essential Factual Elements
>
> [Name of plaintiff] claims that [he/she/it] was harmed by the [product] that [he/she/it] bought from [name of defendant] because the [product] was not suitable for [name of plaintiff]'s intended purpose. To establish this claim, [name of plaintiff] must prove all of the following:
>
> 1. That [name of plaintiff] bought the [product] from [name of defendant];
> 2. That, at the time of purchase, [name of defendant] knew or had reason to know that [name of plaintiff] intended to use the product for a particular purpose;
> 3. That, at the time of purchase, [name of defendant] knew or had reason to know that [name of plaintiff] was relying on [his/her/its] skill and judgment to select or furnish a product that was suitable for the particular purpose;
> 4. That [name of plaintiff] justifiably relied on [name of defendant]'s skill and judgment;
> 5. That the [product] was not suitable for the particular purpose;
> 6. That [name of plaintiff] took reasonable steps to notify [name of defendant] within a reasonable time that the [product] was not suitable;
> 7. That [name of plaintiff] was harmed; and
> 8. That the failure of the [product] to be suitable was a substantial factor in causing [name of plaintiff]'s harm.[5]

The instruction is designed to be tailored to the evidence produced at trial, rather than as a general form for eliciting information. Our ultimate goal will be to present evidence in such a way and of such a nature as to make this task easy for both the court and the jury. At this point, however, we should generalize the elements for our checklist. We will again add in space for facts, evidence, and investigation notes.

---

5. "1232. Implied Warranty of Fitness for a Particular Purpose—Essential Factual Elements," *California Civil Jury Instructions (CACI)*, http://www.justia.com/trials-litigation/docs/caci/1200/1232.html (last accessed September 17, 2011).

Breach of Implied Warranty of Fitness for Particular Use.

1. Buyer bought the product from seller.
   Facts:
   Evidence:
   Investigation:

2. At the time of purchase, Seller knew or had reason to know Buyer
   a. intended to use the product for a particular purpose;
   b. was relying on Seller's skill and judgment to select or furnish
      a product that was suitable for the particular purpose;
   Facts:
   Evidence:
   Investigation:

3. Buyer justifiably relied on Seller's skill and judgment;
   Facts:
   Evidence:
   Investigation:

4. The product was not suitable for the particular purpose;
   Facts:
   Evidence:
   Investigation:

5. Buyer took
   a. reasonable steps to notify Seller
   b. within a reasonable time that the product was not suitable;
   Facts:
   Evidence:
   Investigation:

6. Buyer was harmed; and
   Facts:
   Evidence:
   Investigation:

7. The failure of the product to be suitable was a substantial factor
   in causing the harm.
   Facts:
   Evidence:
   Investigation:

When Buyer told us the story of his purchase of the ring, it did not contain information essential to establishing whether or not there was a basis for a claim of breach of implied warranty of fitness for particular use. For example, he omitted:

> *Ring Buyer explained the purpose of the ring, i.e., it would be both a Christmas and Anniversary gift which Wife would likely wear on a regular basis, not just for special occasions*

and

> *This was not a jewelry store per se, but an "art store" or gallery that included metal-smith art such as rings and other jewelry.*

Each of these statements pertains to Element 2: At the time of purchase Seller knew or had reason to know Buyer (a.) intended to use the product for a particular purpose, and (b.) was relying on Seller's skill and judgment to select or furnish a product that was suitable for the particular purpose. One statement tends to support the element, while the latter tends against the element, but it is necessary for our analysis to apply the elements of the cause of action to *all* facts, not just those that support our client's position.

The first statement also pertains to the "intent" element of a contract: Parties actually intend (a.) to enter into a contract (b.) *for the same bargain* (c.) at the same time. It is possible that the evidence, when fully developed, will indicate that our client thought he was bargaining for a ring that could be worn every day and the store thought it was bargaining for a work of art to be displayed and only occasionally worn.

It is not likely the client intentionally omitted this information. Rather, the client omitted it because he did not realize the significance of the information to the relevant causes of action. In fact, he likely has no idea that causes of action exist in the way that the legal professional does. Thus, it is incumbent upon use to enter into the interview prepared to ask the necessary questions, not place the client in the position of being responsible for providing us with that information.

As a matter of client management and making the client a part of the legal team, it can be helpful to provide the client with a brief explanation of what is needed to make out the particular cause of action much the way the court will do for the jury in jury instructions. This can help focus the discussion and prevent unnecessary, time consuming digressions. It can also trigger client recollections that otherwise have been cast aside as insignificant. There is a danger, however, that some clients will begin to "color" their recollection of the "facts" to meet the requirements of the cause of action.

By the end of the interview our checklist might look like this as it relates to Element 2:

2. At the time of purchase, Seller knew or had reason to know Buyer
    a. intended to use the product for a particular purpose;
    b. was relying on Seller's skill and judgment to select or furnish a product that was suitable for the particular purpose;
    Fact: Client told store's sales person the purpose of the ring— it would likely be worn on a regular basis, not just for special occasions.
    Evidence: Testimony of client. He has no notes of the conversation.
    Investigation: Obtain copies of phone records confirming the call. If possible, obtain a statement from the store salesperson confirming statements.
    Discovery: Ask for all notes, memoranda, etc., in store records relating to this conversation.

Many interviewers may prefer to record the information from the interview in the standard narrative fashion rather than try to integrate the information into the checklist while the client is present. There is no "magic method" in this regard. The essence of the checklist is to elicit and organize information, not to command a particular method of recording it during the interview.

However, completing the checklist in this fashion during the interview allows us to quickly review the information to form yet another checklist—a checklist of items needing follow-up by the client, e.g., that he bring in copies of the phone bill confirming that the phone call to the store was made on the date claimed and the length of that call.

A complete checklist also assists us in the next step of the pre-litigation stage: research and investigation. Like the interview process, research and investigation is most effective when we have prepared and planned. This is the topic of the next section.

Using Cause of Action Analysis to Prepare for and Conduct Pre-Filing Investigation and Legal Research

The basic steps in legal analysis appear quite simple:

(1) Gather the facts,
(2) Determine the applicable law,
(3) Apply the law to the facts, and
(4) Conclude and report (normally using the IRAC method).

Of course as with most aspects of law, they are not nearly as simple as they seem.

First, the process is not as linear as this statement of the steps indicates. In the usual case the gathering of facts starts with the client interview. We have already seen in Section 2.1, however, that even that process should involve some initial determination of applicable law. In our example, the client's reason for making an appointment, *"He wants his attorney to do something about a store that sold him a ring he bought as a Christmas present for his wife,"* provides us with a modicum of facts, but enough for us to make certain assumptions regarding the law, i.e., that various aspects of contract law would likely be helpful in interviewing the client. The interview itself in providing us with further facts leading us to move further into the law—to the warranty of fitness for particular use. This cyclical process should continue throughout the larger litigation process.

Indeed, the investigation and legal research portions of the process should be one of continual refinement, each additional set of facts gathered leading to legal research necessary to refine the determination of the law applicable to those facts and the application of that law to the facts, and the legal research leading us to further evaluate the facts we have and gather whatever additional facts might be necessary. In some instances we might determine that some facts we thought were of importance are not really pertinent to the law applicable to the general body of facts available to us. In others we may find that possible causes of action under consideration are really not viable given the available facts.

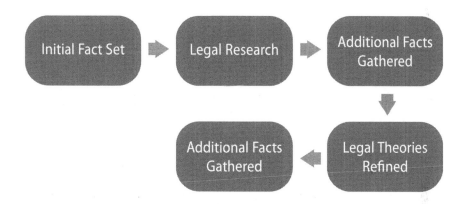

At the beginning stages the gathering of facts will be done through interviewing and investigation. This allows us to refine our legal theories enough to draft initial pleadings—complaints on the plaintiff's side and defenses and/or motions on the defendant's side. Once the litigation process itself has begun, much of the fact gathering will be done through discovery. The role of causes of action in the drafting of pleadings and the discovery stage of litigation will be covered in Chapter Three. The remainder of this chapter will further examine that role in initial legal research and investigation.

The starting point for this examination is the idea that each step of the litigation process should not be conducted randomly, but that we should develop a plan for each step in that process—an investigation plan, a legal research plan, a discovery plan, and a trial plan. Each of those plans should revolve around the causes of action (or the defenses to those causes of action) which forms the basis of that litigation.

Legal Research Planning

Whether you studied legal research as part of a legal research and writing course or learned it through experience, you are likely well aware that legal research is not done well if it is done randomly. In this, as in all things, the legal professional strives to be efficient and effective, not just to get a particular task done. Legal research done according to a plan yields better results in far less time than that done without a plan.

A basic legal research strategy begins with educating oneself on the law pertaining to the legally relevant facts. This, too, can be somewhat circular.

However, this description of basic legal research planning must be imbedded in an overall plan that gives structure to each item needing to be researched. That overall plan gets its structure from the causes of action under consideration. In the last section we saw how the client's initial phone call led to the assumption that knowledge of the cause of action for breach of contract could provide an initial structure for the client interview. We may also have anticipated secondary causes of action such as breach of warranty for particular use, but it may also be that our next step is to take the given set of facts and research whether there are additional causes of action applicable to those facts or that may be applicable if further investigation added certain facts.

Even in the latter case, our research is based on key words and other indicia that emanate towards those causes of action that might be applicable to a given set of facts. In our initial scenario, for example, we may start with the cause of action for breach of contract, but begin researching related causes of action based on our discussion. For example, even if our client does not initially indicate he told the store of the particular use for which the ring was intended, the fact that he made the purchase at a store rather than at a neighborhood yard sale would likely trigger the warranty aspects of contract law. That trigger would lead use to research of breach of warranty causes of action, not to research on causes of action relating to intellectual property.

In general, legal research is done most effectively when the realm in which the research is done is narrowed. We start by narrowing down the applicable law by applying the basic categories into which legal professionals break down law to the facts: civil/criminal, federal/state, substantive/procedural. In our scenario, the initial narrowing directs us towards state civil substantive law. Civil law is further divided into categories such as torts, contracts, and the like, with contracts being the obvious choice for our scenario. Within contracts our topic can be further narrowed to particular causes of action, defenses, or contract alternatives such as quasi-contract, *quantum meriut*, estoppel, and the like. Focusing on causes of action that do or might apply to a given set of facts is the final narrowing.

Let us assume, then, that our narrowing process has led us to three possible causes of action: simple breach of contract, breach of implied warranty of fitness for particular use, and breach of implied warranty of merchantability, research into express warranties not appearing to be warranted given the facts we have. Before proceeding with investigation or litigation we need to pinpoint the requirements for each of those causes of action. In some instances this research may start with certain standard statements of the causes of action in resources such as this handbook, jury instructions, or legal treatises and encyclopedias.

In other cases such as our scenario the research may start with a statute. Since the ring from which the dispute arises is a good, its sale is governed by the Uniform Commercial Code (UCC) which has been adopted (often with some modification) in all fifty states. For example, Article 2 § 2-315. Implied Warranty: Fitness for Particular Purpose, states:

> Where the seller at the time of contracting has reason to know any particular purpose for which the goods are required and that the buyer is relying on the seller's skill or judgment to select or furnish suitable goods, there is unless excluded or modified under the next section an implied warranty that the goods shall be fit for such purpose.

This statement of the warranty provides us with the elements when we analyze it in terms of its basis parts:

- the seller
  - at the time of contracting
  - has reason to know any particular purpose for which the goods are required and
- the buyer is relying on the seller's skill or judgment to select or furnish suitable goods.

Breach of the warranty would obviously require

- the goods were not suitable for the particular purpose
- buyer took reasonable steps to notify the seller within a reasonable time that the goods were not suitable
- buyer was harmed and
- the failure of the goods to be suitable was a substantial factor in causing buyer's harm.

Taken together, this breakdown or analysis of the statute provides us with the elements of the cause of action that we saw in the California Jury Instruction on a cause of action for breach of the warranty of fitness for particular use.[6]

Regardless of where the research starts it should not end with simply obtaining a statement of the elements of the cause of action. It is necessary that the research extend far enough to make sure that we not only know what the elements of the causes of action are, but that we understand them well enough to apply them correctly to the facts we have and use them as guidelines for further investigation of the facts. For example, we say in Section 1 of this Chapter that one sub-element of the offer element of a breach of contract cause of action is "The offer must be certain and definite in its terms." Depending on the facts before us, it may be necessary to gain a greater understanding of what "certain and definite in its terms" means.

In some instances the statutes that give us the elements of a cause of action will also contain definitions of essential terms. Sections 2-103 to 2-106 define many of the words and phrases used in Article 2 of the UCC. Section 2-103 also included an index of other sections that define particular terms and phrases. However, quite often it will be necessary to go outside of the statutes themselves to gain the necessary understanding and it is always avisable to check case law for court interpretation of the elements of a cause of action.

One of the best examples of the last point is a statute and case that takes us to a topic other than one posed by our scenario. Here are the facts of the case as stated by the court:

> On December 7, 1984, Eva Kathleen Philips Ratliff (Eva) executed a last will and testament devising her property to her two children, Kathy Ratliff Watson and William D. Ratliff III, except her personal jewelry, which she left to her granddaughter, Stacy McMurtrey Bufkin (Bufkin).

> Later, Eva made a handwritten note on the envelope of the December 7, 1984 will, which stated:

> > This new will is in my own handwriting. Kathleen P. Ratliff or Mrs. W. D. Ratliff Jr. Enclosed will. This Will is null and void as of feb [sic] 14th, 1992.

---

6. *See* page 28 *supra*.

> Instead, I leave everything that I own in property, cash, CDS, jewelry, car and so forth to my granddaughter Stacy McMurtrey [Bufkin].

Eva died on May 2, 1995. Bufkin offered the holographic will for probate. The only question before the chancery court was whether the writing on the envelope constituted a valid holographic will. The chancery court determined that writing on the envelope did not constitute a valid holographic will.[7]

The issue on appeal was the same—was the writing on the envelope sufficient to meet the elements of a valid holographic will. As noted by the court those elements were contained in a specific statute:

> Holographic wills are creatures of statute recognized in section 95-5-1 of the Mississippi Code. This section provides:

>> Every person eighteen (18) years of age or older, being of sound and disposing mind, shall have power, by last will and testament, or codicil in writing, to devise all the estate … which he or she hath, or at the time of his or her death shall have … provided such last will and testament, or codicil, be signed by the testator or testatrix, or by some other person in his or her presence and by his or her express direction. Moreover, if not wholly written and subscribed by himself or herself, it shall be attested by two (2) or more credible witnesses in the presence of the testator or testatrix.

Breaking this statute down into its elements we can see that the requirements for a valid will can be satisfied by a holographic will (a will wholly in the handwriting of the testatrix) provided:

- The person is
  - 18 years of age or older
  - Of sound and disposing mind, and
- The will be
  - Signed by
    - the person or

---

7. *In the Matter of the Estate of Eva Kathleen Phillips Ratliff,* 95-CA-01120 COA (Miss, 1996).

- some other person
  - in the testator's presences and
  - by his express direction

and
- wholly written by the testator and
- subscribed by the testator.

We can see how this developed. A client came into a law office to see if the writing on the envelope constituted a valid will. (The client is not likely to be familiar with "holographic wills," that term is supplied by the legal professional doing the interview.) The facts seem clear from the interview when the client provides the written documents. At that point it can appear that it is a simple matter of applying the elements of the statute to those facts.

If we have or know the elements we can conduct an intelligent, efficient, and effective interview, soon establishing that the testatrix was over the age of eighteen and that the document was wholly written by the testatrix, including her signature. While it will still be necessary in any formal court proceeding to have some evidence to establish that the testatrix was over the age of 18 and of sound and disposing mind, these elements do not appear to be in contest so there is no need to do extensive research on what "sound and disposing mind" means.[8] However, if there were no controversy there would be no case. Here the issue came down to application of the element requiring that the will be not only wholly written by the testatrix, but "subscribed" by her.

The proponent of the will was able, it appears, to eliminate all of the concerns that arise when a will is wholly in a person's handwriting. There was no issue of fraud, undue influence or the like. Indeed, there seemed to be general agreement that the writing, if effecuated, would accomplish the true intentions of the person doing the writing.[9] The sole issue was application of a par-

---

8. This phrase is, however, quite complex in its meaning and its application. The topic is discussed extensively in Robert E. Mongue, *The Empowered Paralegal: Working with the Elder Client* (Carolina Academic Press, 2010).

9. According to the Court's statement:

> The Appellant's position is that the Court should have found that the writting [sic] on the outside of the envelope constituted the decedent's holographic will regardless of whether or not it meet [sic] each and every statutory criterion. The testimony is replete with eye witness [sic] accounts to the decedent's deliberate intentions to change her previous will and, in effect, void same and to leave all to her granddaughter, the Appellant. Your Appellant would show that the intent of any laws governing wills should be that the wishes of the deceased with regard to the distribution of the assets of the estate be up held [sic] and if it is proven that there was no fraud or undue influence involved then the form of a holo-

ticular element of a particular statute. The legal team for the proponent of the will had done the research, located the applicable statute, analyzed the statute in terms of its elements, and applied those elements to the facts, concluding that the will ought to be declared valid by the courts. From the stand point of our discussion, the problem was, as noted by the appellate court, "argument ignores recent, controlling Mississippi Supreme Court precedent," specifically case law that ruled "Mississippi abides by a bright line rule that requires the testator's signature at the bottom of a holographic will."[10]

The discussion here should not be taken as criticism of the will proponent's legal team's decision to go forward with the case. There can be many reasons for proceeding with a matter when precedent appears to be against your case. There is, however, no justification for proceeding with a matter not knowing that there is precedent contrary to the interpretation of the cause of action on which the legal team is proceeding. Such an occurrence can be avoided if we follow the process suggested here—developing and following a plan of legal research structured by the causes of action that are or may be applicable to the gathered facts in a way that determines which causes of action are indeed applicable to the facts, leads to guidelines for continued investigation, and refines our understanding of the elements enough so that we can apply those elements correctly to those facts.

Investigation Planning

Having refined our elements through legal research, we can continue the investigation of facts. Often, the first step in that investigation is a follow-up interview with the client. Frequently, it will include requesting documents, interviewing witnesses, viewing and photographing the scenes where significant events related to the cause of action occurred, and (less often) sending out a private investigator. Regardless of the methods utilized, investigation of the facts must be done in a planned, organized fashion to be effective and effi-

---

graphic will should survive. *In the Matter of the Estate of Eva Kathleen Phillips Ratliff,* 95-CA-01120 COA (Miss, 1996).

10. The recent court ruling confirmed previously existing law:
The argument has been made that requiring such proof amounts to requiring beneficiaries to "jump through hoops." However, we do not hesitate to rule a holographic will invalid merely because the testator signed his name at the top of the page; similarly, we require that wills not wholly handwritten by the testator be signed by two witnesses. If a holographic will is not signed at the bottom, the will is invalid. See *Baker v. Baker's Estate,* 199 Miss. 388, 24 So.2d 841 (1946).

client. Once again the organizational structure for such planning is embedded in the causes of action being investigated. Even when the next step is a follow-up with the client we want to appear as professional as possible and ask all additional questions at once rather than making repeated phone calls asking just one or two questions.

At this point we have likely refined the elements of the causes of action in a way that fits the set of facts already gathered. In addition, the focus is likely to have shifted from simply gathering facts to thinking in terms of evidence that will support those facts, although evidentiary concerns are never far from our minds even in the initial interview. Our investigation plan thus starts with the elements, seeking both facts that support the elements and evidence that supports those facts as illustrated by the following diagram:

Let's assume, for example, that our client has been injured as a result of a car accident. It would not be productive to send a photographer out to the scene of the accident with only the instruction, "Take lots of pictures." Instead, our investigation plan should be such that we can direct the photographer to take pictures most likely to produce convincing evidence of the particular facts supporting the elements of the causes of action, in this case negligence.

The elements of negligence are duty, breach of that duty, causation, and harm. It is not enough to provide the photographer with a statement of those elements, although it is generally a good idea to provide her with a basic understanding of our ultimate goal, i.e., obtaining evidence of facts that support those elements. At this point in the process we likely have a specific set of facts on which we are at least tentatively basing our action.

Take for instance the duty element. In car accidents the duty is frequently based on statutes or regulations that establish the duties of persons operating motor vehicles on public roads. Based on the facts given to us by our client during the interview, we have established a specific duty on which to base our cause of action: the duty to stop for a stop sign, the duty to drive at or under the posted speed limit, or the duty not to pass in certain zones. Similarly, facts support at least tentatively a claim that the other person breached that duty. The purpose of investigation is to ascertain more facts, but also (and at this point, primarily) to gather evidence supporting existing facts. Thus the photographer's instructions would not be to take as many pictures as possible, but pictures directed at supporting the particular facts on which we will be relying to support each element. Here, those instructions would likely include photographs of the stop sign posted at the other driver's access point to the intersection, together with pictures showing no stop sign posted at our client's access point, or photographs of posted speed limit signs, depending on the particular duty claimed to have been breached.

When we send the photographer out, we hope to do so only once. Thus, we should compile a list of investigation instructions that covers all the evidence we are seeking for each of the facts supporting each of the elements based on our evidence tree (here truncated for reasons of space):

Let's return to our original scenario to see how the investigation plan is developed.

By the end of the interview our checklist might look like this as it relates to Element 2:

1. At the time of purchase, Seller knew or had reason to know Buyer
   a. intended to use the product for a particular purpose;
   b. was relying on Seller's skill and judgment to select or furnish a product that was suitable for the particular purpose;

   Facts: Client told store's sales person the purpose of the ring—it would likely be worn on a regular basis, not just for special occasions.

   Evidence: Testimony of client. He has no notes of the conversation.

   Investigation: 1. Obtain copies of phone records confirming the call.
   2. If possible, obtain a statement from the store salesperson confirming statements.

Other elements on our checklist will have similar listings. For example, the fourth element may look like this:

4. The product was not suitable for the particular purpose;

   Facts: Wife took the ring to a local jeweler for appraisal. Unfortunately the jeweler was unwilling to perform an appraisal because, in his opinion, the settings were faulty and the ring could not be worn on a daily basis.

   Evidence: Wife's testimony
   Appraiser's testimony

   Investigation: 1. Obtain statement from wife
   2. Obtain statement from appraiser
   3. Obtain appraiser's written report
   4. Obtain appraiser's credentials

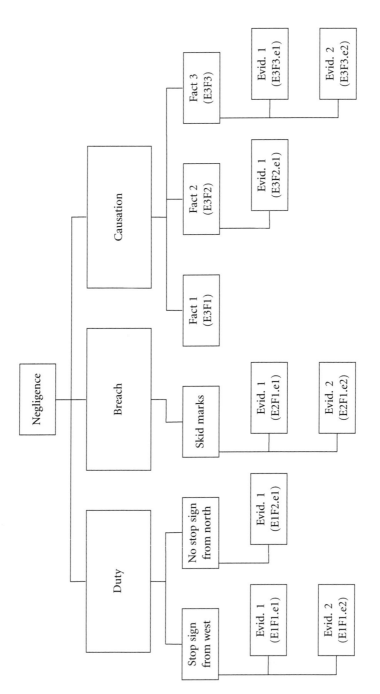

> 5. Check appraiser's participation in prior
> litigation as party or expert witness

By culling the investigation portion of our checklist we can create a independent list of investigation steps:

E2
1. Obtain copies of phone records confirming the call.
2. If possible, obtain a statement from the store salesperson confirming statements.

E4
1. Obtain statement from wife.
2. Obtain statement from appraiser.
3. Obtain appraiser's written report.
4. Obtain appraiser's credentials.
5. Check appraiser's participation in prior litigation as party or expert witness.

This checklist is helpful, but does not constitute a plan.

A plan tells not only what needs to be done, but who is responsible for getting it done and when it will be done. However, the checklist can provide a
basis for such a plan:[11]

From this investigation plan we can then cull several other helpful check
lists, e.g., a list of all tasks to be assigned to an investigator or other responsible person, a list of all items to be obtained from a particular source (e.g., all
areas about which the wife should be questioned), or a list of items that need
to be completed in the first week. Since it is likely that the paralegal will have
overall responsibility for tasks such as contacting the investigator as well as

---

11. A full investigation plan is more complex than illustrated here since this discussion
is limited to the role that causes of action play in developing a plan. One in-depth discussion on formulating a plan of investigation sets out the following steps: (1) Start with what
you already know, (2) Identify the specific goals of your investigation (a) consider the law
of the case and (b) write down the ultimate goals of the investigation, (3) brainstorm for
specifics, (4) identify all possible sources of information, and 5. Organize your plan into a
logical format and chart it. It suggests that step 5 can be accomplished through a chrono-
logical "to-do" list format, a topical format, a sources format, or a cause of action format.
Stephen P. Parsons, *Interviewing and Investigating, 5th Ed.* 263–270 (Wolters Kluwer Law
& Business 2013). The point made here is that the role of causes of action emphasized in
Parsons' step 2b can and should be extended to the entire development of the plan; that
causes of action underpin all of those steps, and that the plan should be done in such a way
as to facilitate moving the information from one format to another as needed.

Task	Responsible Person	Source	When
Obtain copy of phone records confirming the call.	Client Paralegal	1. Client's online access to phone account 2. Request to cellular company	One week Two weeks (start only if 1 is not successful)
Obtain a statement from the store salesperson confirming statements.	Investigator	Store salesperson	Two weeks (check to see if store has known legal counsel and whether there's an ethical problem contacting an agent of the store)
Obtain statement from wife.	Paralegal	Wife	One week
Obtain statement from appraiser.	Investigator	Appraiser	Two weeks (obtain written report first)
Obtain appraiser's written report.	Paralegal	Appraiser	One week

specific responsibility the plan should be integrated with the paralegal's personal "To do" lists and docketing.[12]

Conclusion

Legal research planning and investigation plans are not independent objects generated for their own sake, but are parts of an overall, cyclical refining process designed to allow us to ultimately bring the case to trial with evidence sufficient to convince a factfinder of each of the facts necessary to maintain our cause of action. Thus, the information gained from the investigation may cause us to further refine our statement of the pertinent causes of actions or the applica-

---

12. For extensive treatment of the role of "To Do" lists and personal calendars in being an efficient and effective legal professional *see* Robert E. Mongue, *The Empowered Paralegal: Effective, Efficient, and Professional* (Carolina Academic Press, 2009).

tion of one or more elements to the facts we discover, so our evidence tree should be updated continuously as we obtain additional facts, evidence supporting those facts, or greater understanding of applicable law. We will see how this all comes together in creating a trial notebook in Chapter Four.

Once our initial investigation and legal research plans are complete and fully implemented, we are ready to begin the litigation process by drafting the initial pleadings.[13] Those pleadings as well as other pre-trial aspects of litigation are covered in the next chapter.

---

13. Often attempts at negotiation or settlement are made prior to the initiation of litigation. If those efforts are unsuccessful or if no efforts are made prior to initiation of the litigation, the litigation process itself provides many opportunities for settlement. In most jurisdictions settlement efforts are required as part of the litigation process and in many jurisdictions alternative dispute resolution mechanisms such as mediation are mandatory in certain types of litigation. In this book, the role of causes of action in such settlement efforts is discussed in the context of the pre-trial process in Chapter Three.

Chapter Three

Using the Elements of a Cause of Action in Pre-Trial Litigation

The life of a legal professional involved in litigation revolves around and is governed by rules, primarily rules of civil procedure and rules of evidence with an eye always at least glancing in the direction of rules of appellate procedure. Often the general rules of procedure are modified by local rules of procedure, rules of a particular court, or rules governing particular procedures. The diagram below illustrates the variety of rules in a typical court system.

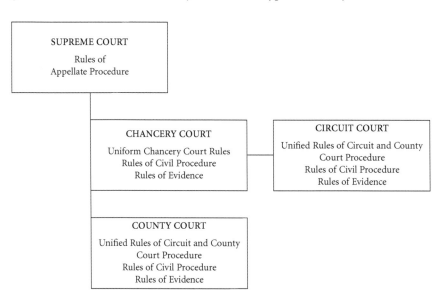

Some legal professionals view these rules as obstacles to be overcome, growing more and more frustrated as rules "prevent" them from doing what they want to do. I prefer to look at such rules as I would a guidebook. This is not to say the rules themselves are just guidelines. They are rules, but they are the type of rules, like those governing sport, that allow the game to be played properly. Baseball with no rules is not baseball. It's just ten people on a field tossing a ball around; the athlete who knows the rules and how best to use them has an advantage over everyone else on the field. The same is true of legal professionals and the rules governing litigation.

Those rules serve as a guidebook to the litigation process from commencement to judgment. They tell us (1) what we can, must, and cannot do along the way to trial; (2) how to do what we do, including formatting and procedure; (3) when we can, must, or cannot do things, and; (4) where to do it.

In this chapter we will examine the role of causes of action in relation to stages of the litigation that are governed by rules—commencement, motions to dismiss for failure to state a cause of action, discovery, and motions for summary judgment—in addition to their role in alternative dispute resolution. As we will see, the rules governing the litigation process are developed around and specifically contemplate causes of action. Thus, like the pre-litigation activities of interviewing, investigation, and legal research (each of which can carry over to the litigation itself) pre-trial litigation requires the legal professional to be engaged in effective planning and preparation performed around the structure established by the causes of action that form the basis for the litigation. This is true not only of the litigation process as a whole, but also of each stage in that process.

Rules of Civil Procedure: A Guidebook for Your Trip to Trial

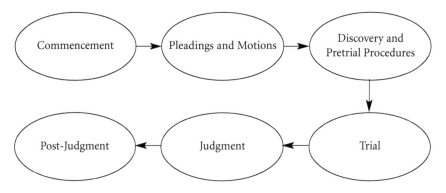

Using Cause of Action Analysis in Drafting the Complaint and Other Pleadings

The Complaint

The Rules of Procedure[1] instruct us that litigation is commenced by a Complaint.[2] Most jurisdictions now allow or require "notice pleading," a short clear, concise statement of the basis for the claim being made against the other party. Some still favor "fact pleadings," more extensive and detailed statements of the claim. Regardless of the type of pleading, the rules do require showing that the pleader is *entitled to relief.*[3] A pleader is only entitled to relief if he can set forth facts that state a viable cause of action.

At this point the pleader is not proving those facts, but must state some facts supporting each element of the causes of action. For example, if the cause of action is for negligence, such as our motor vehicle intersection accident case, but there is no allegation of a breach of duty, then the pleader has not set forth her entitlement to relief even if the complaint details a duty and that defendant's actions caused plaintiff harm. Three out of four is not good enough. While in notice pleading it is often sufficient to make our allegations in fairly conclusory terms, the best pleadings do contain a short, concise, but clear statement of the basis of the claim. This is done by pleading each of the elements of the cause of action.

We can illustrate this using our basic hypothetical scenario. Recall that the elements of a breach of contract cause of action are offer, acceptance, consideration, breach and damages. This means the complaint must aver facts meeting each of the elements of the cause of action, e.g., a complaint for breach of contract must allege: (1) there was an offer by one party (2) that was accepted by another party with (3) consideration passing, (4) a party breached the terms of that contract and (5) the non-breaching party was damaged by the breach.

---

1. References to Rules of Procedure here are to the Federal Rules of Procedure on which most states now base their rules. Since the discussion here is general in nature it is not likely that it would be significantly affected by modification of the rules in your jurisdiction. However, local rules should always be checked before relying on statements made based on the Federal Rules.

2. Rule 7(a), "There shall be a complaint...."

3. *See* Rule 8(a), "General Rules of Pleading-Claims for Relief":
   (a) Claims for Relief. A pleading which sets forth a claim for relief, whether an original claim, counterclaim, cross-claim, or third-party claim, shall contain (1) a short and plain statement of the claim showing that the pleader is entitled to relief ...

While our complaint must comply with other rules regarding captions, formatting, and execution, we will focus here only on the body of the Complaint. Complaints may, according to Rule 8, contain counts setting forth multiple or alternative claims for relief. For our example we will deal only with drafting a count for breach of contract. Other counts such as one for breach of the warranty of fitness for a particular use could be included following the same model.

A complaint drafted to ensure a statement of entitlement to relief based on the cause of action for breach of contract based on our scenario might therefore looks like this:

> NOW COMES RING BUYER, Plaintiff in the above-encaptioned matter, and complains against STORE, Defendant, as follows:
>
> ### COUNT I—BREACH OF CONTRACT
>
> 1. On or about November 28, 2012, Defendant **offered**[4] for sale a ring Stock #1245 in its store located in Portsmouth, New Hampshire;
> 2. On or about December 4, 2012, Plaintiff **accepted** Defendant's offer via a phone call made from his house in Kittery, Maine;
> 3. On said December 4, 2012, Plaintiff paid to Defendant good and valuable **consideration** for the said ring, i.e., Defendant's asking price, via a credit card payment made over the phone from Kittery, Maine;
> 4. Defendant **breached** the contract for sale of the ring by delivering a defective ring which did not meet the terms of the contract;
> 5. The said defect in the ring lowered its value so as to make it worthless, thereby **damaging** Plaintiff in the full amount of the purchase price, $27,000.
> 6. Plaintiff has made demand upon Defendant for said damages, but defendant has refused.
>
> WHEREFORE Plaintiff respectfully demands judgment against Defendant in such sums as are deemed reasonable in the premises and such other relief as this court deems just and equitable.

While it is possible to meet the requirements of Rule 8(a) with more general pleadings,[5] this format has two distinct advantages, both of which are grounded

---

4. In an actual complaint these words would not be in bold type. The emphasis is added here for purposes of illustrating the relationship of the allegations in each paragraph to an element of the cause of action.

5. *See, e.g.,* Form 9, Appendix of Forms, *Federal Rules of Civil Procedure* (Thomson/ West, 2005) which includes only two substantive allegations, one covering all the elements of negligence except harm:

in the rules governing defensive pleadings—answers and Rule 12(b)(6) motions to dismiss.

Responsive Pleadings—The Answer

Rule 8(b)(1)(B) requires that the defendant file a responsive pleading in which she must "admit or deny the allegations asserted against it by an opposing party." By pleading each of the elements, the complaint forces the defendant to admit or deny each element subject to the requirements of Rule 11, i.e., that the "an attorney or unrepresented party certifies that to the best of the person's knowledge, information, and belief, formed after an inquiry reasonable under the circumstances: … (3) the factual contentions have evidentiary support or, if specifically so identified, will likely have evidentiary support after a reasonable opportunity for further investigation or discovery; and (4) the denials of factual contentions are warranted on the evidence or, if specifically so identified, are reasonably based on belief or a lack of information." This helps further refine the issues in dispute.

Let's assume that the defendant agrees a contract existed between the parties, but denies that it breached the contract or that the plaintiff was damaged. The answer would respond to our allegations as shown here:

ANSWER

NOW COMES the defendant in the above-encaptioned matter and answers the plaintiff's complaint as follows:

1. Defendant admits the allegations contained in paragraph one of Count I of plaintiff's complaint.

2. Defendant admits the allegations contained in paragraph two of Count I of plaintiff's complaint.

3. Defendant admits the allegations contained in paragraph three of Count I of plaintiff's complaint.

4. Defendant denies the allegations contained in paragraph one of Count I of plaintiff's complaint.

"2. On June 1, 1936, in a public highway called Boylston Street in Boston, Massachusetts, defendant negligently drove a motor vehicle against plaintiff who was then crossing said highway."

The defendant can deny this allegation without informing the plaintiff whether it is denying the existence of a duty, a breach of duty, or causation. This makes later stages of the litigation more difficult and complex than they need be as the parties work to refine issues in controversy through discovery rather than through pleadings.

5. Defendant denies the allegations contained in paragraph one of Count I of plaintiff's complaint.

6. Defendant admits the allegations contained in paragraph one of Count I of plaintiff's complaint, but denies there was a legal basis for plaintiff's demand.

While we will likely still need to develop evidence regarding the terms of the contract or confirm those terms through discovery, we can focus further research and investigation on those elements that are clearly in controversy— whether the ring was defective and the nature and extent of damage to plaintiff. Here those two issues are closely related and evidence developed for one will also be helpful for the other.

Responsive Pleadings— Rule 12(b)(6) Motion to Dismiss

The defense legal team must also be well versed in cause of action analysis. Any counterclaim or crossclaim filed by a party to litigation requires the same thought. In addition, the rules of procedure allow the defendant to request that the complaint be dismissed for a variety of reasons, including lack of jurisdiction and improper service of process. Our concern here is Rule 12(b)(6) which permits a motion to dismiss asserting "failure to state a claim upon which relief can be granted:" failure to allege that the defendant's conduct satisfies all the elements of a cause of action. Suppose for example that our complaint omitted an allegation that there was consideration for the contract. It would be susceptible to a motion to dismiss that might read like this:

> NOW COMES the defendant and moves that this court dismiss Count I of plaintiff's complaint pursuant to Rule of Procedure 12(b)(6) on the grounds that it fails to state a claim upon which relief can be granted, to wit: there is no allegation of consideration sufficient to establish a contract between the parties.

This motion would be supported by a separate or an incorporated memorandum of law citing the local jurisdiction's requirements for a valid contract (perhaps the state's version of the UCC or case law) and noting the absence of one of those elements.

Responsive Pleadings—Defenses

Rule 8(c) requires certain defenses such as waiver, estoppel, and laches to be raised either by motion or in the answer.[6] Some attorneys for reasons including the press of time preventing full investigation prior to the time limits in which answers must be filed, an over-abundance of caution, or simple laziness have developed a propensity to simply "shotgun" such affirmative defenses, filing something like the following with the answer:

AFFIRMATIVE DEFENSES

1. Plaintiff's complaint is barred by the doctrine of waiver.
2. Plaintiff's complaint is barred by the doctrine of estoppel.
3. Plaintiff's complaint is barred by the doctrine of laches

And so on through all of the affirmative defenses that may possibly pertain to the complaint or even just running through all the defenses mentioned in Rule 8(c). However, this type of pleading runs afoul of the Rule 11 requirements cited above and is now frequently sanctioned by the courts.[7]

Affirmative defenses are defenses rather than causes of action, but the same analysis applies. Each has its own elements. Each of those elements must be supported by facts and it is incumbent upon the legal team to obtain, produce, and have admitted evidence sufficient to establish those facts. For example, in *AC Aukerman Co. v. RL Chaides Const. Co.* the defendant raised affirmative defenses of laches and estoppel. The trial court ruled in favor of AC Aukerman on a motion for summary judgment raising these defenses. The appellate court overturned, basing its analysis on the elements of the defenses noting:

> Two elements underlie the defense of laches: (a) the patentee's delay in bringing suit was unreasonable and inexcusable, and (b) the alleged infringer suffered material prejudice attributable to the delay. The district court should consider these factors and all of the evidence and other circumstances to determine whether equity should intercede to bar pre-filing damages.

---

6. "In responding to a pleading, a party must affirmatively state any avoidance or affirmative defense, including: accord and satisfaction; arbitration and award; assumption of risk; contributory negligence; duress; estoppel; failure of consideration; fraud; illegality; injury by fellow servant; laches; license; payment; release; res judicata; statute of frauds; statute of limitations; and waiver."

7. *See, e.g., Fraser Emp. Fed. Credit Union v. Labbe,* 708 A. 2d 1027 (Me., 1998) where the defendant was sanctioned for raising twenty-three affirmative defenses but was unable to present evidence in support of any of them.

and

> Three elements must be established to bar a patentee's suit by reason of equitable estoppel:
> a. The patentee, through misleading conduct, leads the alleged infringer to reasonably infer that the patentee does not intend to enforce its patent against the alleged infringer. "Conduct" may include specific statements, action, inaction, or silence where there was an obligation to speak.
> b. The alleged infringer relies on that conduct.
> c. Due to its reliance, the alleged infringer will be materially prejudiced if the patentee is allowed to proceed with its claim.[8]

Thus affirmative defenses are subject to the same analysis and process as that discussed for causes of action. From the first contact the defendant's legal team has with the litigation, the team should be thinking in terms of interviewing, legal research, investigation and pleading structured around the causes of action raised in plaintiff's complaint, possible counterclaim causes of action, and affirmative defenses that may legitimately be raised.

Using Cause of Action Analysis to Prepare for and Conduct Discovery

Discovery provides us the opportunity to confirm facts that support disputed elements of our causes of action, determine the basis for the other party's contest of those causes of action, and gather evidence that supports our facts. The Rules of Procedure provide us with a variety of discovery tools, but also constrain our use of those tools. So it is no surprise that an effective discovery plan organized around the elements of causes of action and defenses is essential to successful litigation.

As noted in Chapter 2, discovery planning begins with the initial interview and continues throughout our investigation of our client's claims or defenses. Recall for example our end-of-interview checklist sheet for Element 2 including preliminary thoughts on the use of discovery to complete our evidence tree:

> 2. At the time of purchase, Seller knew or had reason to know Buyer
>   a. intended to use the product for a particular purpose;

---

8. *AC Aukerman Co. v. RL Chaides Const. Co,* 960 F. 2d 1020, 1028 (Federal Circuit 1992).

    b. was relying on Seller's skill and judgment to select or furnish
       a product that was suitable for the particular purpose;
Fact: Client told store's sales person the purpose of the ring—it would
likely be worn on a regular basis, not just for special occasions.
Evidence: Testimony of client. He has no notes of the conversation.
Investigation: Obtain copies of phone records confirming the call.
    If possible, obtain a statement from the store salesperson con-
    firming statements.
    Discovery: Ask for all notes, memoranda, etc., in store records
    relating to this conversation.

Just as we were able to cull an investigation list from our evidence tree, we can form a similar discovery list drawn from our original analysis as refined by our investigation, legal research, and the other party's responsive pleadings. Again, as with the investigation list, more than a simple list is needed.

First, our discovery plan must make the most effective and efficient use of discovery tools possible. Remember, evidence becomes proof when it convinces a jury. Regardless of the intrinsic value of the evidence, it is not convincing unless the jury hears or sees it, understands it and is persuaded by it. So we want to design a discovery plan that is most likely to yield admissible evidence that can be presented to the jury with maximum impact. For example, an x-ray of the titanium rods and pins holding together our client's leg is likely to have more impact than a lengthy medical report of the operation inserting the rods and pins cast in medical terms few outside the medical profession can understand. Similarly, a picture of Store's display window showing dozens of rings on display will be more likely to convince a jury that Store was more than just an art gallery than a deposition statement from Store's owner admitting that Store sold seventy-six rings in the last year.

Our goal is not *just* to gather evidence, but to gather evidence that is most likely to be considered proof of facts supporting disputed elements of our cause of action or defense. In some instances the most effective evidence of a fact may be in the possession of the other party and obtainable only through the use of discovery.

In addition, in most cases a discovery plan must be implemented with an eye to cost benefit analysis. Consider the tools available under the Rules of Procedure:

Rule 30. Depositions by Oral Examination
Rule 31. Depositions by Written Questions
Rule 32. Using Depositions in Court Proceedings
Rule 33. Interrogatories to Parties
Rule 34. Producing Documents, Electronically Stored Information, and Tangible Things, or Entering onto Land, for Inspection and Other Purposes
Rule 35. Physical and Mental Examinations

Each has its own advantages and disadvantages. We can ask the same questions, for example, through written interrogatories to the other party under Rule 33 or through an in-person oral examination. Both ought to produce responses given under oath than can be used to stipulate to facts or impeach testimony at trial. Written interrogatories are far less expensive than the many costs in terms of time, court reporter fees, and transcription fees. However, the other party has thirty days to respond to written questions, giving them plenty of time to consider their words carefully and finding any possible way to answer the question without saying anything meaningful. There is no ability to ask follow-up questions or watch the person's body language while they listen to and answer the question. Thus in many ways a deposition is better than written interrogatories. In developing our discovery plan we must, however, consider whether "the book is worth the candle," i.e., whether the "better" is worth the additional cost.

Second, court case management orders as well as the rules themselves place limits on how and how often we can use each of the discovery tools. Consider, for example, the standard limitations imposed by the case management order in one of my recent cases filed in federal court:

Interrogatories, Requests for Production and Requests for Admissions are limited to 15 succinct questions.
Depositions are limited to the parties and no more than 3 fact witness depositions per party without additional approval of the court.

So once again we have to be selective about which tool we use to gather evidence.

More important, however, is the need to use any given tool effectively. If we can only ask fifteen questions through interrogatories, it is essential that we ask questions designed to yield the information or evidence most important to supporting the facts needed to establish the disputed elements of causes of action or defenses. The plan should consider at least these factors:

What elements are in controversy?

What facts are in controversy?

What evidence exists that must be obtained or confirmed through the other side?

What discovery tools are available?

What are the limitations on those tools?

Factors relating to the type of case and audience (potential jury pool or judge)

What type of evidence is most likely to constitute proof to a factfinder?

The end result is therefore not just a list, but also a plan that results from consideration of these factors. It should state not only what evidence must be obtained through discovery, but the specific tool to be used to obtain that evidence. If a particular fact is important enough it may be appropriate to use more than one tool to obtain different types of evidence supporting that fact. Returning to our example using Element 2, the discovery plan might state:

Element 2:

Fact: Client told store's sales person the purpose of the ring—it would likely be worn on a regular basis, not just for special occasions.

Evidence through discovery:

Request for Production: All notes, memoranda, and other in store records relating to the conversation between Store and Buyer.

Request for Admission: Request that Store admit Buyer made the statement to Store's salesperson.

Deposition of Store Salesperson: Confirm the content of the conversation with Buyer.

Like the investigation plan, the discovery plan can and should lend itself to the creation of a separate list grouping, for example, every Request for Admission or every area that needs to be part of a deposition examination of the store salesperson. The Request for Admission listing can easily be converted into the actual Request and the list of inquiries for the salesperson's deposition imported into a deposition notebook. Since case management orders typically limit the time for completion of discovery, the discovery plan should also be clear as to who is responsible for each aspect of discovery and the deadlines for each item, keeping in mind, for example, that interrogatories and requests for production of documents must be served at least thirty days prior to the discovery completion deadline so that the response deadline is within the discovery period.

Once discovery is completed our evidence tree is essentially complete as shown below, again using the intersection example and again in substantially truncated form:

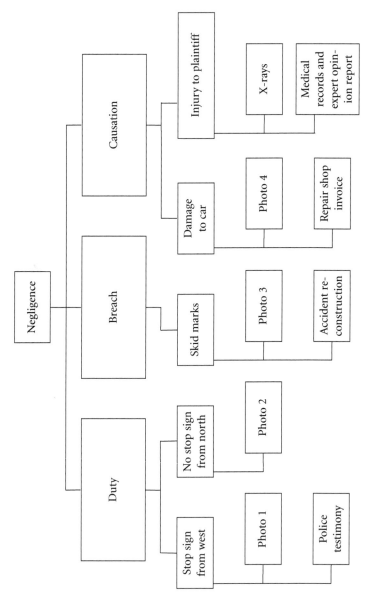

When completed this information is used to prepare for settlement efforts, motions for summary judgment, and trial.

Using Cause of Action Analysis to Prepare for and Conduct Alternative Dispute Resolution

As noted in Chapter Two, efforts at settlement of claims can occur at any point in the pre-litigation or litigation process. There are many different forms that settlement efforts can take — negotiation and mediation being the most common. Each has its advantages and disadvantages and each requires adjustments to the preparation for and conduct of that form based on the form itself, the nature of the case, the disposition and abilities of the client, the styles of the attorneys involved, and so on. Yet there is one key factor common to any successful settlement procedure: cause of action and defense analysis based on the elements of the actions or defenses being maintained by the parties, the facts required to support those elements, and the evidence available to establish those facts to the satisfaction of the factfinder.

Whether plaintiff's counsel is demanding $27,000 for a defective ring or $500,000 for the loss of use of a leg, opposing counsel is unlikely to recommend settlement based solely on her respect for opposing counsel. Nor will such factors weigh for much when plaintiff's counsel is considering a counteroffer from defense counsel. Each will be asking the other questions regarding the type and quality of evidence available to support facts that establish the required elements of a cause of action or a defense. Defendant's counsel is not going to advise his client to pay the $27,000 if he is not convinced there is a substantial risk that the factfinder will find facts leading to a judgment against his client in that amount. Likewise, Plaintiff's counsel will not recommend a reduction in the demand unless she sees a risk that a factfinder may find facts leading to a successful defense.[9]

It is frequently not until discovery is fully complete, therefore, that meaningful settlement efforts can take place. If either counsel wants to engage in meaningful settlement efforts prior to completion of discovery, he must initiate those efforts with a demonstration of the evidence structured around the elements of his causes of action or defenses. This is often done through a settlement brochure.

---

9. There may be other factors considered by both parties. For example, even if defense counsel is fully convinced that plaintiff will be successful, she may make a counteroffer that is slightly less than the demand based on the cost or time savings to plaintiff resulting from a voluntary payment. However, these considerations are normally tangential and less dependent upon the legal analysis.

A settlement brochure in its simplest form may be nothing more than a well-drafted letter, but often they are supported by exhibits demonstrating counsel's ability to produce favorable evidence in an admissible and effective form. Consider the following example from another accident case:

Law Offices of
Saul B. Goodman
123 Maplewood
Sanford, Maine 04043
555-123-4567

March 15, 2013

Appletree Mutual Insurance Company
12 Maine Street
P.O. Box 011
Portland, ME 38655

Re: Don and Betty Draper as Parents and Next Friends of Sally Draper,
a minor
DOI: October 1, 2011
Your Insured: Evel Knieval
Your Claim #:   41B-0223

Dear Sir or Madam:

As you know, I represent Don and Betty Draper as Parents and Next Friends of Sally Draper, a minor, in her personal injury claim arising out of the accident of October 3, 2011. She has completed treatment for her injuries resulting from this accident and the matter is ready for settlement discussion.

LIABILITY

Sally was jogging northbound along East Grand Avenue in Old Orchard Beach with her brother Bobby. Both of the children were surprisingly experienced joggers, given their age, and well versed in safe running techniques. It is almost ironic that they, more careful than many, were the ones affected by your insured.

A bike lane ran along the highway and both children were well inside this lane. Sally was on the outside and Bobby was on the inside, towards the curbing. Sally had on a very light blue sweatshirt that was almost white. A picture of the sweatshirt Sally was wearing is included with this package. The children were jogging against traffic and it was a well-lit area as shown in photographs included with this package.

Your insured, Eval Kneival, was driving southbound when he became distracted while attempting to open a breakfast sandwich, breaching his duty established by 29-A M.R.S.A. Section 2118, and drove into the bike lane and smacked into Sally, the passenger side bumper smashing into her right leg. The impact was very hard and it forced Sally abruptly into Bobby. They both fell to the ground.

Immediately, Sally knew that something was very wrong. As her brother stood by shocked and screaming, Sally squirmed on the side of the road with excruciating pain in her lower right leg and a puncture would on her shin bleeding through her clothes.

Your insured was solely at fault for this collision. Mr. Knieval (1) failed to keep a proper lookout in not observing my client; (2) was inattentive to the driving task; and (3) failed to yield the right of way. As the police report states, he was negligent in all of these ways and more. As a result of your client's negligence, Sally has sustained personal injuries and the balance of her critical sophomore year in high school was thrown into a spin.

MEDICAL TREATMENT

The medical reports included with this package describe the injuries to Sally and the medical treatment required for those injuries. EMS responded immediately to the accident scene. It was obvious that Sally had a deformity to her tibia/fibula on her right leg. Her pain scale was 10 out of 10 and she was given Morphine and Fentanyl. Her leg was put into a splint. She was placed on a gurney and transported Southern Maine Medical Center. Sally had grade one open right tibia and fibula fractures. Copies of her x-rays are included with this package. Immediate surgery was required. Sally faced many risks with this procedure, including infection and damage to her nerves. Sally was brought into the operating room and placed under general endotracheal anesthesia. The operation included irrigation, debridement, and intramedullary rodding using Zimmer 11mm x 34 cm nails. She had an incision to the puncture wound site for drainage. Sally was not discharged from the hospital until October 5, 2011, when she was released under heavy medication, Oxycodone and Ferrous Sulfate. She was also given crutches, as she was non-weight bearing on the right leg.

Of course the surgery and hospital stay was not the end of Sally's ordeal. On October 6, 2011, Southern Maine Visiting Nurses came into Sally's home to start her care. A full assessment was done as to what Sally could and could not do. At this point her "not do" list was long and depressing. Her Dad's home needed modification so she could move around with crutches. Sally received home health assistance through November 2, 2011. Sally had significant edema around the right lower leg area. She also was suffering from off and on nausea.

As you can imagine, Sally was unable to care for herself. She was unable to shower, prepare food, or dress herself. She even had to have assistance to the bathroom, and could not participate in any activities either with her family or outside with her friends. Virtual elimination of independence is one of a teenager's worst nightmares.

Her condition improved over time and she was gradually able to participate in light activities, but nothing strenuous. Dr. Who has decided to leave the hardware in place unless she starts to have symptoms from it and then to address them, which would mean surgery and unknown costs. Sally must be really careful while participating in much-missed athletic activities. Recently she attempted to try out for softball and due to the pain and discomfort she could not continue. She only made it to the first day and realized this was something she just could not do.

Sally has been advised to continue with her home exercise program in order to continue to regain her strength and lessen her persistent symptoms of discomfort. It is not known whether she will need additional treatment, but the probability is there as she still has hardware in place from her initial surgery. She also has significant scarring, as you can see from the pictures, and it is unknown what treatment may be beneficial to help make these scars less noticeable. Sally is very self-conscious and embarrassed by them at this point.

EFFECTS ON LIFESTYLE

This incident has had a negative impact on Sally's life. In many respects she was set back an entire school year. She was significantly depressed, stressed, and upset after the incident. The worst part is that Sally's self-confidence is shattered.

In her freshman year, Sally played basketball, snowboarded, attended school dances, drama club, and other activities and sports. Her sophomore year became nothing more than a list of activities she could not do. Even now she can hardly jog, which is something she used to love to do. As noted above, softball and similar activities are out of the question for the foreseeable future. She also enjoyed the drama club and could not continue with that.

Also at this point, Sally is unsure if she will be able to enter school as a junior next year. She had to drop French class, as the two months she missed placed her so far behind the other students in the class. Sally will also most likely have to repeat other classes, as her grades have not recovered from the two-month gap. Her grades were affected not only by the two-month gap, but also by her inability to get around school due to her disability.

Riding in a car is difficult for Sally and she gets panicky when there are pedestrians around. Driving a car will obviously be difficult as well. Sally also had to cancel her scheduled drivers ed course, yet another way in which the normal course of teenage growth has been disrupted for her.

The scarring would be ugly on an adult woman. For a self-conscious teenager under the constant gaze of her peers, peers who are not always kind in their comments or experienced at hiding their reaction to the ugliness, they are humiliating. Aside from the remaining physical pain, it will be a long time before she can even begin sports that require wearing shorts with any sort of confidence in her stride. Although she loves to swim, the normal enjoyment of being an attractive teenager and young adult in a swimsuit has been eliminated.

While Ms. Draper's condition has improved some, it is clear that she continues to experience pain and thus all of her normal activities continue to be affected. Given her injuries, it is likely she will continue to experience duress in this regard for quite some time. She once was very happy and now feels she just hates her life as it stands. Sally only wants to return to where she was: enjoying life and all of the activities she once did. We can only hope that day will come soon.

This has put a huge burden on Sally's family as well. They have had to juggle schedules to make it to all of her appointments, and meeting with her teachers to help Sally get her school progress back to where it should be. It has been very hard to see Sally go through all of this. It has been especially hard for her brother, who has suffered along with Sally from the moment he stood screaming and watching Sally squirm in pain on the side of the road.

DEMAND

Given the medical treatment and bills of $21,738.68, future medical expenses, terrible scarring, and the residual pain with which she continues to live, I believe Ms. Draper, a minor, is entitled to a fair and reasonable settlement of her claim and make a demand on her behalf in the amount of $521,738.68. I have enclosed copies of the medical records and bills. Please review your file and call me at your earliest opportunity to discuss this matter. I look forward to hearing from you soon.

Very truly yours,

Saul B. Goodman

Because the purpose of the presentation is to convince, the tone has turned from one of analysis to advocacy. The client being hit becomes "impact" as the car "smacked into Sally." This shift in tone is essential when the legal team shifts from pure legal analysis to advocacy.[10] However, the cause of action analysis provides the structure on which the presentation is hung. The facts and evidence gathered through the interview, investigation, and discovery stages and their presentation are organized around the elements of the cause of action.

The elements of the cause of action are not spelled out since we can assume the opposing counsel has done the same legal research as has our legal team. However, each is addressed in the demand letter and supported by evidence in the settlement brochure package. The duty is established by reference to "rules of the road" as specifically set out in an applicable statute.[11] Specific facts describing the breach and the role of that breach in causing harm are set forth.

Because both the pleadings and discovery indicated that the primary issue in contention was the valuation of the harm, much of this demand package fo-

---

10. The importance of the manner of presentation of evidence is discussed more extensively in Chapter 4.

11. 29-A M.R.S.A §2118. Failure to maintain control of a motor vehicle

1. Definitions. As used in this section, unless the context otherwise indicates, the following terms have the following meanings.

A. "Operation of a motor vehicle while distracted" means the operation of a motor vehicle by a person who, while operating the vehicle, is engaged in an activity:

(1) That is not necessary to the operation of the vehicle; and

(2) That actually impairs, or would reasonably be expected to impair, the ability of the person to safely operate the vehicle.

2. Failure to maintain control of a motor vehicle. A person commits the traffic infraction of failure to maintain control of a motor vehicle if the person:

B. Is determined to have been the operator of a motor vehicle that was involved in a reportable accident as defined in section 2251, subsection 1 that resulted in property damage and, at the time the reportable accident occurred, the person was engaged in the operation of a motor vehicle while distracted.

The Maine statute goes beyond those of other states that prohibit driving while texting or using a cell phone, prohibiting any activity that distracts the driver. According to news reports, "State Senator Bill Diamond, Democrat of Windham, said he was moved to introduce the bill after a state trooper reported seeing a woman driving through turnpike toll booths during the Fourth of July weekend while watching the 'Gilmore Girls' on her laptop." "Maine outlaws 'distracted' driving," *Boston.com*, September 13, 2009. http://www.boston.com/news/local/maine/articles/2009/09/13/maine_outlaws_distracted_driving/ (last accessed March 16, 2013).

cuses on the physical damages to the plaintiff.[12] However, the letter makes reference not only to the facts relating to each element, but to the evidence available to demonstrate those facts, especially the evidence included in the package, primarily photographs, x-rays, and medical reports.

Using Cause of Action Analysis in Motions for Summary Judgment

Rule 56 provides a mechanism for resolving cases based on evidence and law without a full trial. Trials are the means used to present evidence to a factfinder when there is a disagreement over what facts are actually proven by the evidence. If there is no substantial disagreement about the facts, a court can apply the law to the facts and determine the outcome. Because the impact of a judgment under the rule is equivalent to that of a judgment after trial but denies a party the right to that trial, the procedures for putting the facts before the court are detailed and complex.

Those procedures may vary depending on the rules of a particular jurisdiction, but the basic formulation of the rule is the same:

> A party may move for summary judgment, identifying each claim or defense—or the part of each claim or defense—on which summary judgment is sought. The court shall grant summary judgment if the movant shows that there is no genuine dispute as to any material fact and the movant is entitled to judgment as a matter of law.

Thus, causes of action and fully developed evidence trees play an essential role in motions for summary judgment.

The motion itself is easy to state and generally somewhat formulaic, mimicking the language of the rule:

> NOW COMES the plaintiff and moves this court to grant summary judgment in its favor and against defendant on Count I of plaintiff's complaint on the grounds that there is no genuine dispute of material fact and plaintiff is entitled to judgment as a matter of law.

However, the motion must be accompanied by a legal memorandum setting out the law and showing how that law is applied to the facts of the case.

---

12. The medical treatment portion of the letter is significantly edited in this example.

The rule requires that with regard to every factual assertion, "A party asserting that a fact cannot be or is genuinely disputed must support the assertion by:

> (A) citing to particular parts of materials in the record, including depositions, documents, electronically stored information, affidavits or declarations, stipulations (including those made for purposes of the motion only), admissions, interrogatory answers, or other materials; or
> (B) showing that the materials cited do not establish the absence or presence of a genuine dispute, or that an adverse party cannot produce admissible evidence to support the fact."

Because the rule allows the opposing party to object if a fact is not supported by admissible evidence, every fact presented must be a form indicating that it would be admissible in evidence if presented in court. Testimony of witnesses can be entered through affidavits made on personal knowledge, but factual assertions can also be supported by directing the court's attention to specific discovery responses such as answers to interrogatories.

The requirement that the moving party demonstrate that there is no genuine issue of material fact is designed to prevent the court from granting summary judgment in instances when a jury or judge should hear both sides of a case and judge matters such as credibility of witnesses. In our basic scenario, for example, summary judgment on the count alleging breach of warranty of fitness for a particular use would not be appropriate if the store salesperson testified at her deposition that buyer never mentioned the particular use to which the ring would be put. This issue is central to an element of the cause of action and cannot be resolved in a summary fashion. A judge or jury must hear both witnesses testify and make a determination which is more credible.[13]

The final product is structured around cause of action analysis and the evidence developed through the evidence tree process. Our legal memorandum would set forth the law we are requesting the court to apply to the facts:

---

13. There need not be total agreement on the facts, but only on material facts, i.e., facts that truly go to whether or not an element of the cause of action is met. For example, if the only disagreement about the conversation between Buyer and the salesperson was whether the conversation lasted nine minutes or twelve minutes, summary judgment may still be appropriate (at least to the elements of notice to Store of the particular use intended by Buyer) since that disagreement is not material to any of the elements of the cause of action.

MEMORANDUM OF LAW IN SUPPORT OF
MOTION FOR SUMMARY JUDGMENT

In Count II of his complaint plaintiff has set forth a claim for relief based on defendant's breach of the implied warranty of fitness for particular use established by 11 M.R.S.A. §2-315. The Supreme Judicial Court has established the elements of that claim, stating "In order to recover upon an implied warranty ... the burden is upon the plaintiff to establish (1) that he made known to the seller the particular purpose for which the goods were required, (2) that he relied upon the seller's skill or judgment, (3) that he used the goods purchased for the particular purpose which he made known to the seller, (4) that the goods were not reasonably fit for the purpose disclosed to the seller, and (5) that he suffered damage by breach of the implied warranty." *Ross v. Diamond Match Company*, 149 Me. 360, 362, 102 A.2d 858, 859 as cited in *Kobeckis v. Budzko*, 225 A. 2d 418 (Me, 1967). As set forth below there is no genuine dispute as material facts establishing each of these elements.

The court's attention would then be directed to the admissible evidence supporting each element. With regard to element one, for example, the court may be directed to (1) Buyer's testimony in a deposition taken by Store's legal counsel describing his statements to Store's salesperson, (2) the telephone records showing the length of his conversation with the salesperson, (3) notes of the conversation produced by Store in response to the Request for Production of Documents, and (4) the specific paragraphs of an affidavit submitted by Buyer's Daughter, attesting that she heard Buyer make those statements while speaking on the phone. Similarly with regard to element four, reference could be made to the testimony of the appraiser given in a deposition regarding the defective nature of the ring setting.

If plaintiff can successfully demonstrate admissible evidence, undisputed in any material respect, for each element of the cause of action, the court will grant his motion for summary judgment. The opposing party's goal is, of course, to prevent this. The path to meeting that goal will also follow cause of action analysis and the associated evidence tree. She may argue that (1) plaintiff has incorrectly stated the elements of the cause of action, perhaps by noting the law has been amended or that there is more recent case law setting forth a different formulation of the elements, (2) that plaintiff has misunderstood or misapplied those elements to the facts, or (3) there is a dispute as to material facts needed to establish one or more of the elements. If she argues the latter, she also will have to support the alleged contravening facts through reference to admissible evidence in the record, for example, specific statements in the deposition of the salesperson denying that Buyer informed her of the particular use to which he intended to put the ring.

Conclusion

Cause of action analysis and evidence trees built on that analysis underlie all stages of pre-trial litigation, from initial pleadings through discovery to efforts to resolve the litigation without trial, including both settlement and motions for summary judgment.

The complaint must contain a short, clear, and concise statement of the plaintiff's claim for relief, best done through allegations addressing each element of the cause of action on which that claim is based. Defendant's response to the complaint must admit or deny each of those allegations, thus defining the issues in controversy. A complaint is subject to a 12(b)(6) motion to dismiss if it fails to state a claim upon which relief can be granted under the law establishing a cause of action.

Effective discovery is structured around the need to gather facts and evidence establishing each of the elements of the cause of action. Only through a well-developed discovery plan based on those elements, can the best use be made of the various discovery tools provided by the rules of procedure given the advantages and disadvantages of each two and the constraints placed on the use of those tools by the rules and by courts in case management orders.

Settlement of claims is virtually impossible unless both parties have performed cause of action analyses, applying the elements of the pending causes of action to the evidence and establishing facts supporting each element. Defense counsel is only likely to recommend settlement if he becomes convinced that there is a risk that plaintiff can present evidence of facts supporting each element in a manner that will persuade a jury. Plaintiff's counsel is likely to recommend acceptance of a counteroffer only if she becomes convinced there is a risk that either (1) on balance a jury may not find that the evidence she can produce with regard to each element is sufficient to meet plaintiff's burden of proof or (2) that defendant can present evidence of facts supporting each element of a defense in a manner that will persuade a jury.

Motions for summary judgment are, by the very nature of the rule that allows them, governed by cause of action analysis. Each such motion must be accompanied by a memorandum of law setting forth the applicable law and a demonstration of admissible evidence, undisputed in any material respect, establishing each element of a cause of action. Opposing counsel seek to prevent summary judgment by showing that plaintiff has incorrectly stated the elements of the cause of action, perhaps by noting the law has been amended or that there is more recent case law setting forth a different formulation of the elements, that plaintiff has misunderstood or misapplied those elements to the facts, or there is a dispute as to material facts needed to establish one or more of the elements.

If neither settlement efforts nor dispositive motions are successful, the case will proceed to trial where cause of action analysis rules the day. This is the topic of Chapter Four.

Chapter Four

Using the Elements of a Cause of Action in Preparing for Trial

From opening statements through closing arguments and jury instructions, trials are the culmination of the cause of action and evidence tree process. In opening statements counsel begin preparing the jury for the task of marshaling evidence around the law of the case by explaining the evidence they will present. In closing arguments counsel, based on the instructions the court will be giving the jury, attempt to persuade the jury that their side has presented the most convincing evidence on each of the elements of each cause of action. In between is the "main event," the presentation of the evidence.

The key to all of this is a trial notebook organized around the causes of action being litigated. In this chapter we will examine closely the development of a trial notebook designed around causes of action, but we will begin by setting some context, i.e., some of the considerations applicable to the presentation of that evidence.

Trial Tactics

The trial attorney must make tactical use of all the weapons available. This can only be done if the case is thoroughly prepared; the facts, law and rules all known, and the evidence all available. There are several excellent books devoted to effective trial tactics, a topic which cannot be covered comprehensively here. However, there are several general tactical considerations which will be helpful to you in understanding what your attorney is doing and how you can most effectively assist the attorney.

Searching for Truth in All the Wrong Places

As discussed in Chapter One, trials are often described as forums in which everyone searches for truth, with truth ultimately being attained in the form of a jury verdict. However, the jury's verdict is based on the evidence presented to it and that evidence may vary dramatically from what actually happened. Not all evidence is admissible at a trial under the Rules of Evidence. Not all evidence has the same relevance. Not all evidence has the same effectiveness. Not all evidence is presented in a way that the jury can understand. And as we have noted previously, facts, evidence and proof are not the same.

Each case involves one or more "causes of action." Each of these causes of action has its own "elements," that is, things that must be proved. An action for breach of contract requires showing that a valid contract was formed, i.e., (a) there was an offer, (b) an acceptance and (c) consideration passed (d) between two or more parties with legal capacity, (e) and the transaction itself was legal. Generally, only evidence that tends to prove or disprove one of those elements is admissible in court. You may recall these explanations from Chapter One where we discussed them in the context of informing your client as part of the legal team, but they bear another look in this context.

Since the search for evidence begins when the case starts, trial tactics considerations start during or even before the initial client interview. From the start, legal professionals need to *know the elements of causes of action in their case* and what is needed both theoretically and practically to prove each one of them. Based on those elements the legal team develops investigation and discovery plans designed around the elements. As the team approaches trial preparation it must be especially aware of the problems with evidence.

- No piece of evidence is "proof positive."
- Any piece of evidence can be made to look other than it is.
- Every piece of evidence is influenced by how it came into existence, how it has been handled and how it has been/is being perceived by the parties, witnesses, attorneys, judge and jury (each of whom bring their own pre-conceptions to the courtroom).
- Often *how* evidence is presented is as important as what evidence is presented.

Presentation Counts—
The Best Dog & Pony Show Wins

Evidence becomes proof when it convinces a jury. Regardless of the intrinsic value of the evidence, it is not convincing unless the jury hears or sees it, understands it, and is persuaded by it. When planning what evidence to present and how to present it, step out of your role as a legal professional and try to assume the role of a juror. This is tricky. It's not enough to say "How would this appear to *me* if *I* were a juror on this case." The jurors are neither likely to have any legal education nor have any knowledge of the case, as you have.

Weeks before the jury pool is even formed the legal team is already planning the evidence presentation and trying to view the evidence from the standpoint of the likely jurors. The same evidence may be viewed differently by a Manhattan jury than by a jury in rural Arkansas. Try to understand the mindset of the likely jurors and present the evidence in a way that is likely to be heard by, remembered by, and persuade *those* jurors.

Demonstrative Aids and Exhibits

Remember some people learn best through audio, but most people these days are visually oriented. Therefore, demonstrative aids are more important than ever. An x-ray is much more effective than a doctor's description of a broken bone. An x-ray combined with the doctor's description is better yet. Photographs of an intersection are better than testimony about the intersection. Damages itemized on a flip chart or slides are more likely to be remembered than your client's testimony about those damages.

Younger juries may react better to animated demonstrative aids. My students delight in telling me how only old people are impressed by PowerPoint presentations. Young people want video clips and sound. This is probably true, but older jurors may be more appreciative of aids that go at a slower pace.

In general, keep in mind that more and bigger are not necessarily better. Use demonstrative aids to emphasize important points—those you want to impress upon the jurors' minds. If used to illustrate every point, they do not assist the jurors in remembering what is and is not important. Too many aids become a jumble of sense impressions, more confusing than clarifying.

Finally, keep in mind the fine line between a *professional* presentation and one that appears *slick*. Jurors respect presentations and presenters that respect them. While much of what is done at a trial is designed to manipulate the jury's minds and hearts, it must be done without the jurors feeling manipulated.

Be Prepared

In many respects trial preparation is the most important aspect of a successful trial. No matter how good a case is, it is likely to lose if the legal team is not prepared to present it <u>and</u> counter the other side's presentation. Often it is the best prepared case that wins, not the best case.

Trial preparation goes beyond preparing exhibits, witness subpoenas and practicing opening statements. The exhibits are not helpful if you can't find them at trial when they are needed. Witnesses can actually be harmful if the attorney does not understand what they add to the presentation and how to extract that value from them in a way the jury will understand and remember.

All of the information necessary to present the case in a winning way must be organized in a way that allows for easy and immediate retrieval. It must be cross-referenced, indexed and available. This will be discussed more in the section on trial notebooks.

Yet even this is not enough. The legal team should be prepared in a way that leaves as little as possible to chance. The team should know not only the case, but also the judge, the jury, the courtroom, the witnesses and the parties.

> *The Judge.* Is the judge conservative or liberal on issues affecting the admissibility of evidence? What are the judge's expectations regarding pre-trial briefs, draft jury instructions, making a record, managing time, managing witnesses and the other details of trial management? If the legal team has not appeared before the judge before, take the time to watch the judge in action a week or so before your trial. If this can't be done, use your network to find out as much as possible about the judge *before* the attorney enters the courtroom.

> *The Jury.* Different jurisdictions have different rules and procedures regarding the information provided about jurors. The legal team must know those rules and procedures and use them. In addition, the team will have many opportunities to observe the jurors both before and after the selection of your jury. Since each member of the legal team has other responsibilities, this one should be shared. Often the paralegal can be the attorney's eyes and ears, watching the body language of the potential jurors while she is conducting *voir dire* of a particular juror. How are they reacting to the questions? How do they look at your client? How do they react to the other attorney? How interested do they appear? The more that is known about the jury, the more the presentation can be keyed to that jury.

The Witnesses and the Parties. Frequently trial preparations focus on what the witnesses or parties are going to say. The well-prepared legal team will also consider everything they can about the witnesses themselves. Include a short biography of the witness or party and notes about impressions obtained during interviews or depositions in the witness section of the trial notebook. Again, much additional information can be obtained during the trial through observation. This is another opportunity for the paralegal to be the attorney's second set of eyes and ears.

The Courtroom. Check out the courtroom in advance. Where can the flip chart stand be placed to maximize visibility by witnesses, the judge and the jury at the same time? Where can the projector be plugged in? How much room and light are available? Will additional tables be needed? How can you leave the counsel table to contact the next witness with the least distraction? Where will the witnesses sit while waiting their turn to testify?

The goal is a professional presentation. The power of the Power-Point presentation on damages during closing argument is greatly diminished if there is no way to position the equipment so that it can be plugged in, even if the court allows time so an extension cord can be found.

Establish a Theme—Tell a Story

The attorney will not simply be presenting the evidence. He'll be telling the jury his client's story. In most cases, his client will be the hero of the story and the other party will be the villain. This can be confusing to a jury because at the same time, the other attorney is telling her client's story and in that story *her* client is the hero and *yours* is the villain. Thus, many trial tactics are designed to narrow and simplify the story. The presentation of evidence should fit that design.

Just as any good storyteller, the attorney will want to establish a theme for the trial. In his story, your client is a hard-working man who is so traumatized by his wife's filing for divorce that he's unable to work; the other client is a gold-digger who has never been interested in anything but the client's money. In the other attorney's story, her client has given up her own career to build her husband's career, only to be cut-off from the benefits of his career when the marriage fell apart. Judgments such as what evidence to use and when to use it or which witnesses to call and what to ask them will be made based on how the evidence or witness' testimony adds or detracts from the theme.

The story and theme must fit your client and your client must be made aware of this theme, how they fit into it and how they fit into the story telling process. The objective cannot be to mold the client or the facts to the story, so the story must be one that "fits" the client and the facts, and will be effective with the jury. The snarling grizzly bear of a client cannot be turned into a teddy bear for trial. The jury will have ample opportunity to see through the smiling veneer to the snarling client. However, once the theme is set, your client will be most helpful if she understands what is being projected to the jury.

The attorney's story will likely come with a "hook." The hook often takes the form of phrases (often alliterative) repeated many times during the trial. "If the glove does not fit, you must acquit" was used as a hook during the O.J. Simpson murder trial. Or the hook may be certain lines of questioning that appear during examination of every witness as well as in the opening statement and closing argument. Perhaps the car accident victim is attempting to blame everything bad about his life on the accident. He refuses to accept personal responsibility for *anything*. The attorney may focus on the jury's own sense of personal responsibility, pointing out that the "victim" blames the police for not fully investigating the accident, the ER personnel for an incomplete record, his doctor for not recognizing the extent of his problem, and the physical therapist for not writing down his complaints.

Often the jury will not remember the intricate details of a doctor's report, but they will remember "the hook." In an effort to keep the story simple but powerful, the attorney may ignore what appears to be important but complicated and confusing evidence in favor of evidence with less importance but more impact.

Litigation Notebooks[1]

The best evidence, the best testimony and the best legal research are of little use at trial unless they are available at trial in way that they can be easily produced and effectively used. The trial notebook makes this possible. A well-organized, indexed and cross-referenced trial notebook can actually make the difference between winning and losing a case. The process starts when the

---

1. This discussion of the development and organization of the trial notebook utilizes our basic contract scenario. For an illustration using a negligence scenario see Robert E. Mongue, *The Empowered Paralegal: Effective, Efficient, and Professional* (Carolina Academic Press, 2009).

file is first opened. From the beginning, the litigation itself should be organized around the elements of the causes of action.

As stated in the previous section, each case involves one or more "causes of action." Each of these causes of action has its own "elements," that is, things that must be proved. As the client initially recounts the events which brought her into your attorney's office, you and the attorney will begin to sort her account into possible causes of action—contract, negligence, breach of warranty and so on. You or the attorney will ask for additional information based on these possible causes of action.

The total body of information will be used to determine whether the facts stated by your client will satisfy the elements of each cause of action. The complaint and the entire litigation process will then be designed around those elements. You will seek evidence through further interviews, investigation and discovery that tends to prove or disprove the necessary elements.

Thus, as we discussed a bit earlier from the start of each case, the legal team must

- *Know the elements of the case* and what is needed both theoretically and practically to prove each one of them.
- Make your client part of the legal team by explaining the process to them in terms they can understand.
- Develop an investigation and discovery plan designed around the elements of your case.

The result of all this work is best maintained in a litigation notebook. In fact, there may be a set of notebooks organized for motion practice, discovery, evidence, and ultimately the trial. Each of these notebooks should be organized in terms of the facts available as evidence to prove the elements of the case and should follow these simple steps:

Step 1: State the cause(s) of action.

Any attempt to analyze and utilize evidence—or the litigation process itself—must start with a clear understanding of the causes of action (civil litigation) or charge (criminal litigation). Therefore, the notebook should start with a statement of the cause of action or charge as it relates to the facts of your case. In our scenario, one cause of action might be stated as, "Defendant breached the implied warranty of fitness for particular use, to wit: after having been informed by plaintiff of the particular use intended by plaintiff, defendant sold plaintiff a ring defective in design and manufacture, making it unfit for everyday use." Each cause of action is a "trunk" for an "evidence tree," an organizational tool discussed in the next section.

Step 2: State the elements which must be proved.

In order to get by a motion for judgment as a matter of law and allow the jury to consider your case, you must submit evidence on each element of the pertinent cause of action or charge. Therefore, for each cause of action or charge, the next step is to set forth the elements. In our scenario we would include:

1. Buyer bought the product from seller.
2. At the time of purchase Seller knew or had reason to know that Buyer
   a. intended to use the product for a particular purpose;
   b. was relying on Seller's skill and judgment to select or furnish a product that was suitable for the particular purpose;
3. Buyer justifiably relied on Seller's skill and judgment;
4. The product was not suitable for the particular purpose;
5. Buyer took
   a. reasonable steps to notify Seller
   b. within a reasonable time that the product was not suitable;
6. Buyer was harmed; and
7. The failure of the product to be suitable was a substantial factor in causing the harm.

Step 3: State the facts in your case which address each element.

You cannot be sure you are submitting evidence on each element unless you know what facts of your client's story fit each element and how they fit that element. In our example, purchase and delivery of the ring satisfy element one, Buyer's statements to Store' salesperson satisfies element two, and so on.

Step 4: State the evidence available that supports each fact.

The existence of a fact cannot be assumed. Each must be "proven" through admissions of the opposing party and/or persuasive evidence presented persuasively to the factfinder. List all sources of evidence for each fact, so that decisions can be made as to which source is the best considering all of the circumstances and so back-up plans can be made in the event that the initially chosen evidence cannot be admitted or is otherwise not as useable as anticipated. In our example, (1) the credit card charge slip, the ring package packing slip, and defendant's admission of paragraph one of the complaint support element one, (2) Buyer's testimony, Daughter's testimony, the phone bills showing the length of the conversation, and Store's internal records support the second element and so on.

Step 5: State the foundation needed to get the evidence admitted unless it is obvious.

In order to get the phone records, it will be necessary to lay a foundation using one or more of the rules of evidence. Rule of Evidence 402[2] makes the general statement that "all relevant evidence is admissible," but limits the general statement with several exceptions, one of which is the other Rules of Evidence. Rule 901 establishes a "Requirement of Authentication or Identification" that can be satisfied by "evidence sufficient to support a finding that the matter in question is what its proponent claims." If the phone records are records kept or accessible to Buyer, it is likely his testimony in this regard will be sufficient. More will be needed if the records are obtained from the cell phone service provider such as being "accompanied by a certificate of acknowledgement executed in the manner provided by law by a notary public or other officer authorized by law to take acknowledgments" under Rule 902(8).

Similarly the daughter's testimony will require a foundation showing that she was in a position to hear her father's end of the conversation with the store's salesperson and was paying attention to the conversation, because Rule 602 requires that a witness only testify regarding matters about which they have personal knowledge.

Step 6: State possible objections to the evidence.

For example, a defense attorney might object to testimony from the daughter on the grounds that under Rule 802 hearsay is not admissible except in certain circumstances provided by other rules or, depending on the age of the daughter, challenging her competency to

---

2. As with Rules of Civil Procedure, references here to Rules of Evidence are to the federal rules. While most states model their rules on the federal rules, there are often significant differences in the individual rules.

testify under Rule 601. For each item of evidence, state the basis for likely objections and the rule(s) that the attorney could use to make the objection, in this example, Rules 802 and 601.

Step 7: State responses to possible objections with reference to the appropriate rule and pertinent case law.

In the above example, the plaintiff's attorney might argue that the daughter's statement is not hearsay as defined by Rule 801 because it is not being offered into evidence "to prove the truth of the matter asserted." The daughter would be reporting on her father's statement, "This ring will be used for everyday use." Her testimony is not offered to prove that the ring was intended for everyday use, but only that her father made the statement while speaking on the phone. This illustrates the importance of aligning our evidence with facts supporting specific elements. Defense counsel's objection may be sustained if the evidence is entered to prove that the ring was to be worn every day, but will be overruled if the evidence is entered to prove element two, that Buyer informed Store of the intended use.

With regard to the possible objection to the daughter's competency, plaintiff's counsel's argument will likely have to range beyond the Rules of Evidence themselves. The federal Rule 601 states that competency to testify "shall be determined in accordance with state law." Thus, counsel is likely to need to provide the court with case law that supports his assertion that the daughter meets the standards for testimony by children. For example, in Mississippi he might cite case law stating,

> In the present case, the trial court examined the minor outside the presence of the jury. The judge questioned the minor regarding her ability to recall the past and her understanding of the importance of telling the truth and listened to her responses to those questions. After questioning and listening to the child, as well as observing the demeanor of the child, the trial court determined that the child's testimony was at least trustworthy enough to be heard. As stated above, the issue of exclusion of a child witness is at the sound discretion of the trial court. *In re EAJ*, 858 So. 2d 205, 208 (Miss, 2003).

The trial notebook should include reference to the specific law counsel will use to overcome likely objections by the opposing party.

Step 8: Cross-reference your evidence to Witness Summary Pages and Exhibit Pages.

Assuming the fact that Store was notified of the particular use intended for the ring will be verified through testimony from the father, the daughter, and the salesperson, and through use of phone records and Store's internal memos, list the required testimony on each of the Witness Summary Pages and reference the relationship of each exhibit to respective witnesses and facts on the Exhibit Page for each exhibit in the exhibit index.

Trial Notebooks

Every successful litigation team has a method for organizing the evidence, court rules, and case law they will accumulate during the litigation process and utilize at trial. Judges and juries expect a lawyer not only to be prepared but to be organized. Every trial team should have a simple method that is effective for that team. The method of organizing the trial notebook will often depend on the type of case, office policy or the preference of your attorney. Most are organized around the trial process itself, beginning with pre-trial motions and ending with post-judgment motions. In between there may be sections for

- Jury selection (e.g., voir dire questions, information on prospective jurors, legal research justifying likely challenges for cause)
- Opening statement
- Direct examination of witnesses
- Legal research and notes for motions at the end of plaintiff's evidence
- Cross examination of witnesses
- Exhibits
- Legal research and notes for motions at the end of defendant's evidence
- Closing arguments
- Jury verdict forms and jury instructions

Notebook dividers with pre-printed trial notebook sections are available from several companies. There are also software systems that assist in creating electronic notebooks.

Regardless of how the notebook is divided into sections, each section must be organized in a way that recognizes the essential goal of the trial—an effective presentation of your client's case in a way that convinces the jury of your client's position on each of the elements.

Evidence Trees

In this section we start by applying the organizational steps to our sample case and build a branch of an evidence tree in trial notebook form. Separate evidence trees should be developed for each count in the complaint.

Step 1: State the cause(s) of action.

The cause of action can be simply stated on the first page for Count II in the notebook:

> Defendant breached the implied warranty of fitness for particular use, to wit: it sold plaintiff a ring defective in design and manufacture making it unfit for everyday use, after having been informed by plaintiff of the ring's particular use

Step 2: State the elements which must be proved.

This statement of the cause of action is, however, only vaguely helpful for purposes of litigation. It may or may not be sufficient to withstand a motion to dismiss and certainly does not provide sufficient structure for designing an interview, investigation and discovery plan, or organizing and presenting evidence during trial. It is the trunk of the evidence tree, but lacks the branches on which the case will hang. We can provide the first, strong branches by listing the elements under the cause of action:

Ring Buyer v. Store—Count II

Cause of Action: Breach of Warranty of Fitness for Particular Use

Defendant breached the implied warranty of fitness for particular use, to wit: it sold plaintiff a ring defective in design and manufacture making it unfit for everyday use, after having been informed by plaintiff of the particular use.

Elements of the Cause of Action:
1. Buyer bought the product from seller.
2. At the time of purchase, Seller knew or had reason to know that Buyer
   a. intended to use the product for a particular purpose;
   b. was relying on Seller's skill and judgment to select or furnish a product that was suitable for the particular purpose;
3. Buyer justifiably relied on Seller's skill and judgment;
4. The product was not suitable for the particular purpose;
5. Buyer took
   a. reasonable steps to notify Seller
   b. within a reasonable time that the product was not suitable;

6. Buyer was harmed; and
7. The failure of the product to be suitable was a substantial factor in causing the harm.

If we fail to introduce evidence on any one of these elements, our case will lose as a matter of law—defense counsel will make and have granted a motion for directed verdict. If we fail to convince the jury on any one of these elements, we lose the case.

Step 3: State the facts in your case which address each element.

Having established the main branches, i.e., the elements, our tree can begin growing as we add the facts from our fact pattern that satisfy each of these elements. Here we use only some of the elements for illustration due to space limitations.

Ring Buyer v. Store—Count II

Cause of Action: Breach of Warranty of Fitness for Particular Use

Defendant breached the implied warranty of fitness for particular use, to wit: it sold plaintiff a ring defective in design and manufacture making it unfit for everyday use, after having been informed by plaintiff of the particular use.

Elements of the Cause of Action:
1. Buyer bought the product from seller.
   Facts: Ring Buyer responded to Daughter's urging and called Store the very next day. The salesperson that answered the phone informed Ring Buyer the ring was not Wife's size, but there would be no difficulty having one custom made in time for Christmas—after all, each ring was custom made by the artist anyway. Ring Buyer gave his credit card number and delivery address to the salesperson. About two weeks later the ring arrived in the mail with the credit card receipt.

2. At the time of purchase, Seller knew or had reason to know that Buyer
   a. intended to use the product for a particular purpose, and
   b. was relying on Seller's skill and judgment to select or furnish a product that was suitable for the particular purpose;
   Facts: Ring Buyer explained that he had not seen the ring, but was following up on his young daughter's admiration for the ring, so he was depending on the knowledge of the Store as to whether the ring was appropriate.
   He then explained the purpose of the ring, i.e., it would be both a Christmas and Anniversary gift which Wife would likely wear on a regular basis, not just for special occasions.
   The salesperson who answered the phone informed Ring Buyer the ring was not Wife's size, but there would be no difficulty having one custom made in time for Christmas—after all each ring was custom made by the artist anyway.

While this illustration is of the steps in a trial notebook it also illustrates how earlier notebooks in the process follow this procedure. Once this step has been completed for each of the elements, we are in a position to develop interview, investigation and discovery plans, each building on the stage prior to it as well as the elements themselves. Simply by reference to this analysis we can establish who we need to interview, e.g., the daughter, the wife, appraiser and which topics need to be covered with each witness. We can also begin to list exhibits which must be obtained through investigation or discovery, e.g., phone bills, store's internal records, credit card receipts, appraiser's report, etc. Later, when investigation and discovery are complete, this same analysis provides the basis for full presentation of the evidence and compiling witness summary pages and exhibit lists.

Step 4: State the evidence available that supports each fact.

The existence each of these "facts" cannot be assumed. Unless the other party has admitted or stipulated to a particular fact, the legal team must produce evidence of each fact; evidence sufficient to convince the jury even if the other side contests that fact. At this point I suggest we move each element onto its own page. This example focuses on Element 2 since that is the one that has been used throughout our discussion. For purposes of this discussion we will assume Store has not admitted any facts, no matter how obvious.

Ring Buyer v. Store—Count II—Element 2

Cause of Action: Breach of Warranty of Fitness for Particular Use

Defendant breached the implied warranty of fitness for particular use, to wit: it sold plaintiff a ring defective in design and manufacture making it unfit for everyday use, after having been informed by plaintiff of the particular use.

Element 2:

At the time of purchase, Seller knew or had reason to know Buyer
   a. intended to use the product for a particular purpose, and
   b. was relying on Seller's skill and judgment to select or furnish a product that was suitable for the particular purpose;

Facts: Ring Buyer responded to Daughter's urging and called Store the very next day. The salesperson that answered the phone informed Ring Buyer the ring was not Wife's size, but there would be no difficulty having one custom made in time for Christmas—after all, each ring was custom made by the artist anyway. Ring Buyer gave his credit card number and delivery address to the salesperson. About two weeks later the ring arrived in the mail with the credit card receipt.

Evidence 1: Testimony of Ring Buyer as to his recollection of the content of the phone call.

Evidence 2: Testimony of Ring Buyer's daughter as to her recollection of hearing her father's statements during the phone call.

Evidence 3: Ring Buyer's phone bill [Exhibit 5] — Indicates the phone call was of sufficient length to cover all claimed by Ring Buyer.

Evidence 4: Store's internal memo of call [Exhibit 8] — While not specific on this issue, it also indicates that the phone call was more than a couple of minutes long and that "customer's concerns" were discussed.

Step 5: State the foundation needed to get the evidence admitted unless it is obvious.

Little is more devastating than being unable to enter otherwise admissible evidence at trial due to lack of proper foundation. Even if the attorney eventually establishes sufficient foundation, floundering around while trying to do so is embarrassing to say the least, and completely unnecessary. The foundation should be easily available to the attorney when the evidence is presented. For purposes of the next three steps it is best to set up a page in the notebook for each piece of evidence:

Ring Buyer v. Store—Count II—Element 2

Cause of Action: Breach of Warranty of Fitness for Particular Use

Defendant breached the implied warranty of fitness for particular use, to wit: it sold plaintiff a ring defective in design and manufacture making it unfit for everyday use, after having been informed by plaintiff of the particular use.

Element 2:

At the time of purchase, Seller knew or had reason to know Buyer
    a. intended to use the product for a particular purpose, and
    b. was relying on Seller's skill and judgment to select or furnish a product that was suitable for the particular purpose;

Facts: Ring Buyer responded to daughter's urging and called Store the very next day. The salesperson who answered the phone informed Ring Buyer the ring was not Wife's size, but there would be no difficulty having one custom made in time for Christmas—after all each ring was custom made by the artist anyway. Ring Buyer gave his credit card number and delivery address to the salesperson. About two weeks later the ring arrived in the mail with the credit card receipt.

Evidence 1: Testimony of Ring Buyer as to his recollection of the content of the phone call

Foundation: 1. Ring Buyer's personal knowledge (Rule 602) is evident from the context.

2. Telephone conversations are authenticated by evidence (from Ring Buyer) that the call was made to the number assigned at the time by the telephone company to a particular business and the conversation related to business reasonably transacted over the phone. (Rule 901(b) (6)).

Evidence 2: Testimony of Ring Buyer's daughter as to her recollection of hearing her father's statements during the phone call.

Foundation: Establish that daughter was in a position to hear the conversation and was attentive to it, i.e., she stood next to her father anxiously awaiting confirmation that the ring had been purchases.

With this information the attorney can easily establish the foundation for this evidence. Unless there is a valid objection, the evidence will be admitted. In a later step we will copy all of the facts, evidence, and foundation statements related to Ring Buyer to his Witness Summary Page, all of those relating to Daughter to her Witness Summary Page, and so on for each witness. We will similarly create pages for each of the exhibits, cross-referencing the witness who will introduce them, the purpose of each, and the foundation for each, etc. This brings us to the next step:

Step 6: State possible objections to the evidence.

This requires that your legal team switch roles and analyze the evidence from the other side—what objections would you make if you were trying to keep this evidence out.

Ring Buyer v. Store—Count II—Element 2

Cause of Action: Breach of Warranty of Fitness for Particular Use

Defendant breached the implied warranty of fitness for particular use, to wit: it sold plaintiff a ring defective in design and manufacture making it unfit for everyday use, after having been informed by plaintiff of the particular use.

Element 2:

At the time of purchase, Seller knew or had reason to know Buyer
  a. intended to use the product for a particular purpose, and
  b. was relying on Seller's skill and judgment to select or furnish a product that was suitable for the particular purpose;

Facts: Ring Buyer responded to daughter's urging and called Store the very next day. The salesperson that answered the phone informed Ring Buyer the ring was not Wife's size, but there would be no difficulty having one custom made in time for Christmas—after all, each ring was custom made by the artist anyway. Ring Buyer gave his credit card number and delivery address to the salesperson. About two weeks later the ring arrived in the mail with the credit card receipt.

> **Evidence 2:** Testimony of Ring Buyer's Daughter as to her recollection of hearing her father's statements during the phone call.
> **Foundation:** Establish that Daughter was in a position to hear the conversation and was attentive to it, i.e., she stood next to her father, anxiously awaiting confirmation that the ring had been purchased.
> **Anticipated Objection 1:** Hearsay—as a witness daughter will be testifying about a statement she heard her father say. Hearsay is prohibited by Rule 802 and no exceptions apply.
> **Anticipated Objection 2:** Competency of the daughter to testify due to her age. (Rule 601)

Having anticipated the objections, we can be prepared for them and have a response set out in the notebook in Step 7.

Step 7: State responses to possible objections with reference to the appropriate rule and pertinent case law.

Ring Buyer v. Store—Count II—Element 2

Cause of Action: Breach of Warranty of Fitness for Particular Use

Defendant breached the implied warranty of fitness for particular use, to wit: it sold plaintiff a ring defective in design and manufacture making it unfit for everyday use, after having been informed by plaintiff of the particular use.

Element 2:
> At the time of purchase, Seller knew or had reason to know Buyer
>   a. intended to use the product for a particular purpose, and
>   b. was relying on Seller's skill and judgment to select or furnish a product that was suitable for the particular purpose;

Facts: Ring Buyer responded to Daughter's urging and called Store the very next day. The salesperson that answered the phone informed Ring Buyer the ring was not Wife's size, but there would be no difficulty having one custom made in time for Christmas—after all, each ring was custom made by the artist anyway. Ring Buyer gave his credit card number and delivery address to the salesperson. About two weeks later the ring arrived in the mail with the credit card receipt. Ring Buyer.

> **Evidence 2:** Testimony of Ring Buyer's Daughter as to her recollection of hearing her father's statements during the phone call.
> **Foundation:** Establish that Daughter was in a position to hear the conversation and was attentive to it, i.e., she stood next to her father, anxiously awaiting confirmation that the ring had been purchased.

Anticipated Objection 1: Hearsay—as a witness Daughter will be testifying about a statement she heard her father say. Hearsay is prohibited by Rule 802 and no exceptions apply.

Response to Objection 1: A statement is not hearsay if it is not offered to prove the truth of the matter asserted. (Rule 801 (c)). Her testimony is not offered to prove that the ring was intended for everyday use, but only that her father made the statement while speaking on the phone.

Anticipated Objection 2: Competency of the Daughter to testify due to her age. (Rule 601).

Response to Objection 2.

The general rule is anyone offered is competent and the objecting party must prove incompetency. (Rule 601). The court can question the minor regarding her ability to recall the past and her understanding of the importance of telling the truth and listen to her responses to those questions. After questioning and listening to the child, as well as observing the demeanor of the child, the trial court can determine whether the child's testimony was at least trustworthy enough to be heard. The issue of exclusion of a child witness is at the sound discretion of the trial court. *In re EAJ*, 858 So. 2d 205, 208 (Miss, 2003).

When case law is cited, copies of the cited case for the attorney, the judge, and the opposing attorney should be available in the notebook

We are almost done! All that's left is *Step 8: Cross-reference your evidence to you Witness Summary Pages and Exhibit Pages.* We will look at the Witness and Exhibit List pages next. For now we'll just indicate here what is cross-referenced where:

Ring Buyer v. Store—Count II—Element 2

Cause of Action: Breach of Warranty of Fitness for Particular Use

Defendant breached the implied warranty of fitness for particular use, to wit: it sold plaintiff a ring defective in design and manufacture making it unfit for everyday use, after having been informed by plaintiff of the particular use.

Element 2:

At the time of purchase, Seller knew or had reason to know Buyer
   a. intended to use the product for a particular purpose, and
   b. was relying on Seller's skill and judgment to select or furnish a product that was suitable for the particular purpose;

Facts: Ring Buyer responded to Daughter's urging and called Store the very next day. The salesperson that answered the phone informed Ring Buyer the ring was not Wife's size, but there would be no difficulty having one custom made in time for Christmas—after all, each ring was custom made by the artist anyway. Ring Buyer gave his credit card number and delivery address to the salesperson. About two weeks later the ring arrived in the mail with the credit card receipt.

Evidence 2: Testimony of Ring Buyer's Daughter as to her recollection of hearing her father's statements during the phone call.

Foundation: Establish that Daughter was in a position to hear the conversation and was attentive to it, i.e., she stood next to her father, anxiously awaiting confirmation that the ring had been purchased.

Anticipated Objection 1: Hearsay—as a witness Daughter will be testifying about a statement she heard her father say. Hearsay is prohibited by Rule 802 and no exceptions apply.

Response to Objection 1: A statement is not hearsay if it is not offered to prove the truth of the matter asserted. (Rule 801 (c)). Her testimony is not offered to prove that the ring was intended for everyday use, but only that her father made the statement while speaking on the phone.

Anticipated Objection 2: Competency of the Daughter to testify due to her age. (Rule 601).

Response to Objection 2.

The general rule is anyone offered is competent and the objecting party must prove incompetency. (Rule 601). The court can question the minor regarding her ability to recall the past and her understanding of the importance of telling the truth and listen to her responses to those questions. After questioning and listening to the child, as well as observing the demeanor of the child, the trial court can determine whether the child's testimony was at least trustworthy enough to be heard. The issue of exclusion of a child witness is at the sound discretion of the trial court. *In re EAJ*, 858 So. 2d 205, 208 (Miss, 2003).

   Cross References:

Witness—Ring Buyer's Daughter
Exhibits—None

Exhibit Lists and Pages

Exhibit lists are important in and of themselves. The format of the exhibit list is often established by the rules of the court or jurisdiction in which the legal team practices. Often it provides spaces for the name of the exhibit, the date of the exhibit, the number of the exhibit, whether it was offered into evidence and whether it was admitted. This is quite useful to attorneys, judges and clerks for purposes of keeping track of exhibits at trial. However, the effective trial notebook will go beyond the standard exhibit list.

A winning trial presentation needs more. Each exhibit must have its own page describing the exhibit and its place in the evidence schematic, and be cross referenced to the facts and witnesses to which it relates. Assume that there are photographs of Store's display window in the Ring Buyer v. Store matter. Let's take a look at the exhibit page for the picture showing the display of dozens of rings. The basic information will include the same information as appears on the exhibit list.

Plaintiff's Exhibit 10
Photo of shop window.
Date taken: February 8, 2013.

This information is available to both sides and the court. However, it is not enough for us to effectively use the information (especially in cases with dozens of exhibits). We want to have that information available to us, but not to have it disclosed to the other side. We'll start with a basic description of the photo and its role in our case.

Plaintiff's Exhibit 10
Photo of shop window
Date taken: January 13, 2013

Description: Photo taken by private investigator two months after the sale of the ring to Ring Buyer. Shows that a major portion of Store's sales efforts related to rings rather than art.

No exhibit can exist on its own. It will only be admitted if the criteria for admissibility are met—identification, foundation, relevance and so on. This is accomplished through one or more witnesses. All of this information should be immediately available to the attorney on Plaintiff's Exhibit 10's exhibit page.

Plaintiff's Exhibit 10
Photo of shop window.
Date taken: January 13, 2013.

Description: Photo taken by private investigator two months after the sale of the ring to Ring Buyer. Shows that a major portion of Store's sales efforts related to rings rather than art.

Foundational witnesses:
Best: **Investigator Thomas Jones**
    He took the photograph, can identify it, testify as to where it was taken and testify as to its accuracy as a representation of what it purports to represent
Second: **Client's Wife**—can I.D. the subject of the photograph and testify as to its accuracy as a representation of what the display looked like when she and daughter entered the store.
Third: **Client's Daughter**—can I.D. the subject of the photograph and testify as to its accuracy as a representation of what the display looked like when she and her mother entered the store.

Testimonial witnesses:

Client's Wife—assist witness in explaining her impression that the store was a jewelry store, not an art store.

Client's Daughter—assist witness in explaining her impression that the store was a jewelry store, not an art store.

Store Owner—possible use to impeach

Store Salesperson—possible use to impeach

Now we're ready for the real meat of the exhibit page—how we actually get the exhibit into evidence and deal with possible objections. Fortunately this does not mean additional work. It is already done through the creation of the Evidence Tree. We simply copy that work here.

Plaintiff's Exhibit 10
Photo of shop window.
Date taken: January 13, 2013.

Description: Photo taken by private investigator two months after the sale of the ring to Ring Buyer. Shows that a major portion of Store's sales efforts related to rings rather than art.

Foundational witnesses:

Best: **Investigator Thomas Jones**

He took the photograph, can identify it, testify as to where it was taken and testify as to its accuracy as a representation of what it purports to represent

Second: **Client's Wife**—can I.D. the subject of the photograph and testify as to its accuracy as a representation of what the display looked like when she and daughter entered the store.

Third: **Client's Daughter**—can I.D. the subject of the photograph and testify as to its accuracy as a representation of what the display looked like when she and her mother entered the store.

Testimonial witnesses:

Client's Wife—assist witness in explaining her impression that the store was a jewelry store, not an art store.

Client's Daughter—assist witness in explaining her impression that the store was a jewelry store, not an art store.

Store Owner—possible use to impeach

Store Salesperson—possible use to impeach

Foundation

Rule 901(b): By way of illustration only, and not by way of limitation, the following are examples of authentication or identification conforming to the requirements of this rule:

(1) Testimony of witness with knowledge. Testimony that a matter is what it is claimed to be.

Possible Objections: (1) Rules 401 and 402—window display is not relevant to any issue in the case.

(2) Rule 403—probative value is substantially outweighed by unfair prejudice and may be confusing to the jury because it shows only one of the store's several display windows.

Response to Objections:

(1) Rule 401—"relevant evidence" is any evidence having any tendency to make the existence of any fact that is of the consequence to the determination of the action more probable or less probable than it would be without the evidence. Photo tends to make the existence of defendant's claim it is really an art store less probable.

(2) The burden is on defendant to show prejudice and confusion. Any prejudice or confusion can easily be averted by a court's limiting instruction and defendant's cross-examination of witnesses.

Citation: "Thus, a trial court presented with a Rule 403 objection to relevant evidence must engage in a balancing process. The more probative the evidence is, the less likely it is that a 403 factor will be of sufficient consequence to substantially outweigh the probative value. On the other hand, the less probative value the evidence has the less significant the 403 factor would have to be to justify exclusion. If one or more of the 403 considerations slightly outweigh probative value, the evidence still must be admitted. To tip the scale is not enough. The 403 factors must, in the language of the rule, "substantially outweigh" probative value before the evidence may be excluded." *Foster v. State*, 508 So. 2d 1111, 1117 (Miss S. Ct, 1987).

Finally we'll tie this page back into the rest of the case through cross-references to the evidence tree and the witness pages.

Possible Objections: (1) Rules 401 and 402—window display is not relevant to any issue in the case.

(2) Rule 403—probative value is substantially outweighed by unfair prejudice and may be confusing to the jury because it shows only one of the store's several display windows.

Response to Objections:

(1) Rule 401—"relevant evidence" is any evidence having any tendency to make the existence of any fact that is of the consequence to the determination of the action more probable or less probable than it would be without the evidence. Photo tends to make the existence of defendant's claim it is really an art store less probable.

(2) The burden is on defendant to show prejudice and confusion. Any prejudice or confusion can easily be averted by a court's limiting instruction and defendant's cross-examination of witnesses.

> Citation: "Thus, a trial court presented with a Rule 403 objection to relevant evidence must engage in a balancing process. The more probative the evidence is, the less likely it is that a 403 factor will be of sufficient consequence to substantially outweigh the probative value. On the other hand, the less probative value the evidence has, the less significant the 403 factor would have to be to justify exclusion. If one or more of the 403 considerations slightly outweigh probative value, the evidence still must be admitted. To tip the scale is not enough. The 403 factors must, in the language of the rule, "substantially outweigh" probative value before the evidence may be excluded." *Foster v. State,* 508 So. 2d 1111, 1117 (Miss S. Ct, 1987).

Cross References:

> Witnesses — Investigator
> > Ring Buyer's Wife
> > Ring Buyer's Daughter
> > Store Owner
> > Store Sales Person

Evidence Tree:

Count I — Breach of Contract

Element 2 — b

Facts — Store accepted Buyer's offer to purchase an "everyday ring."

Witness Lists and Pages

Like Exhibit Lists, the format for Witness Lists is often set by the court or the applicable rule of procedure. Some courts mandate forms. Like Exhibit Lists, Witness Lists themselves contain minimal information intended simply to put opposing parties and the court on notice. Thus, Like Exhibit Lists, Witness Lists themselves are not extremely useful to the attorney conducting the trial. The effective and empowered paralegal will go beyond the standard witness list.

A winning trial presentation needs more. Each witness must have her own page providing the usual identifying information together with information about what evidence she can present with regard to which fact and elements in our evidence tree, which exhibit will be used to assist her testimony and which exhibits she can identify. Again, we will want to include foundational information, possible objections to the witness or his testimony, replies to those objections and the like.

While most of the foregoing information is comparable to information on an exhibit page, there is one sort of information that should be included that does not have a counterpart on an exhibit page. We should include information regarding the witness himself other than simply identifying information. This type of information might include:

- Whether a subpoena will be advisable or required, and, if so, where, when and by whom it should be served;
- Whether the witness needs any special accommodations, such as child care, transportation, sound amplification, wheel-chair access or a translator;
- Possible biases that might affect the witness's testimony such as relationship to a party, an economic interest in the outcome or conviction of a crime that is admissible in court, especially if those biases are noticeable or discoverable by the opposition;
- Special personality traits that might affect testimony or the presentation of testimony such as stuttering, Turret's Syndrome, panic disorder or just excessive nervousness or belligerence.

Much of the information contained on the witness page can be culled from other pages in the notebook. A typical witness page might look like this:

Ring Buyer v. Store: Witness 3

Ring Buyer's Daughter
    Resides with client
    ➔ Witness is a minor
Testimony relevant to: Count II—Breach of Warranty of Fitness for Particular Use
Element 2: Plaintiff buyer advised Defendant seller of particular use intended for the ring and of his reliance on the expertise of the seller.
    Facts: Ring Buyer responded to Daughter's urging and called Store the very next day. The salesperson that answered the phone informed Ring Buyer the ring was not Wife's size, but there would be no difficulty having one custom made in time for Christmas—after all, each ring was custom made by the artist anyway. Ring Buyer gave his credit card number and delivery address to the salesperson. About two weeks later the ring arrived in the mail with the credit card receipt.
    Evidence 2: Testimony of Ring Buyer's Daughter as to her recollection of hearing her father's statements during the phone call.
    Foundation: Establish that Daughter was in a position to hear the conversation and was attentive to it, i.e., she stood next to her father, anxiously awaiting confirmation that the ring had been purchased.
    Anticipated Objection 1: Hearsay—as a witness Daughter will be testifying about a statement she heard her father say. Hearsay is prohibited by Rule 802 and no exceptions apply.
    Response to Objection 1: A statement is not hearsay if it is not offered to prove the truth of the matter asserted. (Rule 801 (c)). Her testimony is not offered to prove that the ring was intended for everyday use, but only that her father made the statement while speaking on the phone.

Anticipated Objection 2: Competency of the Daughter to testify due to her age. (Rule 601).

Response to Objection 2.

The general rule is anyone offered is competent and the objecting party must prove incompetency. (Rule 601). The court can question the minor regarding her ability to recall the past and her understanding of the importance of telling the truth and listen to her responses to those questions. After questioning and listening to the child, as well as observing the demeanor of the child, the trial court can determine whether the child's testimony was at least trustworthy enough to be heard. The issue of exclusion of a child witness is at the sound discretion of the trial court. *In re E*

Cross-References:
   Exhibits—None for this portion of testimony

Conclusion

Like so much of what we do, a good trial notebook requires analysis, thought, preparation and organization. The result of all that effort to accumulate comprehensive vital information in one spot can be overwhelming to the opposing party.

The trial notebook is a system designed specifically to perform this function during a trial. I like to have a similar note book organized around the element-facts-evidence tree for each motion hearing, each deposition and the discovery process as a whole. Ultimately they evolve into and/or are utilized for the trial notebook.

The existence of the information in the file, even in an organized way, does not in itself provide the ease of access to that information needed to do the job during a hearing, deposition or trial. There must be a means of knowing where the information is and how to locate it quickly and accurately.

When it comes to the trial notebook, it is necessary for the system to provide a map showing how each piece of information is connected to every other piece, and how they are all connected to the ultimate goal of proving or disproving to the jury's satisfaction the elements of the causes of action which form the basis of the plaintiff's claims against the defendant. While we have spoken of this primarily in terms of civil actions, it applies in full force to criminal proceedings.

The key to providing "interconnectedness" information is cross-referencing. Each fact should be cross-referenced to the element(s) with which it is associated and the evidence which will be used to prove it. Each exhibit should be cross-referenced to the fact(s) and element(s) to which it relates, to the witnesses who will provide the foundation for its admission, and the witnesses with whom it will be used. Each witness should be cross-referenced to the facts that will be shown by his testimony, the exhibits for which that witness will provide foundation, and the exhibits that will be used to assist their testimony.

In the end, the well-designed trial notebook should allow even an attorney who has little familiarity with a case, working with the paralegal that put the notebook together, to try the case with a modicum of advanced notice.

The trial notebook is the culmination of cause of action analysis and evidence tree development that begins with the initial client interview. It guides the legal team through every stage of the litigation process and provides the legal team with the tools needed for the successful trial.

Part Two

Common Causes of Action, Doctrines, Rules and Defenses

Chapter Five

Contracts

Contract Elements
   1. Offer
   2. Acceptance
   3. Intent/Mutual Assent
   4. Consideration
   5. Legality
   6. Capacity

Contract Causes of Action
   1. Breach of Contract
   2. Breach of Express Contract Warranties
   3. Breach of Implied Warranty of Merchantability
   4. Breach of Implied Warranty of Fitness for Particular Use

Contractual Remedies
   1. Damages
      1.1 Compensatory Damages
      1.2 Punitive Damages
      1.3 Consequential Damages
      1.4 Liquidated Damages
   2. Specific Performance
   3. Rescission
   4. Reformation

Equitable Causes of Action as Contract Alternatives
   1. Promissory Estoppel
   2. Equitable Estoppel
   3. Unjust Enrichment
   4. Quasi-Contractual Remedies: *Quantum meruit* and *Quantum valebant*

Defenses
   1. Duress
   2. Fraud

3. Misrepresentation
4. Undue Influence
5. Unconscionability
6. Mutual Mistake
7. Waiver

Contract Elements[1]

1. Offer

Offer is the first essential element of every valid contract. A valid contract is formed when the parties manifest their mutual assent to the same bargain at the same time. Offer is the statement of one party's willingness to enter into the contract on particular terms. The offeror initiates the contract process by setting the terms of the contract.

A. Elements

1. The offeror must manifest a present contractual intent;
2. The offer must be communicated to the offeree; and
3. The offer must be certain and definite to its terms.

Certain and definite terms may include the following (The UCC contains provision validating certain contracts that lack, for example, a definite time of performance):

    a. The price of the contract
    b. The subject matter of the contract
    c. The parties to the contract
    d. The time of performance for fulfilling the contract

----

1. The common law statement of the elements of a contract, a cause of action, a remedy, and/or a defense may vary from that contained in the UCC. For contracts involving the sale of goods, Article 2 of the UCC as enacted in the appropriate jurisdiction for the relevant statement of elements.

B. Sample Case

In *Hunt v. IBM Mid America Employees Federal*, 384 NW 2d 853, 855–57 (Minn, 1986) an employee complained that he had been wrongfully discharged based on the assertion that the company's employee handbook's statements on employee discipline constituted an offer which he accepted by continuing to work for the company. The court did not agree:

> The parties here do not dispute the material fact that Hunt was an at-will employee. The parties also do not dispute there was no oral or written contract on the duration of Hunt's employment. The complaint, filed in district court by Hunt, lists the employee reference manual as the sole basis for creating an implied contract of employment ... The only question, then, is whether language in the manual was sufficiently definite to raise a triable issue of fact.
>
> Inasmuch as Hunt is relying exclusively on the language contained in the employee manual in his attempt to establish the existence of a contract containing disciplinary and termination procedures, the resolution of whether the language used rises to the level of a contract is for the court. Where, as here, the intent of the parties is totally ascertainable from the writing, construction is for the court. The general rule is that "the construction of a writing which is unambiguous is for the court, particularly when the intention of the parties is to be gained wholly from the writing." Where the issue to be determined is the nature and effect of a writing, the contents of which is not disputed, the general rule is particularly applicable.
>
> In determining whether summary judgment was appropriately granted, we now examine the employee handbook initially given to Hunt when he was first employed. Did the handbook contain sufficiently definite terms, which, when accepted by Hunt by going to work, created a binding unilateral employment contract? Unless it does, the parties concede Hunt was an at-will employee; he was hired for an indefinite term and could be terminated at once.
>
> In *Pine River State Bank v. Mettille*, 333 N.W.2d 622 (Minn.1983), we recognized an exception to the long standing terminable at-will rule when we held that an employee hired for an indefinite term might maintain an action for breach of contract if termination provisions in an employee handbook were sufficiently definite to meet the requirements for the formation of a unilateral contract.

As did the plaintiff employee in *Pine River*, Hunt relies on an employee manual to establish alleged contract rights. As established earlier, he does not allege oral promises relative to the duration of his position, and concedes that at all times he felt free to leave his job.

Examination of the language of the employee manual in this case compared to that in *Pine River* reveals major differences. For example, the disciplinary and discharge section in *Pine River* "set out in definite language an offer of a unilateral contract for procedures to be followed in job termination." In *Pine River* the manual explicitly promises discharge only for an employee "whose conduct does not improve as a result of the previous action taken."

When this definite and specific language is contrasted with the vague language on disciplinary action and discharge in the employee reference manual issued to Hunt by Mid America, the distinction between the two is readily apparent. Mid America's manual fails to provide any detailed or definite disciplinary procedure. The Pine River manual provided a definite, detailed four-step procedure. Moreover, Mid America's manual omits any definite option of a probationary period for an employee before final termination. Here there is no definite language to constitute an offer of a unilateral contract on job termination procedures. Finally, the Mid America manual warns of the possibility of summary discharge: "In the event of a serious offense, an employee will be terminated immediately."

Significantly, the manual neither defines nor gives examples of what is a "serious offense." This vagueness falls far short of the specificity necessary for a contractual offer under principles enunciated in *Pine River*. If this case were to go to trial, a jury would literally be asked to draft new contractual terms and define "serious offense." The jury, then, rather than the employer, would decide what offenses are serious. (Citations and footnotes omitted.)

2. Acceptance

Acceptance is the second element of a valid contract. Prior to acceptance, an offer can be revoked by the offeree or the offeree may reject the offer. Acceptance can be implied from behavior, partial performance, or past dealings. Two important rules apply to acceptance:

A. Mailbox Rule—when offers are accepted through the mail acceptance occurs at the time of dispatching. Rejection, however, is only effective when received. However, the modern trend is to move away from this rule and instead determine the expectation of the parties.

B. Mirror Image Rule — the acceptance cannot alter the offer in any way. Any variance of the offer is considered a counteroffer. This includes anything being added to the offer. This rule may be modified by the UCC in contracts for sale of goods between merchants.

A. Elements

1. Compliance or agreement by one party
2. with the exact terms
3. of an offer.

B. Sample Case

In *Ketcherside v. McLane*, 118 S.W.3d 631 (Mo., 2003) the defendants argued the evidence was insufficient to support a finding that each essential element for the formation of a contract existed, specifically the element of acceptance and the element of intent or mutual assent. The court disagreed.

The plaintiff was contacted to auction the defendant's grocery store equipment. After the plaintiff began promoting the auction the defendant decided to go with another auctioning company. Defendant had told plaintiff the commission terms, time restraints, and the items to be sold:

> In her second point on appeal, Defendant alleges the court erred in finding a breach of contract occurred because "a contract was never formed, due to the absence of acceptance by performance in that ... [the] offer was rescinded before [Plaintiff] began to perform." In this argument, Defendant claims that a unilateral contract was contemplated, but Plaintiff failed to substantially perform before Defendant rescinded, i.e., he did not timely accept the offer. Because both points are interrelated, we discuss them in conjunction ...
>
> "A unilateral contract is a contract in which performance is based on the wish, will, or pleasure of one of the parties. The promisor receives no promise in return as consideration for the original promise. The contractual relationship arises when the conduct of the parties supports a reasonable inference of a mutual understanding that one party perform and the other party compensate for such performance. "An offer to make a unilateral contract is accepted when the requested performance is rendered." The offer cannot be revoked where the offeree has made substantial performance.

Turning to the second point, Defendant claims that Plaintiff failed to accept the offer because he did not substantially perform. We dispatch with this argument by noting that Plaintiff testified he "had everything ready to go," and his "work was done all except the actual auction ... and delivering the sale bills." Moreover, he testified: "The actual auction itself is not the biggest deal. You have more hours spent prior to." He also testified as to the details of his preparatory work. The trial court was free to believe this evidence. There was sufficient evidence to support a finding that Plaintiff substantially performed before Defendant attempted to rescind the offer; consequently, Defendant was not entitled to revoke the offer. (Citations omitted.)

3. Intent/Mutual Assent

Intent is the third element that follows acceptance. Intent is referred to as a meeting of the minds or agreement. For a contract be enforced, the parties must manifest intent to enter into the binding contractual relationship. If all other elements of the contract are satisfied there is no binding agreement if the parties did not intend to enter into the contract. Each party must freely and voluntarily enter into the contract for the contract to be valid. Intent must be present before the parties are entitled to something of legal value. This is often referred to as "mutual assent."

A. Elements

1. Parties actually intend
2. to enter into a contract
3. for the same bargain
4. at the same time.

B. Sample Case

In *Ketcherside v. McLane*, 118 S.W.3d 631 (Mo., 2003) the defendants argued the evidence was insufficient to support a finding that each essential element for the formation of a contract existed, specifically the element of acceptance and the element of intent or mutual assent. The court disagreed.

The plaintiff was contacted to auction the defendant's grocery store equipment. After the plaintiff began promoting the auction the defendant decided to go with another auctioning company. Defendant had told plaintiff the commission terms, time restraints, and the items to be sold:

In Point I, Defendant claims that Walker and Plaintiff were merely negotiating, and they lacked mutuality of agreement because they had not agreed upon many essential terms (the commission, the date of the auction, the equipment to be sold, and the method of advertising). Apparently, Defendant misconstrues our standard of review because this record provides ample evidence to support the judgment.

Plaintiff informed Walker that his commission was ten percent of the total sales made at the auction, and she told him to "get it going" and "I want you to handle the auction." The auction was to be conducted as soon as possible, but before the new tenants were to take possession of the premises. Walker also stated that everything in the store was to be sold. The two further discussed advertising and agreed a limit would be set before spending any amounts on it.

It was reasonable for the court to conclude a contract was formed. Walker told Plaintiff to conduct all steps necessary to get the auction started and that everything was to be sold. Plaintiff told Walker that his commission was ten percent. This disposes of Defendant's contention that the contract lacked two essential terms (price and equipment). Mutuality of agreement is determined by looking to the intentions of the parties as expressed or manifested in their words or acts. (Citations and footnotes omitted.)

4. Consideration

Consideration is the fourth essential element of every valid contract. It is "the bargain" that supports the entire contractual relationship. For a contract to be valid, both parties to the contract must give and receive something of value. It need not be money, but can simply be an exchange of promises.

A. Elements

Each party to a contract must:

1. get something
2. to which the party was not legally entitled and
3. give up something
4. to which the party was legally entitled.

B. Sample Case

Cook v. Heck's Inc., 342 SE 2d 453, 458–9 (W.Va., 1986) considers whether an employee handbook issued by the employer can contain terms sufficient to constitute consideration:

> Courts in other jurisdictions have recently held that an employer may be bound by promises, express or implied, in employee handbooks or policy manuals with respect to job security and termination procedures.
>
> In cases where employees have brought breach of contract actions based on discharge without cause, courts have examined employee manuals looking for promises of job security.
>
> A policy manual that provides for job security grants an important, fundamental protection for workers.... If such a commitment is indeed made, obviously an employer should be required to honor it. When such a document, purporting to give job security, is distributed by the employer to a workforce, substantial injustice may result if that promise is broken ...
>
> In Woolley v. Hoffmann-La Roche, Inc., supra, the Supreme Court of New Jersey examined a personnel policy manual distributed to employees of a large corporate employer. The court concluded that a promise of job security in a policy manual could be viewed as an offer for a unilateral contract and that the employees' continuing to work, when they were under no obligation to continue, would constitute both an acceptance of the offer and the necessary consideration to make the employer's promise binding and enforceable ...
>
> Stating the proposition in general terms, some courts hold that at will employment status is not modified by personnel manuals where there are no promises by the employer that employment will continue for a definite period of time and no contractual or statutory limitations on the employer's right to terminate with or without cause.
>
> This Court has clearly recognized the traditional elements of contract formation. Before a contract can be formed, there must be an offer and an acceptance. The concept of unilateral contract, where one party makes a promissory offer and the other accepts by performing an act rather than by making a return promise, has also been recognized: "That an acceptance may be effected by silence accompanied by an act of the offeree which constitutes a performance of that requested by the offeror is well established."

Consideration is also an essential element of a contract.... Consideration has been defined as "some right, interest, profit, or benefit accruing to one party, or some forbearance, detriment, loss, or responsibility given, suffered, or undertaken by another." A benefit to the promisor or a detriment to the promisee is sufficient consideration for a contract.

Recognizing that a personnel manual may constitute a unilateral contract requires no radical departure from settled principles of contract law. At will employment status may be contractually modified, Bell v. South Penn Natural Gas Co., supra, either to establish a specific duration of the employment or to provide a measure of job security to covered workers. We agree with those courts that have found valuable consideration in the continued labor of workers who have in the past foregone their right to quit at any time. We conclude that a promise of job security contained in an employee handbook distributed by an employer to its employees constitutes an offer for a unilateral contract; and an employee's continuing to work, while under no obligation to do so, constitutes an acceptance and sufficient consideration to make the employer's promise binding and enforceable. (Citations omitted.)

5. Legality

A valid and enforceable contract must be formed for a legal purpose. If the subject matter of the agreement violates statutory law or public policy the court would be unable and unwilling to permit its provisions to be carried out. Even when all the other elements of a valid contract are present, if the subject matter of contract is illegal, no enforceable agreement can exist. There are two categories of illegality of contracts: *malum in se* and *malum prohibitum*.

Malum in se concerns contracts based on acts that are bad in and of themselves. They stem from actions that are generally considered morally reprehensible. Contracts to commit crimes such as prostitution, sale of children, and murder are considered *malum in se* and are entirely unenforceable.

Malum prohibitum encompasses actions that are minor violations of the law and are prohibited by statutory regulation. These contracts are unenforceable, but quasi-contractual relief may be available if the party can demonstrate that to deny the party would unjustly enrich the other party in the agreement. Gambling contrasts, where prohibited by law, are considered *malum prohitum*.

Sample Case

The court in *Benjamin v. Koeppel*, 650 NE 2d 829 (NY, 1995) distinguished between *malum in se* and *malum prohibitum* in determining that an attorney who had not complied with registration requirements could nonetheless recover payment for professional legal services rendered during the period of noncompliance:

> "Illegal contracts are, as a general rule, unenforceable." However, the violation of a statute that is merely *malum prohibitum* will not necessarily render a contract illegal and unenforceable. "If the statute does not provide expressly that its violation will deprive the parties of their right to sue on the contract, and the denial of relief is wholly out of proportion to the requirements of public policy * * * the right to recover will not be denied."
>
> Fee disputes involving persons who have failed to comply with licensing or registration requirements have spawned their own body of case law … " '[W]here the procuring of a license is merely for the purpose of raising revenue it would seem that acts performed without securing a license would be valid. But where the statute looks beyond the question of revenue and has for its purpose the protection of public health or morals or the prevention of fraud, a non-compliance with its terms would affect the legality of the business.' " Two other important tenets that have emerged from the case law are that fee forfeitures are disfavored and that such forfeitures may be particularly inappropriate where there are other regulatory sanctions for noncompliance. As this Court stated in *Charlebois v. Weller Assocs.*, the courts are especially skeptical of efforts by clients or customers to use public policy "as a sword for personal gain rather than a shield for the public good." (Citations omitted.)

6. Capacity

Capacity is the sixth element of every valid contract and refers to the party's legal ability to enter into a binding contractual relationship. The law presumes competence and the burden of proving incompetence is on the party claiming the right to avoid the contract.

A. Elements

In order to enter into a valid contract a party must:

1. Be of legal age and
2. must have mental competence established (depending on the jurisdiction) by

a. Cognitive test—ability to understand nature and consequences of transaction

b. Volitional test—whether person had ability to act reasonably with respect to transaction.

B. Sample Case

Conditions that render parties temporarily incompetent such as Alzheimers and alcoholism provide much fodder for litigation. The conditions themselves do not negate capacity. Rather the court must determine whether the person actually had capacity at the time they entered into the contract. *Gandy v. Ford*, 17 So.3d 189 (Miss. Ct. App. 2009) illustrates this point. The plaintiff participated in four transactions to convey real and personal property to the defendant. Bills of sale and a warranty deed were signed for the conveyance of the property. The plaintiff was an alcoholic, elderly, and was quite eccentric. However, witnesses testified that plaintiff was not drinking at the time that he entered the transactions. The Court concluded that the plaintiff was an individual affected by advanced age, ill health, and chronic drinking, but he clearly remembered the transactions in which he received compensation:

> Although we have reservations about the competency of Ford, due to his age, health condition, habitual drinking, and eccentricities, he was not adjudicated incompetent, nor did the chancellor find him to be incompetent. The chancellor stated in his judgment that "[a]lthough there may have been times due to his drinking or medical problems he was not of capacity to enter into a legal transaction[,] a general incapacity was not shown." ... Although Ford appeared to be somewhat confused at the hearing and had difficulty hearing, Ford testified that he remembered selling the property to Walter, and he remembered receiving $14,000 from Walter. Ford testified that he told Walter, at the time of the transaction, that it was not enough for the property, and he testified that he did not intend for the old tractor to be included in the sale. At trial, Ford lamented that "he would just have to live with it and die with it." Ford also remembered Garland Upton, the lawyer that accompanied Walter to Ford's home in order to notarize the 1992 warranty deed and bill of sale.

Contract Causes of Action

1. Breach of Contract

When one party fails to perform according to a contract, that party is in breach of the contract. If the other party has been damaged by that breach, the other party is entitled to remedies including monetary damages and specific performance.

A. Elements

1. Existence of a valid, enforceable contract and
2. breach of the terms of that contract
3. causing
4. damage to another party to the contract.

B. Sample Case

It can be especially difficult to determine whether a party has breached the terms of that contract when the obligation to perform is subject to conditions. This was the case in *Careau & Co. v. Security Pacific Business Credit*, 222 Cal. App. 3d 1371, 1388–89 (1990). In order to state a cause of action, the plaintiff must allege facts showing that each of the conditions have been satisfied:

> A cause of action for damages for breach of contract is comprised of the following elements: (1) the contract, (2) plaintiff's performance or excuse for nonperformance, (3) defendant's breach, and (4) the resulting damages to plaintiff. What plaintiffs have failed to do here is adequately allege the due satisfaction of several conditions precedent to the formation of a binding contract.
>
> Plaintiffs assert that the letter of August 25 sets forth the terms of a contractual commitment to provide financing. While they acknowledge that the letter contains some conditions, they argue that they have alleged sufficient facts to demonstrate, at least for pleading purposes, that each of such conditions has been satisfied, waived or excused. Defendants, on the other hand, argue that the letter is tentative and nothing more than an expression of intent subject to many conditions, the satisfaction of which plaintiffs have not alleged.
>
> On its face, the August 25 letter is a conditional agreement to provide financing if certain "conditions precedent" are met. The conditions listed are both specific and substantial....

Where contractual liability depends upon the satisfaction or performance of one or more conditions precedent, the allegation of such satisfaction or performance is an essential part of the cause of action. This requirement can be satisfied by allegations in general terms. It is sufficient for a plaintiff to simply allege that he has "duly performed all the conditions on his part." (Citations omitted.)

2. Breach of Express Contract Warranties

Express warranties are created by affirmative acts of the seller that are an affirmation of fact or promise made by the seller which relates to the goods and becomes part of the basis of the bargain. Except for professional opinions which can create a warranty, express warranties are based on factual statements rather than opinions. "Puffing" by sales personnel such as "You'll really enjoy this car" or "The dress looks marvelous on you" does not constitute a warranty.

A. Elements
1. Existence of an express warranty;
2. the goods or services provided did not comply with that warranty; and
3. the failure to comply with the warranty damaged another party.

B. Sample Case
In *Keith v. Buchanan*, 173 Cal. App. 3d 13 (1985), the court held that an express warranty was created, and that actual reliance on the seller's factual representation need not be shown by the buyer. The representation is presumed to be part of the basis of the bargain, and the burden is on the seller to prove that the representation was not a consideration inducing the bargain:

> California Uniform Commercial Code section 2313, regarding express warranties, was enacted in 1963 and consists of the official text of Uniform Commercial Code section 2-313 without change. (3) In deciding whether a statement made by a seller constitutes an express warranty under this provision, the court must deal with three fundamental issues. First, the court must determine whether the seller's statement constitutes an "affirmation of fact or promise" or "description of the goods" under California Uniform Commercial Code section 2313, subdivision (1)(a) or (b), or whether it is rather "merely the seller's opinion or commendation of the goods" under section 2313, subdivision (2). Second, assuming the court finds the language used susceptible to creation of a warranty, it must then be determined

whether the statement was "part of the basis of the bargain." Third, the court must determine whether the warranty was breached

A warranty relates to the title, character, quality, identity, or condition of the goods. The purpose of the law of warranty is to determine what it is that the seller has in essence agreed to sell. "Express warranties are chisels in the hands of buyers and sellers. With these tools, the parties to a sale sculpt a monument representing the goods. Having selected a stone, the buyer and seller may leave it almost bare, allowing considerable play in the qualities that fit its contours. Or the parties may chisel away inexactitudes until a well-defined shape emerges. The seller is bound to deliver, and the buyer to accept, goods that match the sculpted form....

"The determination as to whether a particular statement is an expression of opinion or an affirmation of a fact is often difficult, and frequently is dependent upon the facts and circumstances existing at the time the statement is made." (Willson v. Municipal Bond Co. (1936) 7 Cal.2d 144, 150 [59 P.2d 974].) Recent decisions have evidenced a trend toward narrowing the scope of representations which are considered opinion, sometimes referred to as "puffing" or "sales talk," resulting in an expansion of the liability that flows from broad statements of manufacturers or retailers as to the quality of their products. Courts have liberally construed affirmations of quality made by sellers in favor of injured consumers. It has even been suggested "that in an age of consumerism all seller's statements, except the most blatant sales pitch, may give rise to an express warranty."

Statements made by a seller during the course of negotiation over a contract are presumptively affirmations of fact unless it can be demonstrated that the buyer could only have reasonably considered the statement as a statement of the seller's opinion. Commentators have noted several factors which tend to indicate an opinion statement. These are (1) a lack of specificity in the statement made, (2) a statement that is made in an equivocal manner, or (3) a statement which reveals that the goods are experimental in nature. (Citations omitted.)

3. Breach of Implied Warranty of Merchantability

Article 2, Section 315 of the Uniform Commercial Code imposes a warranty of merchantability applies on all merchants as defined by the Code. Goods to be merchantable must at least: (a) pass without objection in the trade under the contract description; and (b) in the case of fungible goods, be of average quality within the description; and (c) be fit for the ordinary purposes for which such goods are used; (d) run, within the variations permitted by the agreement, of even kind, quality and quantity throughout each unit and among all units involved; (e) be adequately contained, packaged and labeled as the agreement may require; and (f) conform to the promises or affirmations of fact made on the container or label if any.

A. Elements

1. A sale of goods;
2. the seller was a merchant with respect to goods of that kind;
3. the goods were not "merchantable" at the time of sale;
4. the buyer provided the seller notice of the breach of warranty;
5. an economic loss or personal injury occurred as a result of the breach of warranty; and
6. the seller had not specifically excluded or modified the implied warranty.

B. Sample Case

The issue of what goods are not merchantable at the time of sale can be a difficult one to resolve. One issue is whether a specific defect must be shown. *Plas-Tex, Inc. v. US Steel Corp.*, 772 SW 2d 442, 443–4 (Tex, 1989) confronts that issue and notes that while a defect is required, the term "defect" has a different meaning for purposes of this warranty than it does in a strict liability case:

> Fiberex argues that the court of appeals erred in holding that goods must be defective before recovery will be allowed under an implied warranty of merchantability theory ("Goods to be merchantable must be at least such as are fit for the ordinary purposes for which such goods are used."). Fiberex contends that it need not show a defect in the goods, but instead it need only show that the goods were not merchantable, i.e., not fit for the ordinary purposes for which the goods are used.
>
> The majority of the courts of appeals that have considered this issue have concluded that proof of a defect is required. The overwhelming majority of jurisdictions also requires proof of a defect. We likewise hold that proof of a defect is required in an action for breach of implied warranty of merchantability under section.

The defect in an implied warranty of merchantability case is not the same as the defect in a strict products liability case. In the context of an implied warranty of merchantability case the word "defect" means a condition of the goods that renders them unfit for the ordinary purposes for which they are used because of a lack of something necessary for adequacy. In the area of strict products liability, however, the word "defect" means a condition of the product that renders it unreasonably dangerous Practitioners—as well as the courts—should exercise care to see that these terms are used precisely.

A plaintiff in an implied warranty of merchantability case has the burden of proving that the goods were defective at the time they left the manufacturer's or seller's possession. He must show that the goods were unfit for the ordinary purposes for which they are used because of a lack of something necessary for adequacy, i.e., because of a defect. A plaintiff does not, however, have to use direct or expert opinion evidence to show that the goods had a defect; he can instead meet his burden by using circumstantial evidence. To make a prima facie showing of a defect based solely on circumstantial evidence, Fiberex must present evidence that it handled and applied the resin properly.[5] Evidence of proper use of the goods together with a malfunction may be sufficient evidence of a defect. (Citations and footnotes omitted.)

4. Breach of Implied Warranty of Fitness for Particular Use

When the seller (or manufacturer) knows the buyer's particular use and the buyer relies on the seller's expertise or judgment in choosing the product an "implied warranty for fitness for a particular purpose" is created. In other words, the seller warranties that the product will be fit for the buyer's specific use. For example, the seller of a lawn trimmer that could not trim lawn grass would breach the implied warranty of merchantability, but if the buyer told the seller he needed a tool to trim heavy brush and relied on the seller's expertise in selling him the trimmer, the trimmer would have an implied warranty of fitness for trimming heavy brush.

A. Elements

1. Plaintiff bought the product from defendant;
2. at the time of purchase, defendant knew or had reason to know that plaintiff intended to use the product for a particular purpose;

3. at the time of purchase defendant knew or had reason to know that plaintiff was relying on defendant's skill and judgment to select or furnish a product that was suitable for the particular purpose;
4. plaintiff justifiably relied on defendant's skill and judgment;
5. the product was not suitable for the particular purpose;
6. plaintiff took reasonable steps to notify defendant within a reasonable time that the product was not suitable;
7. plaintiff was harmed; and
8. the failure of the product to be suitable was a substantial factor in causing plaintiff's harm.

B. Sample Case

It is not uncommon for a complaint arising from a person's use of a product to contain several causes of action including breach of implied warranty of merchantability and breach of implied warranty of fitness for a particular use. The two, however, are seldom compatible. The former is a warranty for suitability for the use ordinarily made of the product and the latter for a particular use, presumably outside of the ordinary use known to the seller. The court in *Lariviere v. Dayton Safety Ladder Co.*, 525 A. 2d 892 (RI, 1987) emphasizes this need for a particular use and that it be known to the seller:

> The defendant next asserts that plaintiff failed to introduce sufficient evidence to prove the existence of an implied warranty of fitness for a particular purpose.[3] The defendant points to the apparent absence of any evidence produced at trial to establish that the purchaser of the ladder expressed a particular use to defendant or that the purchaser relied on defendant's skill or judgment for selecting or furnishing the ladder. We agree.
>
> An implied warranty of fitness for a particular purpose arises when the seller has reason to know the buyer's particular purpose and that the buyer is relying on the seller's skill or judgment to furnish appropriate goods and the buyer relies on the seller's skill or judgment. *Keenan v. Cherry & Webb*, 47 R.I. 125, 128, 131 A. 309, 311 (1925). This court has distinguished between an implied warranty of merchantability and an implied warranty of a fitness for a particular purpose. In Keenan this court discussed section 15 of the Uniform Sales Act,[4] which contained nearly identical language to our current statutes on implied warranty of fitness for a particular purpose. Id. at 128, 131 A. at 310–11. The plaintiff alleged breach of an implied warranty of fitness for a particular purpose with regard to a fur coat.

Although the court held that the implied warranty of merchantability applied to the coat, the court went on to say that

> "[m]erchantability means that the article sold shall be of the general kind described and reasonably fit for the general purpose for which it shall have been sold. The buyer's particular purpose may be equivalent to nothing more than his general purpose, or it may relate to his more specific purpose. * * * [M]erchantability and fitness for a particular purpose may not be equivalent. * * * Under the Sales Act a dealer who sells articles which ordinarily are used in but one way impliedly warrants fitness for use in that particular way unless there is evidence to the contrary. This is only a warranty of merchantability." *Keenan*, 47 R.I. at 129, 131 A. at 311; see also *Scittarelli v. Providence Gas Co.*, 415 A.2d 1040, 1046 n. 4 (R.I. 1980).

As in *Keenan*, we find sufficient evidence for a jury to find breach of an implied warranty of merchantability. However, in this record there is no evidence that defendant had reason to know of a particular use to which the ladder would be put other than its ordinary use or that the purchaser of the ladder relied on Dayton's skill or judgment for selecting or furnishing the ladder. Therefore, we find that the trial justice erred in his denial of defendant's motion for a directed verdict on plaintiff's claim of breach of implied warranty of fitness for a particular purpose.

Contractual Remedies

1. Damages

1.1 Compensatory Damages

Compensatory damages are monetary awards designed to put the injured party in the same position he would have been in had the contract been in had the contract been completed as originally planned. The Court determines the amount of the monetary loss the injured party suffered because of the breach. These damages are meant to put the plaintiff in the same economic condition she would have been in if defendant had not breached.

A. Elements

Damages that:

1. Fairly compensate
2. for the injury actually sustained

3. as a result
4. of defendant's conduct.

B. Sample Case

Calculating damages can be a difficult task. Court frequently must look to more than one standard in determining what damages are "fair." The damages must be supported by evidence, but need not be mathematically certain. These points and others are made by the court in *VanVoorhees v. Dodge*, 679 A. 2d 1077 (Me.1996):

> Dodge next challenges the court's award of damages based on the breach of his contract with the VanVoorhees. The measure of recovery for defective or incomplete performance of a construction contract is the difference in value between the value of the performance contracted for and the value of the performance actually rendered. *Paine v. Spottiswoode*, 612 A.2d 235, 240 (Me.1992). This difference may be proved either by the diminution in market value or by the amount reasonably required to remedy the defect. Id. See also, *Kleinschmidt v. Morrow*, 642 A.2d 161, 165 (Me.1994) (approving calculation of compensatory damages as the difference between the contract price and the actual total cost to the homeowner of completing the home). The assessment of damages is the sole province of the fact-finder, *Banville v. Huckins*, 407 A.2d 294, 296 (Me.1979), and we will not disturb an award of damages unless there is no basis in the evidence for the award. *McGrath v. Hills*, 662 A.2d 215, 219 (Me.1995). "Although damages need not be proved to a mathematical certainty, an award must be supported by some evidence of the value of the property damaged or expenses incurred." *Currier v. Cyr*, 570 A.2d 1205, 1210 (Me.1990).
>
> In this case, the evidence presented at trial clearly supports the trial court's award of damages. The VanVoorhees presented testimony and documentary evidence that corroborated their claim that at the time of trial the cost of constructing their home was rapidly approaching the $300,000 mark. Exhibits and testimony revealed that prior to Dodge's dismissal the cost of construction was approaching $150,000, that after his termination the VanVoorhees incurred approximately another $144,000 in construction costs, and that they anticipated spending another $10,000 to complete the project. The evidence also supported the court's related conclusion that not all of the additional construction costs could be attributed to Dodge's breach because some

of these costs resulted from the VanVoorhees alteration of the construction plans. Thus, the court's damage award of $73,000 is consistent with the evidence.

1.2 Punitive Damages

Punitive, or exemplary, damages are monetary awards granted by a court for a breach of contract that involves very unusual circumstances. Exemplary damages are intended not only to compensate the injured party but to punish the breaching party. Punishment is not a usual aspect of contract law unless there is a statutory basis for the award under the state's law, although some courts allow recovery of punitive damages if the breach of contract was "tortious" or a tort such as fraud was used to induce a party to enter into the contract. In such cases, the punitive damages may be viewed as actually tethered to the tort, rather than the contract. Since punitive damages arise from the specific elements of a statute or from a related tort, no elements are set forth here.

Sample Case

As the court in *Morrow v. LA Goldschmidt Assoc., Inc.*, 492 NE 2d 181 (Ill, 1986) states, the demarcation between tort and contract is sometimes difficult to make, and occasionally, the conduct complained of can constitute both a breach of contract and a tort:

> At issue is whether counts VIII through XI of plaintiffs' complaint state a cause of action for wilful and wanton misconduct which would, if proved, support an award of punitive damages. Plaintiffs maintain that, in addition to their express and implied warranty claims, they have alleged "a separate tort of wilful and wanton misconduct" which would, if proved, justify an award of punitive damages. Defendants, however, contend that plaintiffs have failed to allege the existence of an independent tort for which punitive damages can be awarded. They argue that the allegations in counts VIII through XI, at most, amount to an intentional breach of contract for which punitive damages are not available....
>
> In support of their claim for punitive damages plaintiffs allege, inter alia, that defendants "inadequately supervised the construction" of the plaintiffs' homes; "knowingly employed incompetent contractors, subcontractors and/or agents who performed the actual construction" of the homes, or were incompetent themselves; and

"wantonly, willfully and/or recklessly failed to inspect" the homes or insure that the units were built "in a good and workmanlike manner and in accordance with the contract specifications." The complaint alleges that defendants' "wanton, willful and/or reckless conduct" is evidenced by their failure to install or to properly install a certain component of the floor-support system since such improper installation "is readily observed and could, and should have been detected by any competent supervisor/inspector familiar with the plans and specifications." Plaintiffs further allege that defendants were aware of the improperly constructed floor-support system as well as other enumerated defects, because similar defects were reported in another unit prior to the closings on plaintiffs' units, and because defendants were informed by various public officials of certain building code violations.... Finally, the complaint alleges that after defendants became aware of the defects in plaintiffs' units and other units in the complex, they "failed to inspect for similar defects and/or properly and adequately correct same."

Both defendants and plaintiffs agree that under Illinois law counts VIII through XI must be construed as alleging a tort in order to properly state a cause of action for punitive damages. As a general rule, punitive damages are not recoverable for breach of contract. The sole purpose of contract damages is to compensate the nonbreaching party, and punitive damages are not available even for a "wilful" breach of contract. The Restatement (Second) of Contracts explains the rule as follows:

> "The traditional goal of the law of contract remedies has not been compulsion of the promisor to perform his promise but compensation of the promisee for the loss resulting from breach. 'Willful' breaches have not been distinguished from other breaches, punitive damages have not been awarded for breach of contract, and specific performance has not been granted where compensation in damages is an adequate substitute for the injured party." Restatement (Second) of Contracts, ch. 16 (introductory note) (1979); see also E. Farnsworth, Contracts sec. 12.8, at 842 (1982).

The rule against awarding punitive damages for breach of contract has been applied to situations, like the present case, where homeowners have sued builders or contractors for construction defects. Courts traditionally have refused to award punitive damages in such cases where the allegations against the builder or contractor amounted to nothing more than a breach of contract.

An exception to the general rule that punitive damages are not recoverable for breach of contract is when the conduct causing the breach is also a tort for which punitive damages are recoverable. That is, punitive damages are recoverable "where the breach amounts to an independent tort and there are proper allegations of malice, wantonness or oppression."

Plaintiffs argue that the allegations in counts VIII through XI state a cause of action for the "tort" of "wilful and wanton misconduct." Defendants, however, argue that plaintiffs have not alleged a separate tort for which punitive damages are available. They note that the complaint does not allege that the defects in workmanship and construction caused personal injury or damage to property other than to the townhouse units themselves. As such, they argue that plaintiffs have incurred only "economic losses" for which there is no tort recovery.

The line of demarcation between tort and contract is sometimes difficult to make, and occasionally, the conduct complained of can constitute both a breach of contract and a tort. Nevertheless, this court held in *Moorman Manufacturing Co. v. National Tank Co.* (1982), 91 Ill.2d 69, that recovery for solely economic losses is more appropriately governed by contract, rather than tort, law principles.

1.3 Consequential Damages

Consequential damages are also called "indirect" damages. Consequential damages include losses buyer incurs which the supplier had reason to know at the time of contracting and which buyer could not reasonably have prevented. These include the recovery of lost revenues or profits suffered as a result of the breach. If the seller provides buyer a defective component for a product the buyer is manufacturing and that defect causes the buyer to lose sales to buyer's customers, the profit buyer would have made had he been able to ship compliant goods constitutes consequential damages. Other types of consequential damages include loss of production, opportunity costs, loss of anticipated cost savings, and lost good will.

A. Elements

Consequential damages are:

1. Indirect damages
2. buyer incurs

3. which the supplier has reason to know or are foreseeable at the time of contracting, and
4. which buyer could not reasonably have prevented that
5. result from defendant's breach.

B. Sample Case

In *Erlich v. Menezes*, 87 Cal.Rptr.2d 886, 981 P.2d 978, 21 Cal.4th 543 (1999), the court was called upon to determine whether emotional distress damages are recoverable for the negligent breach of a contract to construct a house. A jury awarded the homeowners the full cost necessary to repair their home as well as damages for emotional distress caused by the contractor's negligent performance. Since the contractor's negligence directly caused only economic injury and property damage, and breached no duty independent of the contract, the court concluded the homeowners may not recover damages for emotional distress based upon breach:

> In an action for breach of contract, the measure of damages is "the amount which will compensate the party aggrieved for all the detriment proximately caused thereby, or which, in the ordinary course of things, would be likely to result therefrom" (Civ. Code, § 3300), provided the damages are "clearly ascertainable in both their nature and origin" (Civ.Code, § 3301). In an action not arising from contract, the measure of damages is "the amount which will compensate for all the detriment proximately caused thereby, whether it could have been anticipated or not" (Civ.Code, § 3333).
>
> "Contract damages are generally limited to those within the contemplation of the parties when the contract was entered into or at least reasonably foreseeable by them at that time; consequential damages beyond the expectation of the parties are not recoverable. This limitation on available damages serves to encourage contractual relations and commercial activity by enabling parties to estimate in advance the financial risks of their enterprise." "In contrast, tort damages are awarded to [fully] compensate the victim for [all] injury suffered....
>
> In concluding emotional distress damages were properly awarded, the Court of Appeal correctly observed that "the same wrongful act may constitute both a breach of contract and an invasion of an interest protected by the law of torts." ...
>
> The Court of Appeal also noted that "[a] contractual obligation may create a legal duty and the breach of that duty may support an action in tort." This is true; however, conduct amounting to a breach of

contract becomes tortious only when it also violates a duty independent of the contract arising from principles of tort law. "An omission to perform a contract obligation is never a tort, unless that omission is also an omission of a legal duty." (Ibid., quoting Jones v. Kelly (1929) 208 Cal. 251, 255, 280 P. 942.) ...

Plaintiffs theory of tort recovery is that mental distress is a foreseeable consequence of negligent breaches of standard commercial contracts. However, foreseeability alone is not sufficient to create an independent tort duty. " 'Whether a defendant owes a duty of care is a question of law. Its existence depends upon the foreseeability of the risk and a weighing of policy considerations for and against imposition of liability.' Because the consequences of a negligent act must be limited to avoid an intolerable burden on society, the determination of duty 'recognizes that policy considerations may dictate a cause of action should not be sanctioned no matter how foreseeable the risk.' " (Ibid, fn. omitted.) "[T]here are clear judicial days on which a court can foresee forever and thus determine liability but none on which that foresight alone provides a socially and judicially acceptable limit on recovery of damages for [an] injury." In short, foreseeability is not synonymous with duty; nor is it a substitute.

The question thus remains: is the mere negligent breach of a contract sufficient? The answer is no. (Citations omitted.)

1.4 Liquidated Damages

Liquidated damages are reasonable damages that the parties have agreed to in the contract itself. Liquidated damages are specified by the parties it if would be difficult or impossible to compute compensatory damages because of the uncertain nature of the contract or subject matter. The elements of liquidated damages vary somewhat from jurisdiction to jurisdiction, but the ones given here are fairly standard.

A. Elements

Liquidated damages will be enforced if:

1. Actual damages must be difficult to quantify
2. the amount is agreed upon and set in advance
3. the amount is be reasonable
4. the damages are compensation, not a penalty
5. the damages are exclusive (i.e., the only remedy available).

B. Sample Case

Whether a contract provision is for liquidated damages or a penalty is not determined by the label the parties put on it. The court in *Southeastern Land Fund, Inc. v. Real Estate World, Inc.*, 227 SE 2d 340 (Ga, 1976) explained:

> The contract provides: "In the event purchaser defaults hereunder after having paid the additional earnest money [$45,000] ... seller shall be entitled to retain all original earnest money [$5,000] paid hereunder as partial liquidated damages occasioned by such default, to collect the proceeds of the indebtedness owed by purchaser as additional earnest money as further partial liquidated damages occasioned by such default, and to pursue any and all remedies available to him at law or equity including, but not limited to, an action for specific performance of this contract."
>
> If, as the Court of Appeals found, this provision in the contract was a penalty, or is unenforceable as a liquidated damages provision, then the buyer can prevail in asserting a defense to the enforcement of the $45,000 note. If, on the other hand, this is a proper provision for liquidated damages, then the seller can prevail in enforcing the note. Of course, whether a provision represents liquidated damages or a penalty does not depend upon the label the parties place on the payment but rather depends on the effect it was intended to have and whether it was reasonable. Where the parties do not undertake to estimate damages in advance of the breach and instead provide for both a forfeiture (penalty) plus actual damages, the amount, even though called liquidated damages, is instead an unenforceable penalty....
>
> Depending on the language used in the contract and the discernible intent of the parties, the existence of an earnest money provision in a real estate sales contract can have one of three effects in the case of a breach by the buyer. First, the money could be considered as partial payment of any actual damages which can be proven as the result of the buyer's breach. Second, the money could be applied as part payment of the purchase price in the enforcement of the contract in a suit for specific performance by the seller. Third, the money could be liquidated damages for breach of the contract by the buyer. A provision for earnest money cannot, however, under Georgia law, be used for all three results as we shall see....
>
> Of course, Georgia law also recognizes that the parties may agree in their contract to a sum to liquidate their damages. Code Ann. § 20-

1402 provides: "Damages are given as compensation for the injury sustained. If the parties agree in their contract what the damages for a breach shall be, they are said to be liquidated, and unless the agreement violates some principle of law, *the parties are bound thereby.*" (Emphasis supplied.) See also Code Ann. §20-1403.

In deciding whether a contract provision is enforceable as liquidated damages, the court makes a tripartite inquiry to determine if the following factors are present:

"First, the injury caused by the breach must be difficult or impossible of accurate estimation; second, the parties must intend to provide for damages rather than for a penalty; and third, the sum stipulated must be a reasonable pre-estimate of the probable loss."

Another feature implicit in the concept of liquidated damages in addition to the above factors is that both parties are bound by their agreement. A non-breaching party who has agreed to accept liquidated damages cannot elect after a breach to take actual damages should they prove greater than the sum specified. The breaching party cannot complain that the actual damages are less than those specified as liquidated damages. The liquidated damages become the "maximum as well as the minimum sum that can be collected."

The problem that this particular contract provision raises is whether the seller has tried to retain a right to elect to sue for actual damages rather than liquidated damages and in so doing has rendered the purported liquidated damages provision unenforceable. This particular paragraph in the contract provides for "partial" liquidated damages. This can be read that the parties intended for the two "partial" liquidated damages provisions to comprise the whole. However, it is also susceptible to the construction that these two partial liquidated damages were not intended to be the sole damages remedy for this particular breach of contract.

The contract provision that included the retention of the right to elect specific performance as an alternative remedy to damages poses no problem in our analysis as it does not render a valid liquidated damages provision unenforceable....

We think a correct resolution of this issue must be found in the doctrine that "in cases of doubt the courts favor the construction which holds the stipulated sum to be a penalty, and limits the recovery to the amount of damages actually shown, rather than a liquidation of the damages." If the parties intended for the $5,000 and the $45,000 to represent the "maximum as well as the minimum sum that can be collected," from the buyer's breach, the contract should have made it clear that this was the effect intended by these provisions. It is the lingering ambiguity inherent in these provisions of the contract that persuades us to affirm the result reached by the Court of Appeals in construing the contract. (Citations and footnotes omitted.)

2. Specific Performance

Specific performance is a court order requiring the breaching party to perform exactly what she promised under the contract. The subject matter of the contract must be unique. The purchase real property is usually presumed to be unique. If the seller of real property breaches the sales contract, it is normally not sufficient to award damages such as the difference in value between the property subject to the contract and another property. The specific elements vary from jurisdiction to jurisdiction. The elements provided here are from California cases.

A. Elements

Specific performance of a contract may be decreed whenever:

1. Its terms are sufficiently definite;
2. consideration is adequate;
3. there is substantial similarity of the requested performance to the contractual terms;
4. there is mutuality of remedies; and
5. there is inadequate remedy at law, i.e., money damages are not an adequate remedy for the breach.

B. Sample Case

Specific performance is an equitable remedy so the trial court has a great deal of discretion in determining whether the remedy yields an equitable result. However, as the court notes in *EMF Gen. Contr. Corp. v. Bisbee*, 6 AD 3d 45, 51–52 (NY, 2004) the discretion is not unlimited:

> The elements of a cause of action for specific performance of a contract are that the plaintiff substantially performed its contractual obligations and was willing and able to perform its remaining obligations, that defendant was able to convey the property, and that there was no adequate remedy at law....
>
> [T]he trial court concluded, in its position as a court of equity, that both parties came to court with unclean hands, and that the relief of

specific performance would provide a windfall to EMF in view of the enormous increase in the value of the property. We conclude, to the contrary, that no equitable consideration warrants the denial of specific performance here.

Generally, the equitable remedy of specific performance is routinely awarded in contract actions involving real property, on the premise that each parcel of real property is unique. The court has discretion to deny such relief "as equity and justice seem to demand in the light of the circumstances of each case," and the available equitable defenses include serious unfairness, undue hardship, and laches, or unreasonable prejudicial delay. But, "the court's discretion to grant or deny specific performance of a contract for the sale of realty is not unlimited; unless the court finds that granting a decree of specific performance would be a drastic or harsh remedy, or work injustice, the court must direct specific performance"

At the outset, it bears emphasis that there was no unfairness in the deal itself; the contract was fair when entered into. Yet, the passage of time before this action was commenced and the property's increase in value require consideration of a number of rules and cases.

A common fact pattern in which specific performance is denied is discussed in Dobbs's treatise on the law of remedies:

"The speculating land buyer. One of the most common patterns in denying specific performance is the case in which the buyer has contracted in a way that permits him to postpone purchase for a long period for which he has paid no option price. For instance, the buyer may find title defects which give him the right to seek a cure and delay performance accordingly. Or he may obtain extensions for various reasons. If the seller concludes that the buyer has abandoned the contract or breached it and refuses to perform, the buyer may wait for long period before suing for specific performance in order to determine whether the land will increase in value. Any of these devices may be used by buyers as means of getting what in effect is a free option; if the price rises, the buyer will eventually sue for specific performance. If it does not, the buyer drops 53*53 the deal. Many of the doctrines—unfairness, hardship, laches— are invoked in just such cases to defeat the buyer's attempt to get a free ride by denying specific performance." (3 Dobbs, Remedies, supra at 302–303.)

In other words, where it is established that the buyer has made excuses in order to delay closing on the contract, with an actual purpose of waiting to see whether to enforce the contract depending upon whether the market value of the subject property increases or decreases, the courts will not grant specific performance.

3. Rescission

We have all had times when we would like to roll back time and "unwind" something we have done. The unwinding of a contract is possible through the remedy of rescission. When a court grants the remedy of rescission the parties are put back in the position they would have had if the contract had never been formed. Grounds for rescission include fraud, mutual mistake, false representations, and impossibility of performance. This list is not exhaustive. As with other remedies, the elements vary somewhat from jurisdiction to jurisdiction.

A. Elements

1. Making of a contract;
2. existence of fraud, mutual mistake false representations, impossibility of performance, or other ground for rescission or cancellation;
3. that the party seeking rescission
   a. has rescinded the contract and
   b. notified the other party to the contract of such rescission;
4. if the moving party has received benefits from the contract, it should further allege an offer to restore these benefits to the party furnishing them; and
5. the moving party has no adequate remedy at law.

B. Sample Case

A complaint filed by a Jewish religious community seeking rescission of a contract of employment of defendant as its rabbi provided a forum for examination of the appropriateness of the remedy in *Jewish Center of Sussex Cty. v. Whale*, 86 N.J. 619, 432 A. 2d 521 (1981):

> The trial court granted plaintiff's motion for summary judgment, ruling that as a matter of law defendant's failure to disclose to plaintiff his prior criminal record and disbarment from the practice of law amounted to fraudulent concealment.... After discovering these additional facts about defendant, plaintiff's Board of Trustees resolved on April 17, 1978 to rescind the employment contract and so notified defendant in a letter of the same date. Promptly thereafter plaintiff filed suit to rescind the contract and enjoin defendant from entering upon plaintiff's property or performing any functions as rabbi of the

Jewish Center. The verified complaint alleged both fraudulent misrepresentation and fraudulent concealment....

In support of his contention that plaintiff failed to demonstrate that it suffered damage, defendant points out that not only is he a fully qualified rabbi, but prior to the disclosure of his past indiscretions he had performed his rabbinical duties for four months in a manner completely satisfactory to the congregation. He contends that inasmuch as plaintiff failed to prove actual damage, its motion for summary judgment based on fraud must fail. This argument misconstrues the nature of equitable fraud. Actual loss in the financial sense is not required before equity may act; equity looks not to the loss suffered by the victim but rather to the unfairness of allowing the perpetrator to retain a benefit unjustly conferred. See W. Prosser, The Law of Torts 732 (4th ed. 1971). Thus, in awarding an equitable remedy like rescission, the claimant's actual damage is only one factor to be considered. Id. at 733.

Based on this analysis, we hold that the trial court properly granted the remedy of rescission. The defendant's misrepresentation hindered plaintiff's opportunity to discover an episode in his past that reflected unfavorably upon his moral integrity. Because of the unique moral and spiritual relationship between clergy and congregation, revelation of this episode surely would have adversely affected defendant's employment opportunity. Hence, defendant gained an unfair advantage by virtue of this misrepresentation. Furthermore, because of the qualitative nature of the services that defendant was hired to render, mere legal damages cannot make the plaintiff whole. The equitable remedy of rescission is appropriate in this case.

4. Reformation

While rescission "unwinds" a contract, reformation is an equitable remedy that rewrites the contract in a way that better expresses the intentions of the parties. Contracts can be reformed to fix mistakes made in reducing the parties' intentions to writing, not mistakes the parties made in coming to an agreement.

A. Elements

1. A written agreement;
2. a. A mutual mistake or
   b. fraud, or

   c. misrepresentation by a party and a mistake by the other party;

3. The language intended by the parties;
4. A showing of how the parties' performance under the reformed agreement will be affected;
5. The lack of adequate remedy at law.

B. Sample Case

In *Lemoge Electric v. County of San Mateo*, 46 Cal.2d 659, 297 P. 2d 638 (1956) a licensed electrical contractor, brought an action for reformation of a contract with defendant. When defendant announced that the bids of other contractors ranged substantially higher than its bid, plaintiff realized that some material mistake had been made in the preparation of its bid. When the mistake was discovered plaintiff immediately notified defendant and furnished it with work sheets and adding machine tapes showing the error. With knowledge of the mistake and what caused it, defendant accepted the erroneous bid and attempted to bind plaintiff to the consequences of the error. Plaintiff requested that the bid be adjusted to compensate for the error, but defendant refused to allow the correction. It was alleged that the mistake was of such a material and fundamental character that there has been no meeting of the minds of plaintiff and defendant. The court did not allow reformation:

> Once opened and declared, plaintiff's bid was in the nature of an irrevocable option, a contract right of which defendant could not be deprived without its consent unless the requirements for rescission were satisfied. Plaintiff then had the right to rescind, and it could have done so without incurring any liability on its bond. But plaintiff did not rescind. Instead, according to statements made by plaintiff in its briefs and at oral argument, it entered into a formal contract with defendant on the terms specified in the bid and proceeded to perform the required work. It is not claimed that defendant at any time agreed to pay plaintiff an amount greater than the sum designated in the bid. There was no element of fraud or failure to disclose; neither party knew of the error until after the bids were opened, and both parties knew of it before the bid was accepted or the formal contract was executed. The facts alleged do not entitle plaintiff to reformation, and, in view of other facts admitted by plaintiff, there is no reasonable possibility that the complaint can be amended to state a cause of action on any theory.

> The purpose of reformation is to correct a written instrument in order to effectuate a common intention of both parties which was incor-

rectly reduced to writing. In order for plaintiff to obtain this relief there must have been an understanding between the parties on all essential terms, otherwise there would be no standard to which the writing could be reformed. incorporates this principle by providing that, under specified conditions, a written contract which does not truly express "the intention of the parties" may be revised so as to set forth "that intention." ... [T]his language refers to a single intention which is entertained by both parties.

Reformation may be had for a mutual mistake or for the mistake of one party which the other knew or suspected, but in either situation the purpose of the remedy is to make the written contract truly express the intention of the parties. Where the failure of the written contract to express the intention of the parties is due to the inadvertence of both of them, the mistake is mutual and the contract may be revised on the application of the party aggrieved. When only one party to the contract is mistaken as to its provisions and his mistake is known or suspected by the other, the contract may be reformed to express a single intention entertained by both parties. Although a court of equity may revise a written instrument to make it conform to the real agreement, it has no power to make a new contract for the parties, whether the mistake be mutual or unilateral. As we have seen it is not alleged that defendant ever agreed to pay plaintiff an amount greater than the sum designated in the bid, and the complaint therefore does not state facts entitling plaintiff to reformation. (Citations omitted.)

Equitable Causes of Action as Contract Alternatives

1. Promissory Estoppel

This cause of action protects a party who relies on someone else's promise to their detriment when they cannot show all the elements of a valid, enforceable contract. It differs from equitable estoppel in that promissory relates to promises to be fulfilled in the future and equitable estoppel relates to actions/statements about existing or past facts/actions. In most cases, courts avoid injustice by awarding the plaintiff an amount consistent with the value of the promise. Some cases award the plaintiff only an amount necessary to compensate for the actual economic loss. Promissory estoppel can also be raised as a defense.

A. Elements

1. A clear and definite promise
2. made with the intent to induce a particular action
3. justifiable reliance on the promise by the other party
4. which reliance was substantial and of a definite and substantial character and
5. enforcing the promise will serve the best interest of justice.

B. Sample Case

In *Hoffman v. Red Owl Stores, Inc.* 26 Wis.2d 683, 133 N.W.2d 267 (1965) the plaintiffs relied upon the defendant's promises including one that they could purchase a franchise for a promised amount. The plaintiffs relied upon that amount and took the necessary steps to obtain the amount so the store could be purchased. The precise terms of the contract were never established, therefore the plaintiffs could not sue for breach of contract. The court took the opportunity to adopt the Restatement's version of promissory estoppel:

> While it was not necessary to the disposition of the Lazarus Case to adopt the promissory-estoppel rule of the Restatement, we are squarely faced in the instant case with that issue. Not only did the trial court frame the special verdict on the theory of sec. 90 of Restatement, 1 Contracts, but no other possible theory has been presented to or discovered by this court which would permit plaintiffs to recover. Of other remedies considered that of an action for fraud and deceit seemed to be the most comparable. An action at law for fraud, however, cannot be predicated on unfulfilled promises unless the promisor possessed the present intent not to perform. Here, there is no evidence that would support a finding that Lukowitz made any of the promises, upon which plaintiffs' complaint is predicated, in bad faith with any present intent that they would not be fulfilled by Red Owl.
>
> Many courts of other jurisdictions have seen fit over the years to adopt the principle of promissory estoppel, and the tendency in that direction continues. As Mr. Justice MCFADDIN, speaking in behalf of the Arkansas court, well stated, that the development of the law of promissory estoppel "is an attempt by the courts to keep remedies abreast of increased moral consciousness of honesty and fair representations in all business dealings."
>
> ... Use of the word "estoppel" to describe a doctrine upon which a party to a lawsuit may obtain affirmative relief offends the traditional

concept that estoppel merely serves as a shield and cannot serve as a sword to create a cause of action. However, the latter term is still in almost universal use by the courts because of the lack of a better substitute. The same is also true of the wide use of the term "promissory estoppel." We have employed its use in this opinion not only because of its extensive use by other courts but also since a more-accurate equivalent has not been devised.

Because we deem the doctrine of promissory estoppel, as stated in sec. 90 of Restatement, 1 Contracts, is one which supplies a needed tool which courts may employ in a proper case to prevent injustice, we endorse and adopt it.

The court established a three-question test that must be answered in the affirmative for parties to rely upon the promissory estoppel doctrine. Two of the questions are jury questions: (1) Was the promise one which the promisor should reasonably expect to induce action or forbearance of a definite and substantial character on the part of the promisee? (2) Did the promise induce such action or forbearance? The third is a policy decision to be made by the court—Can injustice be avoided only by enforcement of the promise? In *Hoffman* the court found promissory estoppel was proper for the plaintiffs to recover from the defendants.

2. Equitable Estoppel

This doctrine protects an individual from being harmed by another party's voluntary conduct. This conduct may be silence, action or concealment of material facts. Equitable estoppel can be distinguished from promissory estoppel by the fact that it is relying upon a present or past act wherein promissory estoppel relies upon someone's promise to do something in the future. It may also be raised as a defense.

A. Elements
1. Representation by a defendant to plaintiff of a material fact.
2. Representation is contrary to the condition of affairs later asserted by defendant.
3. Plaintiff relies upon representation.
4. Plaintiff suffers detriment by a change in position as a result of the representation and reliance.

B. Sample Case
In *Bowers Window and Door Co., Inc. v. Dearman* 539 So2d 1309 (Miss. 1989), Dearman sought specific performance of an oral contract of employ-

ment or damages for breach of that contract. The court held there was no contract to breach due to the Statute of Frauds and the plaintiffs argued for relief based on equitable estoppel. The defendant objected to the lower court's granting that relief as a means of avoiding the consequences of the Statute of Frauds.

> Bowers does not challenge the chancellor's finding that there were not sufficient writings to bring the employment contract into compliance with the statute of frauds, and for good reason. The chancellor found the writings offered at trial to be insufficient under the statute because there is no written confirmation of the length of employment. Clearly, the length of employment is a substantial term which must be included in a writing being offered to show a contract of employment for a definite term in order for the writing to satisfy the requirement of the statute. Given, therefore, that the writings at issue contains no such reference, the chancellor was correct in concluding that the statute's requirement of a writing was not satisfied in this case.
>
> It becomes necessary, therefore, to consider whether the chancellor erred in applying the doctrine of equitable estoppel to bar Bowers from asserting the statute as a complete defense. That the doctrine of equitable estoppel is a recognized exception to the statue of frauds is established by the case law of this State. Bowers argues that this doctrine has never been held to be an exception to the statute of frauds in employment contract cases; that our prior cases applying the doctrine as an exception have not dealt with subsection (d) of § 15-3-1. However, this argument is contrary to established case law.
>
> In *Shogyo Intern. v. First Nat. Bank of Clarksdale*, 475 So.2d 425, 428 (Miss. 1985), this Court, while finding the statue of frauds inapplicable, held that even were it applicable, "the doctrine of equitable estoppel would take this case outside of the statute of frauds." The *Shogyo* opinion relied for this statement on *PMZ Oil Co. v. Lucroy*, 449 So.2d 201 (Miss. 1984). There this Court held rather clearly that "[e]quitable estoppel ... is a well-established exception to our statute of frauds. Our cases have repeatedly held that, where the elements of equitable estoppel are present, the statute of frauds constitutes no bar to enforcement of that which a party has agreed." 449 So.2d at 206.
>
> Admittedly neither Shogyo nor PMZ involved employment contracts governed by § 15-3-1(d), but in neither case did the Court remotely suggest that the doctrine of equitable estoppel could only be asserted as an exception in certain classes of cases where the statute of frauds is asserted. To the contrary, the Court quite clearly held that

the doctrine may be pled as an exception in any case where the statute is asserted as a defense. (Citations omitted.)

However the court found that while the plaintiff changed his position in reliance on the conduct of defendant, he did not show he suffered a detriment as a result because all plaintiff suffered was leaving an at-will job.

3. Unjust Enrichment

Unjust enrichment is an equitable cause of action that states no individual should be able to profit at another's expense without making restitution for the reasonable value of the benefits that were unfairly obtained. This doctrine can govern many situations wherein a quasi-contract is present. As noted by the court in the sample case, actions brought upon theories of unjust enrichment, quasi contract, contracts implied in law, and quantum meruit are essentially the same.

A. Elements
1. A benefit conferred on defendant
   a. by plaintiff
   b. with the expectation of compensation;
2. Knowledge, acceptance and actual benefit by defendant;
3. Retention of the benefit under circumstances where it would be unjust to do so without payment.

B. Sample Case

In *Paschall's, Inc. v. Dozier*, 407 SW 2d 150 (Tenn, 1966) the complainant furnished certain materials and labor used in the construction of an addition to the defendant's house at the request of defendant's children, both of whom lived in the house. The complainant had attempted to collect the debt from one child, who filed bankruptcy. The complainant commenced an action to secure a mechanic's lien on the defendants' property and to recover a personal judgment against the defendant for the value of the labor and materials furnished. The defendant argued that the complaint on its face showed that there was no special contract with the defendants and that the complainant had lost its right to a mechanic's lien. The appellate court held that privity was not required for equitable causes of action:

> The law recognizes two distinct types of implied contracts; namely, contracts implied in fact and contracts implied in law, commonly referred to as quasi contracts. The distinction between the two has been

explicitly stated by the Court of Appeals in Weatherly v. American Agr. 154*154 Chemical Co., 16 Tenn.App. 613, 65 S.W.2d 592:

> "Contracts implied in fact arise under circumstances which, according to the ordinary course of dealing and common understanding of men, show a mutual intention to contract. Such an agreement may result as a legal inference from the facts and circumstances of the case. * * * 'Contracts implied in law, or more appropriately, quasi or construction contracts, are a class of obligations which are imposed or created by law without the assent of the party bound, on the ground that they are dictated by reason and justice * * *.'"

Actions brought upon theories of unjust enrichment, quasi contract, contracts implied in law, and quantum meruit are essentially the same. Courts frequently employ the various terminology interchangeably to describe that class of implied obligations where, on the basis of justice and equity, the law will impose a contractual relationship between parties, regardless of their assent thereto.

It is well established that want of privity between parties is no obstacle to recovery under quasi contract.

The apparent reason is that such contracts are not based upon the intention of the parties but are obligations created by law. They are founded on the principle that a party receiving a benefit desired by him, under circumstances rendering it inequitable to retain it without making compensation, must do so. (Citations omitted.)

4. Quasi-Contractual Remedies: *Quantum meriut* and *Quantum valebant*

When a plaintiff is successful in an equitable cause of action as an alternative to a contract cause of action, the court must determine what damages are equitable. There are basically three measures of damages: the amount by which the defendant was unjustly enriched, the amount that the goods or services, the amount lost by the plaintiff, and the value of the property or services. While these are closely related, they are not the same and different measures can lead to widely different results.

Take for example the hypothetical of a company that charges $1,000 to install landscaping. Once installed the landscaping raises the value of a house by $1,500. The cost to the landscaper of the shrubs and the labor to install the shrubs is $700. The landowner does the landscaping under conditions that do not satisfy the elements of a contract, but do satisfy the elements of a cause of action for equitable relief. If damages are measured by the amount the home-owner was enriched, the damages are $1,500. If they are measured by the value of the landscaping the damages are $1,000. If they are measured by the loss to the landscaper, the damages are $700. *Quantum meruit* means the value of services rendered. *Quantum valebant* denotes the value of property received.

Sample Case

The various theories for measuring equitable damages are often conflated. The court in *Iowa Waste Systems, Inc. v. Buchanan County*, 617 NW 2d 23, 28–9 (Iowa, 2000) discusses the historical basis for unjust enrichment and *quanum meriut* while distinguishing the two:

> Iowa Waste first claims it was denied equitable relief from the costs it incurred in continuing to perform certain leachate measures after the termination of the operating agreement. Iowa Waste blurs two distinct theories of recovery, *quantum meruit* and unjust enrichment, as its basis for recovery. However despite the years of inseparably connecting these two terms, the two terms are not only markedly different, but not even rooted in the same legal genre. In order to appropriately address both theories we must delve into their respective historical underpinnings and pinpoint where the two theories diverge.
>
> The antiquated term *quantum meruit* literally means "as much as he deserved" and was historically employed in seeking compensation for agreed upon services under the common law writ of assumpsit (meaning "he undertook or promised"). Drake v. Block, 247 Iowa 517, 522, 74 N.W.2d 577, 580 (1956); Distinguishing Quantum Meruit, 71 Fla.B.J. at 88 n. 3. The common writ of assumpsit was not grounded in modern contract law but was simply a remedy designed to hold persons liable for promises not made under the King's seal—whether expressly stated, implied by their actions, or where no promise existed but justice required the at-law imposition of a judicially-created fictional promise. The term *quantum meruit* was pled under the common writ of assumpsit in those situations where services were performed based upon actions implying mutual assent and the party receiving the services refused to pay for them, whereas unjust enrichment, although still pled under the common writ of assumpsit, was utilized in those situations where there was no assent but a promise was equitably imputed to serve justice. The likely historical source of confusion between the two terms lies in their mutual employment under the general writ of assumpsit. However, with the advent of

modern contract law, the two terms diverged and no longer fell under the same general cause of action. Rather, *quantum meruit* became grounded in the realm of pure contract, whereas unjust enrichment was placed in the equitable sphere of quasi contract.

In modern contract law, there have traditionally been two types of contracts—express and implied. "When the parties manifest their agreement by words, the contract is said to be express." When there "is merely a tacit promise, one that is inferred in whole or in part from expressions other than words on the part of the promisor" it is said to be implied in fact. Thus, the antiquated term *quantum meruit* is actually used to denote a particular subclass of implied-in-fact contracts—an implied-in-fact contract to pay for services rendered. Recovery, therefore, on a claim of *quantum meruit* is guided by all present notions of contract law. True to its contractual roots, one may recover under a claim of *quantum meruit*, or more accurately a breach of an implied-in-fact contract, for the reasonable value of the services provided and the market value of the materials furnished.

Unjust enrichment on the other hand is not grounded in contract law but rather is a remedy of restitution. As it is not grounded in pure contract law such remedies are often referred to as quasi contracts or implied-in-law contracts.

A quasi-contractual obligation is one that is created by law for reasons of justice, without any expression of assent and sometimes even against a clear expression of dissent. If this is true, it would be better not to use the word "contract" at all. Contracts are formed by expressions of assent. Quasi contracts quite otherwise. The legal relations between contractors are dependent upon the interpretation of their expressions of assent. In quasi contract the relations of the parties are not dependent on such interpretations.

Unjust enrichment is the modern designation for the doctrine of quasi contracts or contracts implied in law. Damages under a claim of unjust enrichment are limited to the value of what was inequitably retained. (Citations omitted.)

Defenses

Promissory and equitable estoppel, discussed above, can both be raised as defenses as well as causes of action. In addition, the following defenses are commonly raised.

1. Duress

Duress is a defense for someone who is claiming a contract is not valid and, therefore, the individual should not be held responsible. In essence the party raising the defense is attempting to note that there was truly intent to enter into a contract. Duress results from threatening or causing actual physical harm to someone so that they enter into a contract, threatening or causing economic harm and psychological threats. The standard for determining duress is judged by how a reasonable person in similar circumstances would react. Because the threats must be wrongful, normal negotiations in the setting of terms of the contract do not constitute duress. For example, while it may cause the other party stress, stating, "If you do not sign this contract, I will take my business elsewhere" does not constitute duress when the party making the statement has the legal right to do business elsewhere.

A. Elements

1. A wrongful threat
2. by one party
3. intended to induce action by the other party
4. reasonably causes other party to take that action.

B. Sample Case

In *Lebeck v. Lebeck*, 881 P.2d 727 (N.M. 1994) the trial court found that a wife's claim of duress (among other defenses) was not sufficient to challenge a prenuptial agreement contract. The court held that a lawful demand to do what the demanding party has the right to do (in this case, not marry the wife if she does not sign the contract) is not sufficient to claim duress nor does a threat to do a legal act or subject the party to the legal consequences of a refusal constitute duress:

> In the present case, Wife claims that she signed the agreement as a result of undue influence, coercion, overreaching, and misrepresentations exerted by Husband. She offers as proof of this claim the fact that she wanted to marry to "legitimize" her daughter, so when Husband presented her with the agreement he had drafted several days prior to the wedding and told her he would not marry her without such an agreement being in place, she felt she had to sign it.
>
> The fact that Husband personally drafted the agreement does not indicate that the agreement was unfair or improper, particularly where, as here, Wife had it reviewed by independent counsel. Neither is the

short amount of time between executing the agreement and the date of the wedding sufficient to demonstrate that Husband was exercising undue influence, coercion, or overreaching. "The mere shortness of the time interval between the presentation of the premarital agreement and the date of the wedding is insufficient alone to permit a finding of duress or undue influence." We thus conclude that the short time interval and Husband's statement that he would not marry without a prenuptial agreement are not sufficient in themselves to compel a finding that the agreement was unfair.

Wife further claims that Husband's actions forced her to sign the agreement under duress. We are not persuaded. A lawful demand or a threat to do that which the demanding party has a right to demand is not sufficient to support a claim of duress. "A threat to do a legal act or subject the party to the legal consequences of a refusal to make an agreement, is not duress...." (Citations omitted.)

2. Fraud

Fraud may be raised as a defense to a contract or contract alternative cause of action. A party can avoid the contract because of a lack of intent or fulfill the contract when induced to enter the contract through fraud. Silence can constitute a false statement when there is a duty to disclose. There are two kinds of contractual fraud 1) fraud in the execution relates to the nature of the agreement being entered and 2) fraud in the inducement which relates to the party's motivation to enter into the contract. See "11. Fraud and Misrepresentation" in "Intentional Torts" for elements and a sample case.

3. Misrepresentation

When one party makes a false statement to another party to induce that party to enter into a contract, the induced party may raise misrepresentation. There are different types of misrepresentation in contract law: 1. fraudulent misrepresentation occurs when one party intentionally deceives the innocent party. 2. negligent misrepresentation occurs when one party makes a statement while having no reasonable basis on which to make it. 3. innocent misrepresentation occurs when one party makes a false statement to the other party without having knowledge that the statement is false. The defense of misrepresentation may make the contract voidable. See "11. Fraud and Misrepresentation" in "Intentional Torts" for elements and a sample case.

4. Undue Influence

Undue influence is a defense raised in contract actions that claims outside pressures negated the free will of the contracting party, so that the party lacked the necessary mental capacity for a valid contract. It raises the question of whether an individual is acting freely. The law generally regards one party as "dominant." However, this does not just mean that one party has more resources, exercises its leverage, or negotiates better than the other. The advantage being reference is one that rises from a special relationship between one party and the other, for example, an attorney-client relationship, doctor-patient relationship, or caregiver-dependent person relationship.

A. Elements

1. A party who is dominant
2. due to a confidential, fiduciary, or other special relationship
3. exercises undue influence or the other party to that relationship
4. to induce that party into entering into a contract.

B. Sample Case

Undue influence is frequently raised as a defense to enforcement of prenuptial agreements, but is almost as frequently unsuccessful because husbands and wives are not considered to be in a confidential relationship prior to marriage. As the court in In re Marriage of Dawley, 17 Cal.3d 342, 551 P. 2d 323, 131 Cal. Rptr. 3 (1976) explains, if there is no such relationship, something more is needed:

> Betty contends that the antenuptial agreement is tainted by undue influence. The issue of whether or not undue influence has been exerted frames a question of fact.... From the trial court's conclusion that Betty freely and voluntarily entered into the antenuptial agreement we therefore imply a finding that her consent was not procured by undue influence.
>
> Substantial evidence supports the implied finding negating undue influence. Parties who are not yet married are not presumed to share a confidential relationship; the record demonstrates that Betty did not rely on the advice and integrity of James in entering into the antenuptial agreement.
>
> Betty points out that even in the absence of a confidential relationship, a contract may be tainted by undue influence if one party takes "a grossly oppressive and unfair advantage of another's necessities or

distress." We appreciate that Betty was compelled to enter into the antenuptial agreement by her unplanned pregnancy and her fear that she would lose her job, but James, threatened with a paternity suit and likely loss of his position, was in no position to take advantage of her distress. Perhaps reflecting this rough equality of bargaining power, the Dawleys' antenuptial agreement was in no way "oppressive or unfair." Both James and Betty secured their earnings and property acquired with those earnings as separate property, and James agreed to support both Betty and her daughter during the period when Betty would not be working.

We therefore conclude that substantial evidence supports the trial court's finding that the agreement was not procured by undue influence. (Citations and footnote omitted.)

5. Unconscionability

Unconscionability may be raised as a defense to void a contract. This is a difficult concept. A contract that is so *unusually* shocking and unfair that it offends the conscience of the court. Simple unfairness is not the test. In essence, it is a contract that no person who is mentally competent would enter into and that no fair and honest person would accept. Unconscionability requires two elements, both of which must be present in order to make a contract invalid — procedural unconscionability and substantive unconscionability.

A. Elements
1. Procedural unconscionability may be shown by either:
    a. Inequality in bargaining power which can appear from (i) terms unreasonably favorable to other party, (ii) terms hidden in the contract, or (iii) a plaintiff with a low education or limited mental capacity, or
    b. unfair surprise.
2. Substantive unconscionability may be shown by (i) an allocation of risks or costs so unbalanced that it cannot be justified by the circumstances, or (ii) great price disparity.

B. Sample Case
The "nature of this often-amorphous legal doctrine" was discussed in *A & M Produce Cop. v. FMC Corp.*, 135 Cal. App. 3d 473, 186 Cal. Rptr. 114 (1982):

The major issues in this case involve the validity of FMC's purported disclaimer of warranties and limitation on the buyer's ability to recover consequential damages resulting from a breach of warranty. Resolution of both these issues turns largely on the proper application of the doctrine of unconscionability, which the trial court utilized in precluding enforcement of the warranty disclaimer and the consequential damage limitation. Although FMC concedes that California Uniform Commercial Code section 2719[4] allows a court under proper circumstances to declare a consequential damage limitation unconscionable, it argues that unconscionability is inapplicable to disclaimers of warranty, being supplanted by the more specific policing provisions of section 2316. We conclude otherwise, however, and turn our attention to the nature of this often-amorphous legal doctrine, outlining the analytic framework to be used in determining whether a particular contractual provision is unconscionable....

Acknowledging that a limitation on consequential damages may be unconscionable FMC asserts the trial court erred in applying that doctrine to the disclaimer of warranties. It contends unconscionability is irrelevant to warranty disclaimer provisions, having been eliminated by the specific statutory requirements of section 2316. Alternatively, FMC suggests the California Legislature's failure to adopt the general Uniform Commercial Code section on unconscionability (§ 2-302) as part of California's Uniform Commercial Code precludes the trial court's reliance on the doctrine in this instance.

While FMC's argument is not without force, we conclude that an unconscionable disclaimer of warranty may be denied enforcement despite technical compliance with the requirements of section 2316. Unconscionability is a flexible doctrine designed to allow courts to directly consider numerous factors which may adulterate the contractual process. Uniform Commercial Code section 2-302 specifies that "any clause of the contract" may be unconscionable. The policing provisions of section 2316 are limited to problems involving the visibility of disclaimers and conflicts with express warranties. But oppression and unfair surprise, the principal targets of the unconscionability doctrine, may result from other types of questionable commercial practices. Moreover, the subtle distinction between an "implied" warranty and an "express" warranty may do precious little to mitigate the exploitation of a party with inferior bargaining power. Yet as long as the warranty remains "implied," section 2316's policing provisions are ineffective.

FMC's contention regarding the status of the unconscionability doctrine in California is similarly unpersuasive. Unconscionability has long been recognized as a common law doctrine which has been consistently applied by California courts in the absence of specific statutory authorization. And although the Legislature did not adopt section 2-302 as part of California's version of the Uniform Commercial Code the identical language, complete with accompanying commentary, was recently enacted as section 1670.5 of the Civil Code. The only significant difference is that section 1670.5, placed under the "Unlawful Contracts" heading of division 3, part 2, title 4 of the Civil Code, applies to all contracts rather than being limited to those sales transactions governed by the Commercial Code. We think the trial court properly entertained A & M's arguments directed at the unconscionability of both the consequential damage exclusion and the warranty disclaimer. (Citations and footnotes omitted.)

6. Mutual Mistake

A mutual mistake defense requires a mistaken assumption of material fact by both parties. A mistaken assumption is a fact that both parties believed to be true at the time the contract was signed. However, due to whatever circumstance, this fact was or is no longer true. As a result, one party cannot perform the contract as originally intended. These mistakes are factual ones as opposed to the value of the subject matter as the value of the subject matter can never be the basis for rescission of the contract. For example, if you and I agree that I will build a deck extending 30 feet from your house, both of use believing that your property line is at least 30 feet from the house, but it turns out the boundary line is only 20 feet from the house we are both operating under a mistake of fact regarding the location of the line and the legality of building the deck.

A. Elements
1. Both parties
2. were acting under
3. the same misunderstanding of
4. the same material fact
5. when the agreement was executed, and
6. the mistake was of the type that could not be foreseen.

B. Sample Case

Proving a mutual mistake can be difficult because if a lawsuit is necessary it is unlikely that the opposing party will agree there was a mistake. This was the downfall of the defense in *Lancaster v. Lancaster*, 530 SE 2d 82, 86–7 (NC 2000). In this case the wife claimed mutual mistakes were made in the separation agreement she had with her husband. The Court held:

> Ms. Lancaster alleges four different areas of contention: (1) She and Mr. Lancaster agreed that $18,000 of their savings account would be used to pay for their daughters' education; however, no provision was made for these funds in the separation agreement; (2) both parties agreed that Mr. Lancaster's retirement plans would be divided equally by a qualified domestic relations order; however, the parties disagree as to which separation date should be used and therefore, the amount of benefits to be divided; (3) the balance of the parties' saving and checking accounts, after deducting $20,000 of Mr. Lancaster's separate property and $18,000 for the daughters' education, would be split evenly; but apparently, it was not split evenly; and (4) the parties intended to divide their furniture equally but did not do so. Ms. Lancaster alleges that these "mutual mistakes" should be rectified by this Court, since the separation agreement did not reflect the true intentions of the parties.
>
> It is well established that the existence of a mutual mistake as to a material fact comprising the essence of the agreement will provide grounds to rescind a contract. "A mutual mistake of fact is a mistake 'common to both parties and by reason of it each has done what neither intended.'" Although Ms. Lancaster argues that the separation agreement contains "mutual mistakes," Mr. Lancaster offers no such argument, thereby negating the contention that the alleged mistakes were "mutual." Moreover, Ms. Lancaster's attempts to rescind or alter the contract are barred by the parol evidence rule, which forbids the admittance of evidence used to alter the written terms of a contract. The parol evidence rule provides that when parties have formally and explicitly expressed their contract in writing, that contract shall not be contradicted or changed by prior or contemporaneous oral agreements. Ms. Lancaster attempts to add or change four terms of the separation agreement by arguing that she and Mr. Lancaster really agreed to terms other than those expressly written in the agreement. However, the parol evidence rule bars that evidence. (Citations omitted.)

7. Waiver

Waiver as a defense can take the form of written provisions included in a contract giving up a right, e.g., waiver of warranties and waiver of certain remedies. However, waiver can also arise as an equitable defense that arises after the execution of the contract. Waiver can be implied from conduct indicating a clear intent to waive one's rights.

A. Elements

1. Plaintiff knew defendant had an obligation to perform;
2. plaintiff demonstrated an unequivocal and conscious intention to abandon those rights.

B. Sample Case

Waiver is akin to estoppel in that it is used to prevent one party from taking advantage of another party's reliance on the first party's conduct to the second party's detriment. As the court in *Gilbert Frank Corp. v. Fed. Ins. Co.*, 70 NY 2d 966 (1988) suggests, there must be clear evidence that one party acted in a way that would lull the other into sleeping on or abandoning their rights:

> Evidence of communications or settlement negotiations between an insured and its insurer either before or after expiration of a limitations period contained in a policy is not, without more, sufficient to prove waiver or estoppel. (Waiver is an intentional relinquishment of a known right and should not be lightly presumed.) Plaintiff offers no evidence from which a clear manifestation of intent by defendant to relinquish the protection of the contractual limitations period could be reasonably inferred. Nor do the facts show that defendant, by its conduct, otherwise lulled plaintiff into sleeping on its rights under the insurance contract. Indeed, since the conduct complained of occurred subsequent to expiration of the limitations period, plaintiff could not have relied on that conduct in failing to timely commence its action. (Citations omitted.)

Chapter Six

Negligence

Negligence Causes of Action
1. Negligence
2. Gross Negligence
3. Negligence *per se*
4. Negligent Infliction of Emotional Distress

Negligence Doctrines and Rules
1. *Res ipsa loquitur*
2. Public Duty Doctrine
3. Good Samaritan Doctrine
4. Emergency Rule
5. Substantial Factor Rule
6. Foreseeability Test for Proximate Cause

Negligence Defenses
1. Contributory Negligence
2. Comparative Negligence
3. Assumption of Risk
4. Waiver (Written Assumption of Risk)
5. Good Samaritan Immunity
6. Sovereign Immunity

Negligence Causes of Action

1. Negligence

Negligence is broadly defined as the failure to exercise reasonable care, given a particular set of circumstances, resulting in harm to a person or property.

This may involve doing something carelessly or failing to do something that should have been done. Key factors in negligence are *reasonableness* and *foreseeability*.

A. Elements

1. The defendant owed a <u>duty</u> of care to the victim.

A duty is an obligation. In most instances there is a duty to take reasonable steps so that our actions do not cause harm to other people. The trier of fact, determining how the reasonable person would have acted, determines what is reasonable under the circumstances. Sometimes the duty is imposed by statute or by the actor assuming responsibility over that considered reasonable under the circumstances.

2. The defendant must also <u>breach</u> that duty. The plaintiff must allege and prove by a preponderance of the evidence that a breach occurred. If the elements of the doctrine *res ipsa loquitur*, which is Latin for "the thing speaks for itself," are met, the burden of proof is shifted to the defendant. In order for the legal doctrine of *res ipsa* to be applicable, all elements of *res ipsa* must be met. For more information on the legal doctrine of *res ipsa loquitur*, please refer to the "Doctrines and Rules" section.

3. This breach must be the <u>cause</u> of injury to the victim. There are many different legal theories of causation. Even if the plaintiff can demonstrate that the injury would not have happened "but for" the defendant's actions, the courts will generally not find the defendant liable unless the injury was a reasonably foreseeable consequence of the defendant's conduct. Some courts make this determination based on "substantial factor" analysis, i.e., a determination of whether defendant's actions were a substantial factor in causing the injury rather than just one link in a chain of events leading to the injury.

4. Resulting in damage or <u>harm</u> to the victim. In order to prove damage, the plaintiff must have suffered an actual loss as a result of the injury. This loss is most often measured monetarily.

B. Sample Case

In *Newell v. Southern Jitney Jungle Co.*, 830 So.2d 621 (Miss. 2002), the plaintiff was at her place of employment when her estranged husband entered and caused her injury. She claimed her employer was negligent by not providing proper security. The court considered the traditional concepts of intervening and superseding cause, and refused to place a burden on a business for the criminal acts of a third party when the action of the third party was not reasonably foreseeable.

2. Gross Negligence

While ordinary negligence can be defined as the failure to exercise a reasonable care in a situation that causes harm to a person or property, gross negligence differs in the degree of carelessness. Punitive damages can be awarded if the degree or amount of negligence can be proven to a higher degree than ordinary negligence.

A. Elements

1. A set of circumstances, which, together, constitute a clear and present danger;
2. an awareness of such danger; and
3. a voluntary act or omission in the face that constitutes conscious disregard of that danger, which is likely to result in injury.

B. Sample Case

The Court of Appeals in Florida laid out the differences in degrees between ordinary, gross and culpable negligence in *Glaab v. Caudill*, 236 So.2d 180 (Fla. App. 1970). In this case, the defendant was driving a car with the plaintiff riding as a passenger. The two women were going to pick up dinner for their families. While driving the speed limit, the defendant took her eyes off the road and both of her hands off the wheel to retrieve a bag of drinks that had spilled. This court outlined the three elements of gross negligence as (1) a set of "circumstances which, together, constitute an 'imminent' or 'clear and present' danger amounting to more than [the] normal or usual"; (2) a "chargeable knowledge or awareness of the imminent danger"; (3) the act or omission must show a "conscious disregard of consequences." The court differentiated gross negligence from ordinary negligence by changing the phrase in the third element "conscious disregard" to a "careless disregard" and defines culpable or criminal negligence as a "willful or wanton disregard."

3. Negligence *per se*

Negligence *per se* occurs is when a defendant violates a statute or ordinance which establishes a duty or standard of care. When violation of the established duty causes injury to the plaintiff, defendant is presumed negligent and must present effective negligence defenses to avoid liability. In order to be successful in a negligence *per se* claim, a plaintiff must be within the class intended to be protected by the law, the action must fall inside the area for which the law was created and the violation must be the proximate cause of the injuries. Because this is a statute or ordinance based tort, the statutes and laws of the individual state in which it occurred must be reviewed to determine the standard of care and the class of persons intended to be protected.

A. Elements

1. Violation of a public duty,
2. enjoined by law for the protection of a person or property,
3. proximate cause,
4. resulting in injury.

B. Sample Cases

In *Thomas v. McDonald*, 667 So. 2d 594 (Miss. 1995), the plaintiff claimed the defendant did not have the statutorily required warning lights when it was stalled in the highway, resulting in a crash and injury. The court defined negligence *per se* as a violation of a statute combined with injury as a proximate result of that violation. The court reiterated the fact that in order to recover, the plaintiff must be a member of the class the statute was designed to protect and the harm he/she suffered must be the type the statute intended to prevent.

In some states, violation of a statute is treated as *prima facie* negligence rather than negligence *per se*. See, for example, *Moore v. Skyline Cab Co.*, 134 W.Va. 121, 59 S.E.2d 437 (1950).

4. Negligent Infliction of Emotional Distress

Emotional distress consists of mental anguish caused by a tortfeasor, that is an individual or business entity that breaches a duty causing injury. Emotional distress may include fright, anxiety, shock, grief, mental suffering, shame, embarrassment, and emotional disturbance. Since emotional distress is subjective in nature, the courts have limited the circumstances under which this tort can be maintained as a cause of action. These vary by state and include:

1. The impact rule—the plaintiff must have experienced physical impact to recover any damages.
2. Physical manifestation rule—the plaintiff must have experienced physical symptoms associated with mental anguish in order to recover any damages.

3. The zone of danger rule—a bystander witness of an injury to another person who was not physically impacted may still recover if they were immediately threatened by the negligence.
4. The family relationship rule—this requires the witness bystander be a member of the physically injured person's close family in order to recover damages.
5. Sensory perception rule—the bystander must have perceived the injury with his/her own senses.

A. Elements

1. Outrageous conduct by the tortfeasor, which
2. the tortfeasor should have anticipated would have produced
3. significant and reasonably foreseeable emotional injury to the victim; when
4. the tortfeasor breached his duty of reasonable care to avoid causing such emotional harm to the victim; and
5. the victim was a reasonably foreseeable plaintiff.

B. Sample Case

Entex v. McGuire, 414 So.2d 437 (Miss. 1982) set the standard in Mississippi for determining whether a defendant has a duty to a bystander plaintiff. The factors that the court considered included (1) whether the plaintiff was located near the scene of the accident (2) whether the shock resulted from a direct emotional impact upon plaintiff from the sensory and contemporaneous observance of the accident and (3) whether the plaintiff and victim were closely related.

Negligence Doctrines and Rules

1. *Res ipsa loquitur*

This doctrine relates to the proof required in establishing a breach of duty. The evidentiary burden shifts to the defendant if its elements are met.

A. Elements

1. An injury is alleged to have been negligently inflicted
2. the harm is shown not to occur in the usual course of everyday conduct unless
3. a person who controls the instrumentality likely to have produced that harm fails to exercise due care to prevent its occurrence.

B. Sample Case

The Oklahoma Supreme Court explains the doctrine of *res ipsa loquitur* this way in *Harder v. FC Clinton, Inc.*, 948 P. 2d 298 (Okla, 1997):

> *Res ipsa loquitur* is a pattern of proof which may be followed when an injury is alleged to have been negligently inflicted and the harm *is shown not to occur* in the usual course of everyday conduct unless a person who controls the instrumentality *likely to have produced that harm* fails to exercise due care to prevent its occurrence. The purpose of the *res ipsa loquitur* evidentiary rule is to aid a plaintiff in making out a prima facie case of negligence in circumstances when direct proof of why the harm happened is beyond the power or knowledge of the plaintiff. Once the foundation facts for *res ipsa loquitur* are established, *negligence may be inferred* from the injurious occurrence without the aid of circumstances pointing to the responsible cause. The burden of producing further evidence (going forward with proof), but not the ultimate burden of persuasion, is then shifted to the defendant.
>
> *Whether a case is fit for the application of res ipsa loquitur presents a question of law.* It is a judicial function to determine if a given inference may be drawn from a proffered set of circumstances. When, at the close of the plaintiff's case the evidence does not demonstrate a sufficient balance of probabilities in favor of negligence, or the issue still rests on conjecture, submission on *res ipsa loquitur* consideration is not the plaintiff's due.
>
> The effect of the *res ipsa loquitur* evidentiary rule is merely to raise a rebuttable inference which allows a plaintiff to take the case to the jury and thus avoid a directed verdict for the defendant. Where the *proof is conflicting or subject to different inferences,* some of which are in favor of and others against the applicability of *res ipsa loquitur,* the question must be left to the jury. It is only when one of the foundation facts is *irrefutably negated* that the necessary prop may be deemed knocked out from under the *sine qua non* predicate for application of the *res ipsa* proof pattern. [Footnotes omitted. Emphasis in original.]

2. Public Duty Doctrine

In order for a public officer to be liable to an individual for negligence, that officer must owe that individual a duty which is more than the duty that the officer owes the public in general.

A. Elements

1. A public officer
2. acting in the capacity of his office
3. owing a duty to the general public of the same nature as the duty claimed to have been breach by the individual.

B. Sample Case

In *Sapp v. City of Tallahassee*, 348 So. 2d 363 (Fla, 1977) officers assigned to a "stake-out" of a building because of violence that had taken place there failed to investigate suspicious activity by two men who assaulted an employee of the building. The victim sued the city, claiming that by its agents engaging in the stake-out with the purpose of preventing violence, it had undertaken a special duty to the employees of the building over that owed to the general public. The court confirmed that, "It is clear before a municipality may be held liable for the negligence of its employees, there must be shown the existence of a special duty, something more than the duty owed to the pubic generally," but concluded "a situation where police authorities undertook a responsibility to particular members of the public, exposing them, without adequate protection, to risks which then materialize into actual injury."

Some courts have begun rejecting the public duty doctrine. See, for example, Drake v. Drake, 618 NW 2d 650 (Neb, 2000) where the court states, "In *Maple v. City of Omaha*, 222 Neb. 293, 384 N.W.2d 254 (1986), we concluded that the 'public duty doctrine' had no place in Nebraska law. The public duty doctrine provided that a government official or employee owed no duty of care to the general public in the absence of an undertaking of a special or private duty. See *id.* In rejecting the public duty doctrine, we adopted the rationale of the Arizona Supreme Court in *Ryan v. State*, 134 Ariz. 308, 656 P.2d 597 (1982), that "'the parameters of duty owed by the state will ordinarily be coextensive with those owed by others.'" *Maple*, 222 Neb. at 300, 384 N.W.2d at 260.

3. Good Samaritan Doctrine

The Good Samaritan Doctrine holds that a person can voluntarily take on a duty that he or she would not otherwise have. It should not be confused with the immunity a person can be granted under Good Samaritan statutes (see Negligence Defenses). The "Good Samaritan Doctrine" is enunciated in *Restatement (Second) of Torts*, §§ 323 and 324A. Section 324A.

A. Elements

One who:

1. undertakes
   a. gratuitously or
   b. for consideration
2. to render services which he should recognize as necessary for the protection of a third person or his things
3. to another,
4. causing physical harm resulting from his failure to exercise reasonable care to protect his undertaking,

is liable to the that person if

5. a. his failure to exercise reasonable care increases the risk of such harm, or
    b. he has undertaken to perform a duty owed by the other to the third person, or
    c. the harm is suffered because of reliance of the other or the third person upon the undertaking.

B. Sample Case

Plaintiffs complained the Union "failed to develop an adequate program for inspection and for safety, ... failed to inspect," and "failed to require other safety devices to be used." The trial court in *Rawson v. United Steelworkers of America*, 726 P. 2d 742 (Ida, 1986) started with the premise that there was no duty to act as a Good Samaritan, but that while breach of contract is not in itself a tort, a contract can give rise to a duty. However, it analyzed the plaintiff's claims in terms of the three aspects of the fifth element cited above and concluded that the plaintiffs' claims failed. The appellate court disagreed, holding that both premises were incorrect and stating "The record establishes that the Union's safety undertaking was not the act of a 'Good Samaritan' but was, in fact, a substantial part of the Union's offering in consideration of the workers' membership and payment of dues" and "the cause of action is premised upon the Union negligently performing those safety functions which it did, in fact, undertake," while confirming that "mere nonfeasance, even if it amounted to willful neglect to perform a contract, is insufficient to establish duty in tort."

4. Emergency Rule

A person who is confronted with an emergency that is not of his or her own making is excused from liability for harm resulting if he or she does not take the best course of action in dealing with the emergency unless the choice is so hazardous that an ordinary prudent person would not have made it under the circumstances. It is based on the premise that such a situation leaves the actor with no time for thought and requires a speedy decision based largely upon impulse.

A. Elements

A person:

1. who is confronted by a situation
   a. not of his or her own making
   b. that is sudden or unexpected combination of circumstances which calls for immediate action

is not negligent for choosing something other than the best responsive action if

2. the action chosen is not so hazardous that an ordinary prudent person would not have made it under the circumstances.

B. Sample Case

The court in *DiCenzo v. Izawa*, 723 P. 2d 171 (Haw, 1986) explains:

> [T]he appearance of an emergency "does not invoke a different standard of care than that applied in any other negligence case." *Martin v. City of New Orleans*, 678 F.2d 1321, 1325 (5th Cir. 1982). "The conduct required is still that of a reasonable person under the circumstances, as they would appear to one who was using proper care, and the emergency is to be considered only as one of the circumstances." ... In other words, "[t]he doctrine of sudden emergency cannot be regarded as something apart from and unrelated to the fundamental rule that everyone is under a duty to exercise ordinary care under the circumstances to avoid injury to others. A claim of emergency is but a denial of negligence." Lawrence v. Deemy, 204 Kan. 299, 306, 461 P.2d 770, 774 (1969); see also Restatement of Torts (Second) §296. Moreover, an emergency of his own making obviously does not shield the negligent person from liability.... And when one "engages in an activity in which [emergencies] are likely to arise," he "must be prepared to meet them."

5. Substantial Factor Rule

The Substantial Factor Rule relates to the cause element of negligence. It is generally applied in cases of concurrent liability, i.e., cases where the harm is the result of the negligence of two or more defendants. The Rule states that such defendants will be liable for negligence if the harm could have resulted from either of their actions alone and thus each was a substantial factor in causing the harm.

A. Elements

1. Two or more tortfeasors
2. commit negligent acts
3. each of which are sufficient to cause the resulting harm
4. resulting in harm to a third party.

B. Sample Case

There has been confusion over whether the Substantial Factor Rule eliminates the need to apply the "but for" test in cases involving multiple tortfeasor. This issue was tackled directly by the court in *Callahan v. Cardinal Glennon Hosp.*, 863 SW 2d 852 (Mo, 1993.) The court notes the different treatment of the Substantial Factor Rule by the Restatement and by some legal scholars. The court deals with the issue using the classic law school example of two fires:

> The law school example of the latter type of case is where two independent tortfeasors set fires on opposite sides of the mountain, the fires burn toward the cabin at the top, and either is sufficient to destroy the cabin. Under these circumstances, the "but for" test fails to accurately test for causation in fact because the absence of either fire will not save the cabin. Applying the "but for" causation test to fire number one results in the conclusion that the cabin would have burned even if fire number one had not occurred because fire number two would have burned the cabin. For the same reason, applying the "but for" causation test to fire number two leads to the conclusion that the cabin would have burned even if fire number two had not occurred because fire number one would have burned the cabin. Nevertheless, it is obvious that both fires are causes in fact. This limited circumstance, hereinafter called a "two fires" case, is the only situation where the Restatement (Second) would not require a "but for" test. The confusion arises because the Restatement (Second) labels

all cases where legal cause is present as substantial factor cases. Thus, under the Restatement's approach the vast majority of cases, although called substantial factor cases, are required to meet a "but for" causation test.

The court concludes, "In summary, there is nothing inconsistent or different about applying a 'but for' causation test to a circumstance involving multiple causes. The 'but for' causation test operates only to eliminate liability of a defendant who cannot meet this test because such defendant's conduct was not causal. The fact that the conduct of a particular defendant either does or does not meet 'but for' causation has no impact on the remaining defendants. The remaining defendants rise or fall on their own 'but for' causation test."

6. Foreseeability Test for Proximate Cause

Even when we can say that harm would not have resulted but for a negligent act of a defendant, that act may not meet the causation element of the negligence cause of action. That element requires the act be the "proximate cause" of the harm. Whether an act is a proximate cause of a harm depends on the foreseeability test, i.e., whether the result was foreseeable, the result arose in a foreseeable manner, and the person harmed was a member of the class of people foreseeable as potential victims of the act.

A. Elements

A proximate cause occurs when the harm resulting from a negligent act is:

1. A foreseeable result of the act
2. arose in a foreseeable manner, and
3. affected a foreseeable victim.

B. Sample Case

Just how foreseeable the harm must be is not just a matter of probability. The New Jersey Supreme Court noted in *Caputzal v. Lindsay Co.*, 222 A. 2d 513 (NJ, 1966),

> Foreseeability is not solely a mere matter of logic, since anything is foreseeable, but frequently involves questions of policy as well. When it does, the matter is one for determination by the court and not by the fact-finder. *Goldberg v. Housing Authority of City of Newark*, 38

N.J. 578 (1962); *Morril v. Morril*, 104 N.J.L. 557, 561 (E. & A. 1928). Chief Justice Weintraub makes the point well in Goldberg. There the plaintiff, a tradesman, was attacked and robbed by unknown persons in a multi-building, high-rise public housing development operated by the defendant. He sought to establish liability for his injuries on the thesis that the defendant had a duty to provide police protection. In finding no such duty as a matter of law, the Chief Justice said:

> "The question whether a private party must provide protection for another is not solved merely by recourse to 'foreseeability.' Everyone can foresee the commission of crime virtually anywhere and at any time. * * *

The question is not simply whether a criminal event is foreseeable, but whether a duty exists to take measures to guard against it. Whether a duty exists is ultimately a question of fairness. The inquiry involves a weighing of the relationship of the parties, the nature of the risk, and the public interest in the proposed solution." (38 N.J., at p. 583)....
Many years ago a case in this State hit it on the head when it was said that the determination of proximate cause by a court is to be based "'upon mixed considerations 78*78 of logic, common sense, justice, policy and precedent.'" *Powers v. Standard Oil Co.*, 98 N.J.L. 730, 734 (Sup. Ct. 1923), affirmed o.b. 98 N.J.L. 893 (E. & A. 1923).

Negligence Defenses

1. Contributory Negligence

Contributory negligence is an affirmative defense to negligence by a defendant based on plaintiff's own negligence. The defense states that the plaintiff's conduct failed to meet the standards required of a person with due regard for that person's own safety or protection. It is draconian in its effect, barring any recovery on the part of contributorily negligent plaintiff, regardless of the relative fault of the plaintiff and defendant. A plaintiff even one percent at fault for her own injuries would be barred from recovering from a defendant ninety nine percent at fault.

This defense is no longer favored in most jurisdictions, having been replaced by the defense of comparative negligence. (See below.) Thus, the same case is used to illustrate the reasoning of one court in making the transition.

The elements are essentially the same as those for a negligence cause of action, although cast in slightly different terms.

A. Elements

A plaintiff is unable to recover from a defendant for harm if the plaintiff:

1. engaged in conduct that falls below that which a ordinary prudent person would take for his own safety or protection and
2. the conduct contributes to the plaintiff's own harm.

B. Sample Case

The South Carolina Supreme Court replaced the contributory negligence defense with the comparative negligence defense in *Nelson v. Concrete Supply Company*, 399 SE 2d 783 (SC, 1991), a short opinion adopting the reasoning of the South Carolina Court of Appeals in *Langley v. Boyter*, 284 S.C. 162, 325 S.E. (2d) 550 (Ct. App. 1984). That opinion sets out in detail the history and basis for both contributory and comparative negligence defenses and goes on to note:

> Since the doctrine was first adopted in this country, numerous exceptions have eroded the scope of its application. One exception is the rule that the negligence of the plaintiff is no defense when the defendant's conduct is willful, wanton or reckless. Woods, The Negligence Case § 1:6. See also Davenport v. Walker, 280 S.C. 588, 313 S.E. (2d) 354 (S.C. App. 1984), citing Oliver v. Blakeney, 244 S.C. 565, 137 S.E. (2d) 772 (1964) (simple contributory negligence is not a defense to reckless or willful misconduct).
>
> The most important exception is the doctrine of last clear chance which originated in the case of Davies v. Mann, 10 M. & W. 546, 152 Eng. Rep. 588 (1842). Woods, The Negligence Case § 1:7.... Application of this exception has resulted in enormous confusion among, and even within, the various states. See W. Prosser, Law of Torts § 66 at 428 (4th ed. 1971). The courts in South Carolina have not escaped difficulty in applying the doctrine of last clear chance. See, e.g., Thomas v. Bruton, 270 F. Supp. 33, 35 (D.S.C. 1967) ...
>
> To paraphrase John Locke, there is nothing less powerful than an idea whose time is gone. In our opinion, the doctrine of contributory negligence is an idea whose time is gone in South Carolina. It is extinct almost everywhere it once existed. It no longer exists in England, the country of its birth. It survives only in parts of this country, where it is threatened and endangered. Indeed, the doctrine of contributory negligence exists today as the Ivory-Billed Woodpecker of the common law.

The continued existence of the doctrine of contributory negligence as presently applied in South Carolina cannot be justified on any logical basis. It is contrary to the basic premise of our fault system to allow a defendant, who is at fault in causing an accident, to escape bearing any of its cost, while requiring a plaintiff, who is no more than equally at fault or even less at fault, to bear all of its cost. As our Supreme Court has observed, "There is no tenet more fundamental in our law than liability follows the tortious wrongdoer." Fitzer, 282 S.E. (2d) at 231.

2. Comparative Negligence

Comparative Negligence, like contributory negligence, is an affirmative defense based on the claim that plaintiff was at least partially responsible for her own injury. The elements do not differ from those of contributory negligence. Rather, it is the effect of the defense that differs. While a successful contributory negligence defense bars plaintiff's recovery, comparative negligence compares the relative fault of the parties in one of three approaches:

1. The pure comparative approach, which allocates damages in the same percentage as the allocation of fault. If the defendant is 70% responsible and the plaintiff 30% responsible, the plaintiff recovers 70% of the damages;
2. The 50/50 approach, which allows the plaintiff to recover damages based on the allocation of fault provided that plaintiff's fault is less than 50%. If the plaintiff's allocated fault is equal to or more than defendant's, she cannot recover; and
3. The 50/49 approach, in which plaintiff's recovery is barred if his allocation of the fault exceeds defendant's, but can still recover 50% of the damages if his fault is equal to the defendant's.

A. Elements

A plaintiff is unable to recover from a defendant for harm if the plaintiff:

1. engaged in conduct that falls below that which a ordinary prudent person would take for his own safety or protection; and
2. the conduct contributes to the plaintiff's own harm.

B. Sample Case

Maine adopted comparative negligence by way of a statute which, at least at the time of its enactment, was unique in the United States as it adopted the

English rule, stating "the damages recoverable in respect thereto shall be reduced to such extent as the jury thinks just and equitable having regard to the claimant's share in the responsibility for the damage." 14 M.R.S.A. 156 (1965). The Maine Supreme court delineated the duties of the jury under that statute in *Wing v. Morse*, 300 A. 2d 491 (Me, 1973):

> The jury should be told that if it determines, in the apportionment process that the claimant's responsibility for the damage is less than that of the defendant, it should proceed to the last step in the apportionment process.
>
> Having determined the relative departure from the standard of a reasonable man, the factfinder is finally directed by the Act to reduce the damages recoverable by the plaintiff to such extent as the factfinder thinks just and equitable, having regard to the complainant's share in the responsibility for the damages.
>
> By the use of the term "as the jury thinks just and equitable," the Legislature intended that the factfinders, representing as they do the judgment of the community, should bring that judgment into play in determining the amount of reduction from the total damage to make, limited only by the direction they must have "regard to the claimant's share in responsibility for the damage," i.e., the blameworthiness of the causative fault.

3. Assumption of Risk

Assumption of risk occurs when a plaintiff has knowingly or willingly exposed himself or his property to the possibility of harm. It is a complete defense in some jurisdictions, meaning that it totally bars recovery in the same way as contributory negligence. (See above.)

A. Elements
1. Voluntary assumption
2. of a known risk
3. with full appreciation of the dangers involved in that risk.

B. Sample Case
Some court opinions appear to treat assumption of risk and contributory negligence as essentially equivalent. However, in *Spurlin v. Nardo*, 114 SE 2d 913, 930 (W.Va, 1960) the West Virginia Supreme Court make the distinction between them clear stating,

Contributory negligence and assumption of risk are not identical. The case of *Hunn v. Windsor Hotel Co.*, 119 W.Va. 215, 217, 193 S.E. 57, distinguishes between the two, wherein it is stated: "The essence of contributory negligence is carelessness; of assumption of risk, venturousness." This matter is also discussed in 38 *Am.Jur.*, Negligence §172, wherein it is stated: "The defense of assumption of risk is closely associated with the defense of contributory negligence. One who does not exercise ordinary care for his own safety is said, speaking broadly, to assume the risk, that is, take the chance, of being hurt. The defense of assumption of risk is not incompatible with contributory negligence; the two defenses may arise under the same state of facts. Some courts regard the defenses as interchangeable. However, there is a clear distinction between the defense of assumption of risk and the defense of contributory negligence, notwithstanding they may arise under the same set of facts and may sometimes overlap. There is a line of demarcation which, if carefully scrutinized and followed, will allow the court to differentiate between them. Assumption of risk rests in contract or in the principle expressed by the ancient maxim, 'volenti non fit injuria,' whereas contributory negligence rests in tort. The former involves a choice made more or less deliberately and negatives liability without reference to the fact that the plaintiff may have acted with due care, whereas the defense of contributory negligence implies the failure of the plaintiff to exercise due care. As stated in some decisions, assumption of risk is a mental state of willingness, whereas contributory negligence is a matter of conduct."

4. Waiver (Written Assumption of Risk)

Waivers are contractual exclusions of negligence liability, essentially written agreements to waive or release the right to sue for negligence in a particular situation. Landowners will frequently post signs warning of danger and declaring that they are not responsible for injuries occurring on their property as a result of that danger. Such signs go to the element of "known risk" in an assumption of risk defense. Written exclusions such as those written on the back of a ski lift ticket excluding liability for risks known to be associated with a sport such as being hit by a foul ball in baseball are similar in nature. However, at times people will sign a written contract whereby they agree to waive liability in exchange for the ability to, for example, participate in an activity. In these instances the elements of the defense must include both those of assumption of risk and those of contracts.

A. Elements

1. Voluntary assumption
2. of a known risk
3. with full appreciation of the dangers involved in that risk
4. as part of a contract. (See Elements of a Contract *infra.*)

B. Sample Case

Written waivers will generally be strictly construed by the courts as illustrated by a case in which the parents of the plaintiff had signed a waiver that stated, *inter alia,* "I fully understand that *Bowdoin College, its employees or servants will accept no responsibility for* or on account of *any injury or damage sustained by Brian* arising out of the activities of the said THE CLINIC. *I do, therefore, agree to assume all risk of injury or damage* to the person or property of Brian arising out of the activities of the said THE CLINIC." The Maine court in *Doyle v. Bowdoin College,* 403 A2d 1206 (Me. 1979) cited a Pennsylvania case for the principle that:

> contracts providing for immunity from liability for negligence must be construed strictly since they are not favorites of the law ... such contracts 'must spell out the intention of the parties with the greatest of particularity'... and show the intent to release from liability 'beyond doubt by express stipulation' and '[n]o inference from words of general import can establish it'... such contracts must be construed with every intendment against the party who seeks the immunity from liability ... the burden to establish immunity from liability is upon the party who asserts such immunity. *Employers Liability Assurance Corp. v. Greenville Business Men's Association,* 423 Pa. 288, 224 A.2d 620, 623 (1966).

Then the court examined the written waiver to conclude,

> The documents executed by Leonard and Margaret Doyle contain no express reference to defendants' liability for their own negligence. Though the documents state that Bowdoin College will not "assume" or "accept" any "responsibility" for injuries sustained by Brian, such language merely indicates an unwillingness to shoulder any additional obligation, which the College would not otherwise bear. This is the reasonable interpretation of the language since it would be an inappropriate use of words for Bowdoin College to be intending to refer to its responsibility for injuries caused by its own *negligent conduct* as a liability that is not "assumed" or "accepted." Whether "assumed" or "accepted", or not, Bowdoin College has such responsibility in any event because the *law* had imposed it.

5. Good Samaritan Immunity

Good Samaritan immunity is immunity provided by a statute to persons who voluntarily choose to aid others who are ill or injured. To encourage persons with no legal duty to do so to assist an ill or injured person, states have enacted laws providing immunity against liability for negligence. The elements of this immunity will, of course, depend on the statute granting it. Idaho's statute is typical:

> I.C. §5-330. Immunity of persons giving first aid from damage claim. That no action shall lie or be maintained for civil damages in any court of this state against any person or persons, or group of persons, who in good faith, being at, or stopping at the scene of an accident, offers and administers first aid or medical attention to any person or persons injured in such accident unless it can be shown that the person or persons offering or administering first aid, is guilty of gross negligence in the care or treatment of said injured person or persons or has treated them in a grossly negligent manner. The immunity described herein shall cease upon delivery of the injured person to either a generally recognized hospital for treatment of ill or injured persons, or upon assumption of treatment in the office or facility of any person undertaking to treat said injured person or persons, or upon delivery of said injured person or persons into custody of an ambulance attendant.

A. Elements

(Based on the Idaho statute)
Immunity is granted to any person or persons, or group of persons, who:

1. in good faith
2. being at, or stopping at the scene of an accident
3. offers and administers first aid or medical attention to an injured person
4. to any person or persons injured in such accident
5. without gross negligence in the care or treatment of that person
6. prior to
   a. delivery of the injured person to either a generally recognized hospital for treatment of ill or injured persons, or
   b. assumption of treatment in the office or facility of any person undertaking to treat said injured person or persons, or
   c. upon delivery of said injured person or persons into custody of an ambulance attendant.

B. Sample Case

In *Dahl v. Turner*, 458 P. 2d 816 9 (NM, 1969) the issue of whether defendant was entitled to immunity depended on the court's interpretation of the elements of New Mexico's Good Samaritan Statute. Plaintiff had wrecked his own automobile. Defendant came upon the accident scene. She helped plaintiff pick up his belongings from the highway and visited with plaintiff approximately fifteen minutes. Other than a cut on his arm which had bled plaintiff appeared "perfectly normal and uninjured" to Defendant. However, there is evidence that plaintiff wasn't aware that "he had rolled his car" and didn't seem to know where he had been or where he was going. Plaintiff didn't want to go to a doctor, but did want to be taken to a friend at a motel in Silver City. Defendant agreed to give plaintiff a ride to Silver City since that was her destination anyway. While traveling to Silver City, Defendant "was kind of worried about him [plaintiff] because he had never ridden with me and I was scared he would be scared to ride with me." On the way to Silver City Defendant was involved in a motor vehicle accident. Plaintiff sued Defendant for injuries arising from that accident. Defendant raised the defense of immunity under the Good Samaritan law.

According to the court:

> The pertinent part of § 12-12-3, supra, reads:
> "No person who shall administer emergency care in good faith at or near the scene of an emergency, as defined herein, shall be held liable for any civil damages as a result of any action or omission by such person in administering said care, except for gross negligence;"
> Section 12-12-4, supra, defines emergency to mean:
> "an unexpected occurrence involving injury or illness to persons, including motor vehicle accidents and collisions, disasters, and other accidents and events of similar nature occurring in public or private places."
> Section 12-12-3, supra, refers to "emergency care" and the "scene of an emergency as defined herein." The wording of the definition of emergency in § 12-12-4, supra, indicates that definition applies only to the second use of the word "emergency". The meaning of "emergency" in the term "emergency care" is not defined.
> The only "care" which [Defendant] can be said to have administered to plaintiff was the providing of transportation.... If [Defendant] was administering "care" in providing transportation to plaintiff, such care was not emergency care within the meaning of the statute. There are no facts indicating a pressing necessity for such transportation; no facts indicating that the transportation was immediately called for.

6. Sovereign Immunity

Sovereign immunity is the doctrine that the sovereign, originally the king but now "the government," cannot be sued for torts without its permission. Most jurisdictions have mitigated this doctrine with statutes authorizing some types of tort lawsuits called "Torts Claims Acts." The immunity, with some exceptions, applies to the governmental officials committing the torts as well as the government entity on behalf of whom the official acted.

The immunity is granted for "governmental actions," i.e., actions performed for the general public good normally associated with governmental agencies such as fire and police protection. It is not granted for "proprietary actions," i.e., actions that are performed by governmental agencies but are generally associated with the private sector, such as providing utilities. This distinction is often very difficult to make.

A. Elements

Sovereign Immunity is a defense when the negligent action is committed by:

1. A governmental agency
2. engaged in a governmental function.

B. Sample Cases

Sovereign immunity is immunity from suit rather than just immunity from liability. This is made clear in *Shay v. Rossi*, 253 Conn. 134, 166–68 (Conn, 2000) a case where the court also sets forth the rationale for the doctrine:

> The modern rationale for the doctrine, however, rests on the more practical ground "'that the subjection of the state and federal governments to private litigation might constitute a serious interference with the performance of their functions and with their control over their respective instrumentalities, funds and property.' J. Block, 'Suits Against Government Officers and the Sovereign Immunity Doctrine,' 59 *Harv. L. Rev.* 1060, 1061 (1946)." *Pamela B. v. Ment*, 244 Conn. 296, 328, 709 A.2d 1089 (1998). This rationale suggests that the doctrine protects the state from unconsented to litigation, as well as unconsented to liability.
>
> Although we have never explicitly delineated this particular aspect of the doctrine in final judgment terms, our sovereign immunity cases implicitly have recognized that the doctrine protects against suit as well as liability—in effect, against having to litigate at all. In *Bergner v. State*, 144 Conn. 282, 286, 130 A.2d 293 (1957), we recognized the

distinction between immunity from suit and from liability, and held that a statutory waiver of sovereign immunity constituted a waiver of suit and provided "a remedy to enforce such liability as the general law recognizes." See also *Babes v. Bennett*, 247 Conn. 256, 271, 721 A.2d 511 (1998) (where state sued pursuant to statutory waiver of sovereign immunity in action for negligence of state employee operating state owned vehicle, state not immune from reallocation of damages pursuant to General Statutes §52-572h [g]); *Struckman v. Burns*, 205 Conn. 542, 559, 534 A.2d 888 (1987) (statutory waiver of sovereign immunity from suit was not waiver of immunity from prejudgment interest); State v. Chapman, 176 Conn. 362, 366, 407 A.2d 987 (1978) (statutory waiver of sovereign immunity from suit was not waiver of immunity from costs). These cases demonstrate that the state's waiver of its immunity from liability only arises after a prior determination that it has waived its immunity from suit, and that a waiver of immunity from suit does not necessarily imply a waiver of immunity from all aspects of liability.

Some courts no longer accept this rationale and have eliminated the judicially created and maintained doctrine of sovereign immunity, forcing the legislature to establish the immunity by statute. See, for example, *Davies v. City of Bath*, 364 A. 2d 1269 (Me, 1976):

No purpose would be served here by restating our reasons for holding that governmental immunity is no longer a rational judicial doctrine. See Bale v. Ryder, supra. Throughout the United States, the doctrine has been so discredited that an overwhelming majority of jurisdictions has abolished it either by judicial decision] or 1273*1273 by statute. When the conditions of society change to such an extent that past judicial doctrines no longer fulfill the needs of a just and efficient system of law, we should not be bound by the constraints of stare decisis. As we noted in *Moulton v. Moultion*, 309 A.2d 224, 228 (Me. 1973),

"'stare decisis' will ultimately become a self-defeating principle if, in functioning to achieve stability in the law, it operates so inflexibly as to deny to judges the power to move ahead amidst the onrushing currents of change in the present when, in standing still restrained by the bonds of the past, they must fall behind into a cultural lag of unfairness and injustice."

We will no longer dismiss actions in tort brought against the State or its political subdivisions solely on the basis of governmental immunity. (Footnotes omitted.)

Chapter Seven

Strict Liability and Other Special Liability Actions

Strict Liability
   1. Animal Owners Liability—Wildlife
   2. Animal Owners Liability—Domestic Animals
   3. Abnormally Dangerous Activities
   4. Strict Products Liability

Other Special Liability Actions
   1. Products Liability—Negligence
   2. Product Liability—Breach of Warranty
   3. Premises Liability
   4. Premises Liability—Attractive Nuisance
   5. Vicarious Liability
   6. Motor Vehicle Vicarious Liability

Doctrines and Rules
   1. Vicious Propensity Rule
   2. Frolic and Detour Rule
   3. Coming and Going Rule
   4. Dangerous Instrumentality Doctrine

Defenses

———————

Strict Liability

Strict liability is liability without fault. This type of liability is applied to owners of animals, abnormally hazardous activities, and products liability.

1. Animal Owners Liability — Wildlife

Modern absolute liability arose in common law involving private ownership of wild animals. Owners are strictly liable for the injuries that their wildlife inflicts — fault is irrelevant. It does not matter that the owner exercised every precaution to safeguard others from harm.

A. Elements

Defendant has:

1. a wild animal (*ferae naturae*)
2. under his dominion and control, and
3. that animal causes
4. injury to another person or another person's property.

B. Sample Case

In *Woods-Leber v. Hyatt Hotels of Puerto Rico, Inc.*, 124 F. 3d 47 (C.A., 1st Cir 1997) a hotel guest sued the hotel after she was bitten by a wild mongoose at their facility. The guest contracted rabies and had to undergo a series of painful inoculations. The Court of Appeals agreed with the district court and found the hotel not liable because it could not have reasonably expected such an attack. Although the hotel's "verdant grounds are bordered on the west by a mangrove swamp, which is under the protection of the Commonwealth's Department of Natural Resources," and thus prone to entry by wildlife, the Court noted, "In order to prevail on an Article 1805 claim, a plaintiff must show, at a bare minimum, that the defendant owned, possessed, or used the wild animal. *See Ferrer v. Rivera*, 56 P.R.R. 480, 482 (1940); Redinger v. Crespo, 18 P.R.R. 106, 111 (1912). This customarily involves a showing that the defendant exercised control over the animal." Other causes of action may be available against the hotel, but since the element of dominion and control was not supported by the evidence, summary judgment was granted on behalf of the hotel.

2. Animal Owners Liability—Domestic Animals

Domesticated animals are animals generally considered to be "tame" and therefore harmless—dogs, cats, horses and the like, rather than an individual animal normally considered wild that has been "tamed." Many jurisdictions have statutes that change the common law when a victim is bitten by a dog. There is a common perception that there is a "one bite free" rule with regard to domestic animals, i.e., that animals such as dogs are allowed to injure one person without liability to its owner, but once that injury has occurred the owner can be held strictly liable. This is a misconception that is likely drawn from the "vicious propensity rule" (see below) that covers any domestic animal that displays vicious propensities, whether those propensities have actually resulted in injury to a person or property. Once that propensity is known to the owner, the injured person need not show negligence on the part of the owner.

A. Elements

Defendant has:

1. a domestic animal (*domitae naturae)*
2. that the defendant knows or reasonably should know has displayed vicious tendencies
3. under his dominion and control, and
4. that animal causes
5. injury to another person or another person's property.

B. Sample Case

Courts typically do not focus on the word "vicious," but on the concept of the animal being abnormally dangerous for an animal of its type. In *Bauman v. Auch*, 539 NW 2d 320 (SD, 1995) the court concluded that:

> more than sufficient evidence was presented to put the matter before the jury: (1) When its owner rode her at the beginning of each riding season, he used a special piece of equipment to restrain her: a tie-down, a device which kept her from getting her front legs off the ground. He used the tie-down because Krissy will "try to act up," "try to challenge you a bit," because "she's spirited, see." (2) Krissy was flighty, high-strung and nervous according to another individual who had ridden her before. (3) A farrier who had regularly shoed Krissy for years said she was "one of the top four or five worst horses" that he ever did. She had an "explosive personality," was not "totally trustworthy,"

and would throw her head back and "go crazy." "It was scary to work on her." On several occasions this farrier advised its owner to sell Krissy because she was dangerous, she was going to hurt somebody and she was not going to get better. (4) A neighbor familiar with Krissy testified that in his opinion the horse's characteristics were not normal for her breed; she was "unruly and extremely flighty." (5) Krissy's owner was familiar with these characteristics, and yet he never mentioned to his son, Bob, an inexperienced rider, that he should use a tie-down.

It arrived at this conclusion applying existing South Dakota law:

> South Dakota law on liability for injuries caused by domestic animals has been long established; the approach is similar to the Restatement. A person possessing a domestic animal "known to be of vicious tendencies" is liable for such injuries as may be caused by the animal, regardless of the degree of care exercised by the owner in restraining and controlling the animal or the precautions taken by the owner of the animal to prevent its doing injury. This liability is subject to the defenses of contributory negligence and assumption of the risk. Anderson v. Anderson, 41 S.D. 32, 36, 168 N.W. 852, 852–53 (1918). The owner must have seen or heard enough to convince a person of ordinary prudence of the animal's inclination to commit the class of injury charged against it. Warwick v. Mulvey, 80 S.D. 511, 127 N.W.2d 433, 434 (1964). Where proof is made of mischievous propensities which cause injury to another, of which the owner knew or should have known, liability follows. Id.

The court noted, "As the above quoted law indicates we should not unnecessarily focus attention on the word 'vicious,' a term more applicable to a dog, than to a horse." Instead the court concentrated on the language of the Restatement, "dangerous propensity abnormal to its class."

3. Abnormally Dangerous Activities

Common examples of abnormally dangerous activities include the use of explosives, flammable substances, noxious gases, poisons, hazardous wastes. Statutes usually shield public utilities distributing electricity and natural gas, private contractors that work for the government, municipal zoos or parks that maintain wild animals. Statutory immunities most often include governmental activities involving uses of explosives, chemicals or energy service.

These immunities reflect public policy objectives to balance necessary public services against an individual's right to be compensated for injury.

A. Elements

1. The activity creates a high risk of substantial injury to an individual or her property.
2. The risk could not be removed through the use of reasonable care.
3. The activity is not commonly undertaken.
4. The activity was inappropriately undertaken in the place where the injury occurred.
5. The hazards associated with the activity outweigh the benefits that the activity brings to the community.

B. Sample Case

In re Hanford Nuclear Reservation Litigation, 521 F. 3d 0128 (C.A., 9th Cir 2008) a group of citizens sought compensation for injuries they claimed were related to the abnormally dangerous chemical the defendants manufactured. The chemical being manufactured was plutonium, to be included in the development of an atomic bomb, although the defendant claimed that the chemicals used were within federally authorized levels. The Court of Appeals list the factors from the RESTATEMENT (SECOND) OF TORTS § 520 stated above in determining whether this activity constituted an abnormally dangerous activity. The Court stated that it did not have to weigh each element listed. However, one element alone is not sufficient to find an activity abnormally dangerous. The Court of Appeals agreed with the lower court, in that several of these factors applied and that given the totality of the circumstance, the nuclear plant could be held strictly liable for harm to the citizens.

4. Strict Product Liability

Products liability is any form of liability arising out of the use of a defective product. There are three causes of action which can be brought, depending on the facts: strict liability, negligence, or breach of warranty.

Strict liability is liability without fault. As it applies to products liability, this legal concept states that the seller of the product is liable for a defective or hazardous product that threatens a consumer's well-being, health or safety. Because one of the possible defenses to this tort is adequate warning of the possibility of danger, we now see an abundance of warnings on just about every product

sold. Other possible defenses are the negligent use of the product with knowledge of the defect and misuse of the product.

A. Elements

1. The Defendant manufactured, sold, or leased the product in question;
2. the Defendant was in the business of manufacturing, selling, or leasing
   such products;
3. the product was defective and because of the defect, the product was unreasonably dangerous to a person [or to the property of a person] who uses,
   consumes, or might be reasonably expected to be affected by the product;
4. the product was defective
   a. at the time it was manufactured, sold, or leased by the Defendant, or
   b. when the product left the Defendant's control;
5. plaintiff was a person who used, consumed, or could have reasonably
   been affected by the product; and
6. plaintiff sustained personal injuries and/or damage to property directly
   caused by the defect in the product.

B. Sample Case

Strict liability decisions are often intertwined with product liability statutes.
Wolf v. Stanley Works, 757 So.2d 316 (Miss. App. 2000) is such a case. Plain-
tiff was injured by an automatic sliding glass door that closed prematurely.
The court started with the Mississippi statute that states:

> (a) The manufacturer or seller of the product shall not be liable if
> the claimant does not prove by the preponderance of the evidence
> that at the time the product left the control of the manufacturer or
> seller:
> (i)1. The product was defective because it deviated in a material
> way from the manufacturer's specifications or from otherwise identi-
> cal units manufactured to the same manufacturing specifications, or
> 2. The product was defective because it failed to contain ade-
> quate warnings or instructions, or
> 3. The product was designed in a defective manner, or
> 4. The product breached an express warranty or failed to conform
> to other express factual representations upon which the claimant jus-
> tifiably relied in electing to use the product; and
> (ii) The defective condition rendered the product unreasonably
> dangerous to the user or consumer; and

(iii) The defective and unreasonably dangerous condition of the product proximately caused the damages for which recovery is sought. Miss.Code Ann. § 11-1-63 (Supp.1999).

The court also noted, "A plaintiff has the burden of showing that the defect that allegedly was the proximate cause of injury existed at the time that the product left the hands of the manufacturer, and that the defect rendered the product unreasonably dangerous. Accordingly, the proof must support that no material change in that product occurred after leaving the manufacturer's control." Because the business in which the door was located had replaced a sensor, this element was not met.

Other Special Liability Actions

1. Product Liability—Negligence

In a negligent product liability tort, the same basic elements of negligence apply, which are duty, breach, causation and harm.

A. Elements

1. Duty—The manufacturer/distributor/retailer/seller owes a duty to use reasonable care to any foreseeable plaintiff.
2. Breach—A breach of that duty can include a lack of reasonable care in supplying the product, a negligent design in which the manufacturer knew or should have known of the dangers, and negligent manufacturing of the product.
3. Causation—The breach causes harm.
4. Harm—The plaintiff is harmed or their property is harmed.

B. Sample Case

In *Ward v. Hobart Mfg Co.*, 450 F.2d 1176 (5th Cir. 1971), the plaintiff sought to recover for severe injury to her hand that occurred when she was cleaning a meat grinder manufactured by the defendant. The district court found defendant liable on two grounds: (1) negligence in the design of the grinder and (2) negligence in failing to warn of the danger involved in using the grinder. The appellate court started with basic negligence analysis, "(1) plaintiff must be protected under some rule of law against defendant's conduct (duty); (2) defendant's conduct must have violated this duty (breach); (3) plaintiff's injury must be the result of defendant's conduct (causal relationship); and (4) plaintiff must have suffered a loss (damage). Only when items (1) and (2) are shown is it possible to proceed to a consideration of item (3) since a duty and a breach of that duty are essential to a finding of negligence under the traditional and accepted formula. A defendant's act or failure to act may be the cause in fact of another's injury, but if the act was not negligent there is no liability." (Footnotes omitted.) It then concluded that the defendant had not been negligent in either design of the product or in warning the plaintiff of danger, stating:

> Without question Hobart was under a duty to design a reasonably safe meat grinder. Hobart does not contest this obligation; it does contest the district court's finding that its design was unreasonable. Such a determination must not be made in the abstract; it is necessary to measure the reasonableness of a product's design against objective standards. The criteria most frequently applied have been: (1) the conformity of defendant's design to the practices of other manufacturers in its industry at the time of manufacture; (2) the open and obvious nature of the alleged danger; and (3) the extent of the claimant's use of the very product alleged to have caused the injury and the period of time involved in such use by the claimant and others prior to the injury without any harmful incident. (Footnotes omitted.)

2. Product Liability — Breach of Warranty

This cause of action can be confusing. Technically a breach of warranty claim is not a true strict liability claim to the extent that the latter is grounded in tort law and the former is based in contract law. A warranty in products liability is a promise or guaranty, which can be either expressed or implied, that the product being sold will perform in a specific manner for a certain period of time. Proof of fault is not necessary once the warranty has been breached. This tort has its basis in contract law and is typically governed by the Uniform Commercial Code (UCC). A version of the UCC has been passed in every state, although there may be differences in each state. A thorough evaluation of the statutes in one's state should be performed to decide if this law applies. A possible defense to this tort is misuse of the product.

A. Elements

1. A contract exists between a purchaser and a seller of a product;
2. subject to an express or implied warranty (including warranty of merchantability);

3. the product fails to comply with the warranty;
4. the failure to comply with the warranty caused; and
5. injury to the plaintiff or the plaintiff's property.

B. Sample Case

Denny v. Ford Motor Co., 662 N.E.2d 730 (NY App. 1995) attempts to clarify the confusion that arises from blending breach of warranty with products liability. The case involved injuries that occurred with a Ford Explorer rollover. The plaintiff sued on both strict product liability and breach of warranty claims. The court took the opportunity to speak on the distinction and viability of the two claims:

> In this proceeding, Ford's sole argument is that plaintiffs' strict products liability and breach of implied warranty causes of action were identical and that, accordingly, a defendant's verdict on the former cannot be reconciled with a plaintiff's verdict on the latter. This argument is, in turn, premised on both the intertwined history of the two doctrines and the close similarity in their elements and legal functions. Although Ford recognizes that New York has previously permitted personal injury plaintiffs to simultaneously assert different products liability theories in support of their claims (see, Victorson v. Bock Laundry Mach. Co., 37 N.Y.2d 395, 400), it contends that the breach of implied warranty cause of action, which sounds in contract, has been subsumed by the more recently adopted, and more highly evolved, strict products liability theory, which sounds in tort. Ford's argument has much to commend it. However, in the final analysis, the argument is flawed because it overlooks the continued existence of a separate statutory predicate for the breach of warranty theory and the subtle but important distinction between the two theories that arises from their different historical and doctrinal root.
>
> When products liability litigation was in its infancy, the courts relied upon contractual warranty theories as the only existing means of facilitating economic recovery for personal injuries arising from the use of defective ... the courts posited the existence of an implied warranty arising as an incident of the product's sale and premised a cause of action for consequential personal injuries based on breaches of that warranty ...
>
> Eventually, the contractually based implied warranty theory came to be perceived as inadequate in an economic universe that was dominated by mass-produced products and an impersonal marketplace.... the warranty approach remained unsatisfactory, and the courts shifted

their focus to the development of a new, more flexible tort cause of action: the doctrine of strict products liability

The establishment of this tort remedy has, as this Court has recognized, significantly diminished the need to rely on the contractually based breach of implied warranty remedy as a means of compensating individuals injured because of defective products ...

Nonetheless, it would not be correct to infer that the tort cause of action has completely subsumed the older breach of implied warranty cause of action or that the two doctrines are now identical in every respect ...

Although the products liability theory sounding in tort and the breach of implied warranty theory authorized by the UCC coexist and are often invoked in tandem, the core element of "defect" is subtly different in the two causes of action. Under New York law, a design defect may be actionable under a strict products liability theory if the product is not reasonably safe.... This standard demands an inquiry into such factors as (1) the product's utility to the public as a whole, (2) its utility to the individual user, (3) the likelihood that the product will cause injury, (4) the availability of a safer design, (5) the possibility of designing and manufacturing the product so that it is safer but remains functional and reasonably priced, (6) the degree of awareness of the product's potential danger that can reasonably be attributed to the injured user, and (7) the manufacturer's ability to spread the cost of any safety-related design changes ...

In other words, an assessment of the manufacturer's conduct is virtually inevitable, and, as one commentator observed, "[i]n general, * * * the strict liability concept of 'defective design' [is] functionally synonymous with the earlier negligence concept of unreasonable designing" ...

It is this negligence-like risk/benefit component of the defect element that differentiates strict products liability claims from UCC-based breach of implied warranty claims in cases involving design defects. While the strict products concept of a product that is "not reasonably safe" requires a weighing of the product's dangers against its over-all advantages, the UCC's concept of a "defective" product requires an inquiry only into whether the product in question was "fit for the ordinary purposes for which such goods are used" (UCC 2-314 [2] [c]). [4] The latter inquiry focuses on the expectations for the performance 259*259 of the product when used in the customary, usual and reasonably foreseeable manners. The cause of action is one involving true "strict" liability, since recovery may be had upon a showing that the product was not minimally safe for its expected purpose—

without regard to the feasibility of alternative designs or the manufacturer's "reasonableness" in marketing it in that unsafe condition.
(Citations omitted.)

3. Premises Liability

The elements of a cause of action for premises liability are the same as for
simple negligence. What makes it "special" is the various modes of duty courts
apply in the first elements. At one point, all courts differentiated between the
duty owed to trespassers, licensees, and invitees. If the individual is a trespasser,
the defendant would owe a very limited duty not to cause intentional, willful,
or wanton harm. If the person has permission to be on the premises, otherwise
known as a licensee, then the property owner should correct any known dangers on the property. If someone is an invitee, the landowner has the highest
duty of reasonable care toward that person. This invitation may be expressed
or implied. Courts have, however, begun to eliminate the distinction and imposed traditional negligence theory duty with regard to all persons on the land.

A. Elements

1. The defendant owed a duty to the plaintiff
   (A) Differentiating jurisdictions
      a. Plaintiff was a trespasser so the duty was to do no intentional will-
        ful or wanton harm
      b. Plaintiff was a licensee so the duty was to take reasonable care to dis-
        cover and correct known harms
      c. Plaintiff was an invitee
   (B) Non-differentiating jurisdictions
      Plaintiff was owed a duty of reasonable care
2. the premises owner/occupier breached that duty;
3. the owner/occupier's breach was the cause
4. of injury to the plaintiff.

B. Sample Cases

Leffler v. Sharp, 891 So.2d 152 (Miss. 2004) demonstrates some of the problems that can arise when there is a differentiation of duty based on the status
of the plaintiff. The Court was asked to determine whether and when status
changed from invitee to trespasser, with a corresponding change in duty owned
by the premises owner. Upon entering the premises the plaintiff was an invitee. However, once he exited the public portion of the establishment and en-

tered into an area that was marked "no entrance," his status changed to trespasser and the defendant owed no duty to him.

Poulin v. Colby College, 402 A. 2d 846, 851 (Me, 1979) shows the reasoning in those jurisdictions where the differentiated duty method has been abandoned in favor of traditional negligence analysis:

> The justification for abandoning the historical common law distinctions between invitees and licensees is found in the evolution of our society from a culture centered on the land to one grounded in an urban, industrialized setting ... We can find no reason for denying a plaintiff the opportunity to recover damages for injuries sustained due to the negligence of a landowner merely because the former was a licensee and not an invitee. This is especially so in situations where the burden is no greater on the landowner to exercise reasonable care in providing reasonably safe premises for licensees than for invitees. We, therefore hold, as have those jurisdictions noted above, that an owner or occupier of land owes the same duty of reasonable care in all the circumstances to all persons lawfully on the land. This does not require an owner or occupier to insure the safety of his lawful visitors. Rather it merely extends the protection previously afforded invitees to those persons who had heretofore been classified as licensees.

4. Premises Liability — Attractive Nuisance

Owners/occupiers of premises owe a special duty to children, even in jurisdictions where trespassers are treated differently than other persons on the premises under the attractive nuisance doctrine. As with other historical forms of premises liability, courts are also abandoning the attractive nuisance doctrine in favor of traditional negligence analysis. There is a four-part test which may hold a landowner liable for an unknown child on their property as indicated in the Elements below.

A. Elements

The owner/occupier of premises will be liable for injuries occurred by children on their premises when:

1. the property is under the custody and control of the defendant;
2. defendant knows or should have known of the condition on the property;
3. the premises must
   a. allure children and

b. endanger;
4. the presence of children must be reasonably anticipated; and
5. the danger posed to the children outweighs the cost of making the condition safe.

B. Sample Cases

In *Cope v. Doe*, 464 NE 2d 1023 (Ill, 1984) the court explained the doctrine and its reasons for moving to the standard foreseeability of harm analysis:

> Prior to this court's decision in *Kahn v. James Burton Co.* (1955), 5 Ill.2d 614, the "attractive nuisance" doctrine governed the liability of owners or parties in possession or control of premises upon which a trespassing child was injured. Under the doctrine, liability was imposed for injuries to the child caused by a condition which attracted him to defendant's premises. In such cases, the courts employed the fiction that the child was an invitee because the defendant, by maintaining a condition that was attractive, enticed the child to enter the premises. It followed then that there was a duty to take reasonable precautions to protect the child from injuries.
>
> The attractive nuisance doctrine however is no longer the law in Illinois. Recognizing that "irreconcilable conclusions" resulted from applying the doctrine, the court in Kahn held that "the only proper basis for decision in such cases dealing with personal injuries to children are the customary rules of ordinary negligence cases." (5 Ill.2d 614, 624.) The significance of this decision is that it discarded the notion that the dangerous condition had to lure children onto the premises, and it established the rule that foreseeability of harm to the child is the test for liability. Moreover, the common law categories of trespasser, licensee and invitee, as they pertain to an injured child's status, are no longer relevant in determining liability. 5 Ill.2d 614, 625.

5. Vicarious Liability

Vicarious liability is the liability of one person for the negligent conduct of another who is acting on their behalf. The parties involved are considered the principal and the agent. This is often the case in employer and employee relationships. However, employment is not an essential element. The legal doctrine that covers the employer/employee relationship is known as *respondeat superior*. This is Latin for "let the master answer." The doctrine of *respondeat superior* can be applied when the employee is acting under the scope of employment of their employer. Those who hire independent contractors are generally not vicariously liable for the contractors' negligence. Under the doctrine of motor vehicle vicarious liability a vehicle owner is generally vicariously liable for the negligence of an authorized driver of their vehicle.

A. Elements

A principal is liable if:

1. an agent commits a tort and
2.   a. agent acts with actual authority, or
    b. principal ratifies agent's actions, or
    c. principal is negligent in selecting, supervising, or otherwise controlling agent, or
    d. principal delegates duty to take care of others to agent, or
    e. agent acts within scope of employment, or
    f. agent acts with apparent authority on or purportedly on behalf of principal.

B. Sample Case

Petrovich v. Share Health Plan, 719 NE 2d 756 (Ill, 1999) deals with the interesting issue of an HMO's vicarious liability for medical malpractice. The plaintiff brought a medical malpractice action against a physician and others for their alleged negligence in failing to diagnose her oral cancer in a timely manner. The plaintiff also named her health maintenance organization (HMO) as a defendant. The central issue was whether the plaintiff's HMO may be held vicariously liable for the negligence of its independent-contractor physicians under agency law. The plaintiff contended that the HMO is vicariously liable under both the doctrines of apparent authority and implied authority. The court identified five theories, including vicarious liability, under which HMOs could potentially be held liable for medical malpractice:

> Indeed, the national trend of courts is to hold HMOs accountable for medical malpractice under a variety of legal theories, including vicarious liability on the basis of apparent authority, vicarious liability on the basis of respondeat superior, direct corporate negligence, breach of contract and breach of warranty ... Our appellate court has also expressed the view that HMOs are subject to liability under the five legal theories listed above.

The issue in the case was whether an HMO could be vicariously liable for independent contractors. The court held that it could, based on the doctrine of apparent authority, stating, "To establish apparent authority against an HMO for physician malpractice, the patient must prove (1) that the HMO held itself out as the provider of health care, without informing the patient that the care is given by independent contractors, and (2) that the patient justifiably relied upon the conduct of the HMO by looking to the HMO to provide health care services, rather than to a specific physician."

The court also found a basis for liability in implied authority:

> Implied authority is actual authority, circumstantially proved. One context in which implied authority arises is where the facts and circumstances show that the defendant exerted sufficient control over the alleged agent so as to negate that person's status as an independent contractor, at least with respect to third parties. The cardinal consideration for determining the existence of implied authority is whether the alleged agent retains the right to control the manner of doing the work. Where a person's status as an independent contractor is negated, liability may result under the doctrine of *respondeat superior*. (Citations omitted.)

6. Motor Vehicle Vicarious Liability

Motor vehicle vicarious liability imputes liability to the owner of a motor vehicle to third persons for injuries caused by negligent operation or use of the motor vehicle by a person to whom the owner entrusted the vehicle. The cause of action is often governed by statute. There can be separate causes of action under a state statute and under the common law of negligent entrustment, i.e., the statute may create a cause of action based simply on entrustment by the legal owner but if all the elements of the statute are not met, the plaintiff may still have a cause of action, alleging that the particular entrustment was negligent on the part of the owner.

A. Elements

A defendant may be held liable through motor vehicle liability when:

1. he is
   a. legal owner of a motor vehicle or
   b. has dominion and control over a motor vehicle
2. he entrusts the vehicle (gives authority to drive to) another person
3. the other person negligently causes
4. injury to
5. a third party.

B. Sample Case

Florida courts have recognized motor vehicle vicarious liability since 1920 as part of a larger "dangerous instrumentality doctrine." Florida's Fourth District Court of Appeals explained the development of the tort in *Morales v. Coca-Cola Co.*, 813 So. 2d 162, 165 (Fla, 2002):

> Under Florida's dangerous instrumentality doctrine, the owner of a motor vehicle is liable to third persons for injuries caused by the negligent operation or use of the motor vehicle by the person to whom the owner entrusted the vehicle. See *Southern Cotton Oil Co. v. Anderson*, 80 Fla. 441, 86 So. 629, 637 (1920). The doctrine is based upon the view that motor vehicles are dangerous instrumentalities when operated upon the public highways; consequently, the owners of motor vehicles are obligated to ensure that their vehicles are properly operated when on the public highway under their authority. See *Barth v. Miami*, 146 Fla. 542, 1 So.2d 574 (1941). Since adopting the dangerous instrumentality doctrine in 1920, Florida courts have repeatedly applied the doctrine, with very few exceptions. Recently, the Florida Supreme Court reaffirmed the important public policies underlying its adoption. See *Aurbach v. Gallina*, 753 So.2d 60, 62 (Fla.2000) (quoting *Kraemer v. Gen. Motors Acceptance Corp.*, 572 So.2d 1363, 1365 (Fla. 1990)). As Justice Grimes wrote in Kraemer:
>
> > The dangerous instrumentality doctrine seeks to provide greater financial responsibility to pay for the carnage on our roads. It is premised upon the theory that the one who originates the danger by entrusting the automobile to another is in the best position to make certain that there will be adequate resources with which to pay the damages caused by its negligent operation. If Florida's traffic problems were sufficient to prompt its adoption in 1920, there is an all the more reason for its application to today's high-speed travel upon crowded highways.

Doctrines and Rules

1. Vicious Propensity Rule

The Vicious Propensity Rule is a rule applied in determining whether or not the owner of a domestic animal such as a dog, cat, or horse, should be strictly liable for harm done by the animal. It states that since domestic animal are normally presumed to be harmless, the owner of a domestic animal will only be strictly liable for harm done by the animal if the owner knows or should reasonably know that the animal has demonstrated a vicious propensity. See "Strict Liability—2. Animal Owners Liability—Domestic Animals" above for a sample case.

2. Frolic and Detour Rule

The Frolic and Detour Rule is a rule setting forth an exception to vicarious liability. While an employer is responsible for the negligence and intentional torts of its employees committed while the employee is working, the employer is not liable if the employee was pursuing personal activities substantially outside of the normal course of employment, even if the activities occur during the work day.

A. Elements

Conduct:

1. of an employee
2. outside the scope of employment
3. solely for the benefit of the employee.

B. Sample Case

A California Court of Appeals addressed the difficulty in determining the difference between a mere detour and a personal frolic in *O'Connor v. McDonald's Restaurants*, 220 Cal. App. 3d 25 (1990):

> The central issue before us is of some antiquity. In 1834 Baron Parke addressed the issue: "The master is only liable where the servant is acting in the course of his employment. If he was going out of his way, against his master's implied commands, when driving on his master's business, he will make his master liable; but if he was going on a frolic of his own, without being at all on his master's business, the master will not be liable." (*Joel v. Morison* (1834) 6 Car. & P. 501, 503, 172 Eng.Rep. 1338, 1339.)
>
> Unfortunately, as an academic commentator observed in 1923, "It is relatively simple to state that the master is responsible for his servant's torts 30*30 only when the latter is engaged in the master's busi-

ness, or doing the master's work, or acting within the scope of his employment; but to determine in a particular case whether the servant's act falls within or without the operation of the rule presents a more difficult task." (Smith, Frolic and Detour (1923) *23 Colum.L.Rev.* 444, 463.)

Here we must determine whether the superior court properly concluded as a matter of law that Evans's activity in attending the gathering at Duffer's house constituted a complete departure from a special errand for McDonald's (a frolic of his own) rather than a mere deviation (a detour).

Whether there has been a deviation so material as to constitute a complete departure by an employee from the course of his employment so as to release employer from liability for employee's negligence, is usually a question of fact. (*Loper v. Morrison* (1944) 23 Cal.2d 600, 605 [145 P.2d 1].)

"In determining whether an employee has completely abandoned pursuit of a business errand for pursuit of a personal objective, a variety of relevant circumstances should be considered and weighed. Such factors may include the intent of the employee, the nature, time and place of the employee's conduct, the work the employee was hired to do, the incidental acts the employer should reasonably have expected the employee to do, the amount of freedom allowed the employee in performing his duties, and the amount of time consumed in the personal activity. [Citations.] While the question of whether an employee has departed from his special errand is normally one of fact for the jury, where the evidence clearly shows a complete abandonment, the court may make the determination that the employee is outside the scope of his employment as a matter of law. [Citations.]" (*Felix v. Asai, supra*, 192 Cal. App.3d at p. 932–933.) [Enumeration of paragraphs omitted.]

Note: Restatement (Second) of Agency §228 comment *d* (1958) contains an extensive list of factors to be considered in determining whether an employee acted within her scope of employment.

3. Coming and Going Rule

The Coming and Going Rule relieve employers of responsibility for torts of their employees committed while going to and coming from work, i.e., the employees' normal commute. It does not apply when employees are engaged in work errands on the way home, such as delivering mail to the post office or filing documents with a court.

A. Elements

Conduct:

1. of an employee
2. occurring while going to work or returning from work
3. while not engaged in work-related activities.

B. Sample Case

In *Luth v. Rogers and Babler Construction Company*, 507 P. 2d 761, 763–765 (Alaska, 1973) the employee was employed by defendant as a flagman on a road construction project. At the time of the accident, he was returning home from his jobsite after completing his work. Since he did not live near the jobsite, he commuted approximately 25 miles to work by car every day. The Master Union Agreement under which he worked provided for payment of $8.50 daily additional remuneration, since the jobsite was located a considerable distance from the business's home base. All of the company's employees on this particular construction project received the additional remuneration, whether they commuted or lived near the jobsite. Defendant contended that it could not be liable on the basis of *respondeat superior*, since the employee was not acting within the scope of his employment at the time of the accident. The trial court directed a verdict in favor of defendant. The appeals court reasoned:

> Under the doctrine of *respondeat superior*, an employer is liable for negligent acts or omissions of his employee committed in the scope of his employment. However, Rogers attempts to avoid liability for Jack's negligence by relying on the so-called "going and coming" rule. Under this rule, an employee is ordinarily considered outside the scope of his employment while going to and from work. Some courts justify this rule by reasoning that ordinarily the employment relationship is suspended and thus the employer has no right to control the employee from the time the employee leaves his work until he returns. Others reason that while commuting the employee is not rendering service growing out of, or incidental to, his employment....
>
> [R]esolution of scope of employment questions will "depend primarily on the findings of fact in each case" and that the "factual determination generally is left to the jury." For example, in determining

the applicability of a particular exception to the going-and-coming rule, the Supreme Court of Washington stated:

> The "exceptions" to the general rule, to which appellants refer, generally, if not invariably, spring from the particular facts and circumstances of the cases out of which they arise. And, in those instances where there is any valid evidentiary dispute, *conflict* or *interpretative* issue surrounding the employment status of an employee, while going to or coming from his day's work, the applicability of a recognized exception to the general rule becomes a question of fact to be resolved by the trier of the facts. It is only when the dispositive facts relative to the questioned employer-employee relationship are without dispute, *or are such as to lend themselves to but one conclusion*, that they compel a given determination. (Emphasis added by court.)
>
> Moreover, the Restatement recognizes that scope of employment questions are jury issues where conflicting inferences can be drawn from undisputed facts. [Footnotes omitted.]

Note: Restatement (Second) of Agency § 228 comment *d* (1958) contains an extensive list of factors to be considered in determining whether an employee acted within her scope of employment.

4. Dangerous Instrumentality Doctrine

This common law doctrine provides that the owner of property with an inherently dangerous condition is liable for any injuries caused by that condition. The version that holds the owner of a dangerous tool is liable for injuries arising from the tool's use is sometimes referred to as a "Florida Doctrine," because Florida somewhat famously extended it to establish vicarious liability for the owners of motor vehicles in 1920 (see "6. Motor Vehicle Vicarious Liability" above,) but it is not exclusive to Florida.

A. Elements

1. The owner/occupier of premises
2. brings or artificially creates on those premises
3. a condition or thing dangerous to children
4. under circumstance when he should reasonable anticipate children will be exposed to the danger but
5. fails to take reasonable care to prevent harm to children
6. resulting in harm to a child or to children.

B. Sample Case

The doctrine is explained and applied in *Tolbert v. Gulsby*, 333 So. 2d 129 (Ala, 1976):

> This doctrine is based on a "straight" negligence theory and arguably developed as a reaction to the restrictive use of the attractive nuisance theory. See Fulford, The 133*133 Tort Liability of Possessors of Property to Trespassing Children in Alabama, supra. The doctrine is set out in Thompson v. Alexander City Cotton Mills Co., 190 Ala. 184, 191, 67 So. 407, 410 (1914), which quotes Thompson on Negligence, section 1030 (1880):
>
> > "We now come to a class of decisions which hold the landowner liable in damages in the case of children injured by dangerous things suffered to exist unguarded on his premises, where they are accustomed to come with or without license. These decisions proceed on one or the other of two grounds: (1) That, where the owner or occupier of grounds brings, or artificially creates something thereon, which, from its nature, is especially attractive to children, and which, at the same time, is dangerous to them, he is bound, in the exercise of social duty and the ordinary offices of humanity, to take reasonable pains to see that such dangerous things are so guarded that children will not be injured by coming in contact with them. (2) That, although the dangerous thing may not be what is termed an 'attractive nuisance' (that is to say, may not have especial attraction for children by reason of their childish instincts), yet where it is so left exposed that they are likely to come in contact with it, and where their coming on contact with it is obviously dangerous to them, the person so exposing the dangerous thing should reasonably anticipate the injury that is likely to happen to them from its being so exposed, and is bound to take reasonable pains to guard it, so as to prevent injury to them."
>
> .... Under this doctrine the standard is one of reasonableness: should defendant have reasonably anticipated that injury would result from the condition he created on his property?

Defenses

Whether and how a particular defense can be raised in response to strict liability or other special causes of action discussed above varies with the cause of action and the jurisdiction. In general, the defenses are the same as those raised to the standard negligence cause of action: 1. Comparative Negligence, 2. Contributory Negligence, 3. Assumption of Risk, 4. Waiver (Written assumption of risk), and 5. Sovereign Immunity. For discussion of these defenses see "Defenses" in the "Negligence" section.

Chapter Eight

Intentional Torts

Intentional Tort Causes of Action
1. Assault
2. Battery
3. Intentional Infliction of Emotional Distress
4. Invasion of Privacy
   4.1 Invasion of Privacy—Unreasonable Intrusion
   4.2 Invasion of Privacy—Appropriation
   4.3 Invasion of Privacy—Public Disclosure of Private Facts
   4.4 Invasion of Privacy—False Light in the Public Eye
5. Trespass
   5.1 Trespass to Land
   5.2 Trespass to Chattel
   5.3 Toxic Trespass
6. Conversion
7. Defamation
   7.1 Libel/Slander
   7.2 Slander of Title
   7.3 Commercial Disparagement
8. Nuisance
   8.1 Private Nuisance
   8.2 Public Nuisance
9. False Imprisonment
10. Sexual Harassment
11. Fraud and Misrepresentation
   11.1 Fraud
   11.2 Misrepresentation (Negligent Misrepresentation)
12. Malicious Prosecution/Abuse of Process

Doctrines and Rules
1. Transferred Intent Doctrine
2. Actual Malice Rule

3. Defamation *per se*
4. "Coming to Nuisance" Doctrine

Defenses
1. Consent
2. Self-Defense
3. Defense of Others
4. Defense of Property
5. Privilege

Intentional Tort Causes of Action

Intent as it applies to intentional torts can best be described as the state of mind which brings about a result that trespasses on the interests of another person or their property. Many intentional torts are also considered crimes, but often have different names and different elements. For example, the same act may be the tort of battery and the crime of assault depending on the elements of each. There are differences between civil torts and crimes. Civil torts are "wrongs" against a person or their property and crimes are wrongs against society. The state initiates charges of crimes, while individuals or groups bring suits for torts. The type of intent required is generally also different. For the civil tort of trespass, for example, one need not have the intent to trespass on the land of another; only the intent to go upon a particular piece of land is required if the other elements of trespass are met.

1. Assault

Assault is the intentional threat, show of force, or movement that reasonably makes a person feel they are danger of a physical attack or harmful physical contact. Actual physical contact is not necessary, whereas in battery physical contact or touching is required. This intentional tort involves the immediate threat that an un-consented contact is about to occur. The rights being protected by this tort involve an individual's right to control what touches him or her. Also, it protects the individual from the fear that un-reasonable or un-consented contact will take place. There must be an immediate threat of contact; therefore threats at a distance and conditional threats do not qualify. Some of the possible defenses against assault are self-defense, defense of others, defense of property, and consent.

A. Elements

1. The tortfeasor attempts to make un-consented harmful or offensive contact.
2. The victim is apprehensive for his safety. Apprehension means that a person reasonably fears for their physical safety in anticipation of being struck by the un-consented, harmful or distasteful contact.
3. The threat of contact is imminent. This fear arises from the likelihood that something or someone is about to strike.

B. Sample Case

An assault is not a mere threat of physical harm as explained by the court in *Cucinotti v. Ortmann*, 399 Pa. 26, 28–31 (Pa, 1960). Plaintiffs alleged:

> 2.) … [T]he defendants threatened the plaintiffs with threats of violence that the defendants would commit immediate bodily harm upon the plaintiffs, and would strike the plaintiffs with blackjacks and would otherwise hit them with great force and violence.
> 3.) At the time as aforesaid, the plaintiffs were put in great fear by the offer of the defendants to commit bodily harm upon them.
> 4.) As a result of the offers by the defendants to commit immediate bodily harm upon the plaintiffs, the plaintiffs were placed in fear that a battery would be committed against them.

The trial court dismissed for failure to state a claim. The appellate court agreed:

> Generally speaking, an assault may be described as *an act* intended to put another person in reasonable apprehension of an immediate battery, and which succeeds in causing an apprehension of such battery. See 1 Harper & James, Law of Torts § 3.4 (1956). Words in themselves, no matter how threatening, do not constitute an assault; the actor must be in a position to carry out the threat immediately, and he must take some affirmative action to do so. Bechtel v. Combs, 28*28 70 Pa. Superior Ct. 503 (1918); 1 Restatement, Torts § 31; Harper & James, supra, § 3.5 …
> There is still no allegation indicating that the blackjacks were produced with such a show of force as to place plaintiffs in immediate

fear of harmful bodily contact. Nor is there any indication of a connection in time between the showing of the blackjacks and the asserted threats of violence. The two incidents might very well have occurred at different times on the same day. It simply has not been alleged that defendants have indulged in any act that amounts to an offer to commit a battery. That the defendants had in their possession blackjacks does not convert unactionable words into an actionable trespass unless the blackjacks were displayed and produced in such a manner as to amount to an offer to commit a battery.

2. Battery

The intentional tort of battery occurs when someone physically contacts another and that contact is offensive or harmful to the one being contacted. Battery takes assault a step further and requires the actual, physical contact by one person to another. This contact may be made on an extension of the person's body. The victim must not have given any expressed or implied consent to the contact, because consent is a possible defense to this tort. For example, football players consent to the physical contact of the sport and students moving from class to class in a crowded hall impliedly consent to the almost inevitable incidental contact. Other possible defenses are self-defense, defense of others, and defense of property.

A. Elements

1. Nonconsensual physical contact. Actual touching is necessary. However, contact does not have to be made with their body. Extensions of the person can translate into touching the actual person. Battery can only occur if the victim did not consent to it. This consent can be expressed or implied.

2. Offensive or harmful contact. "Harmful" is easier to define than "offensive." Conduct one person considers acceptable or even wanted, another may consider offensive. Acceptability of certain contact may even vary from one time to another for the same person depending on the person making the contact and other circumstances. Whether or not a particular instance of contact is offensive under the circumstances is determined the reasonable person standard. Reasonableness is often based upon the victim's actions in conjunction with the tortfeasor's actions.

3. The tortfeasor's intent to touch another person. A harmful or offensive contact with a person, resulting from an act intended to cause him to suffer such a contact, is a battery.

B. Sample Case

A defendant's liability for the harm resulting from a battery extends to consequences which the defendant did not intend and could not reasonably have foreseen. This point was made by the court in *Caudle v. Betts*, 512 So. 2d 389 (La, 1987):

> The present case is one in which the plaintiff employee sought to recover damages as the result of an intentional tort, a battery committed upon him by his employer's principal owner and chief executive officer. The trial court found that the chief executive had intentionally shocked the employee with an auto condenser as a practical joke without the employee's consent or approval but that the serious injury to the employee's occipital nerve which resulted was neither foreseeable nor intentional. From this the trial court concluded that no intentional tort occurred ... A harmful or offensive contact with a person, resulting from an act intended to cause the plaintiff to suffer such a contact, is a battery. *Cage v. Wood*, 484 So.2d 850 (La.App. 1st Cir.1986); ... Restatement (Second) of Torts, American Law Institute § 13 (1965); ... The intention need not be malicious nor need it be an intention to inflict actual damage. It is sufficient if the actor intends to inflict either a harmful or offensive contact without the other's consent. *Karl J. Pizzalotto, M.D., Ltd. v. Wilson*, 437 So.2d 859 (La.1983); ...
>
> The original purpose of the courts in providing the action for battery undoubtedly was to keep the peace by affording a substitute for private retribution. F. Stone, Louisiana Civil Law Treatise, Tort Doctrine, § 125 (1977). The element of personal indignity involved always has been given considerable weight. Consequently, the defendant is liable not only for contacts that do actual physical harm, but also for those relatively trivial ones which are merely offensive and insulting. W. Prosser and W. Keeton, The Law of Torts, § 9 (5th ed. 1984); *Harrigan v. Rosich*, 173 So.2d 880 (La.App. 4th Cir.1965).
>
> The intent with which tort liability is concerned is not necessarily a hostile intent, or a desire to do any harm. Restatement (Second) of Torts, American Law Institute § 13, (comment e) (1965). Rather it is an intent to bring about a result which will invade the interests of another in a way that the law forbids. The defendant may be liable although intending nothing more than a good-natured practical joke, or honestly believing that the act would not injure the plaintiff, or even though seeking the plaintiff's own good. W. Prosser and W. Keeton,

The Law of Torts, § 9 (5th ed. 1984); see *Newman v. Christensen*, 149
Neb. 471, 31 N.W.2d 417 (1948); ...

Bodily harm is generally considered to be any physical impairment
of the condition of a person's body, or physical pain or illness. Restatement (Second) of Torts, American Law Institute § 15 (1965). The
defendant's liability for the resulting harm extends, as in most other cases
of intentional torts, to consequences which the defendant did not intend, and could not reasonably have foreseen, upon the obvious basis
that it is better for unexpected losses to fall upon the intentional wrongdoer than upon the innocent victim. W. Prosser and W. Keeton, The
Law of Torts, § 9 (5th ed. 1984); Restatement (Second) of Torts, American Law Institute § 16, n. 22 (1965); F. Harper and F. James, The Law
of Torts, § 3.3, n. 32, 33 (2nd ed. 1986). (Some citations omitted.)

3. Intentional Infliction of Emotional Distress

The tort of intentional infliction of emotional distress is designed to protect persons from others' efforts to cause shock, fright or other psychological
trauma. One owes a duty to others not to intentionally inflict emotional distress. The victim must have suffered mental anguish rather than physical injury as it is the psychological harm that this tort remedies. The misdeed must
be so outrageous that a reasonable person would suffer severe emotional injury. Minor annoyances do not fall under this tort. Injuries to the mind or
emotions are easier to prove if there are physical symptoms like documented
shock, illness, or some other sort of physical manifestation.

A. Elements

1. Intentional or reckless action by the tortfeasor;
2. outrageous or extreme conduct by the tortfeasor
3. that causes
4. severe mental anguish in the victim. The test for anguish revolves around
   the way a reasonable person of ordinary sensibilities would react to the
   actions.

B. Sample Case

Maine was relatively late in recognizing this tort. It did so *Vicnire v. Ford
Motor Credit Co.*, 401 A. 2d 148, 154–55 (Me, 1979), but ultimately concluded
that the plaintiff had not met all the elements of the tort because the distress
resulting from defendant's acts was not of the nature required:

We now adopt the rule of liability stated in the Restatement of Torts. We expressly recognize that a defendant may be liable for engaging in extreme and outrageous conduct and intentionally or recklessly inflicting severe mental distress on a plaintiff. Specifically, in order to recover for the intentional infliction of emotional distress, a plaintiff must establish that (1) the defendant intentionally or recklessly inflicted severe emotional distress or was certain or substantially certain that such distress would result from his conduct, *Restatement (Second) of Torts* § 46, Comment i; (2) the conduct was so "extreme and outrageous" as to exceed "all possible bounds of decency" and must be regarded as "atrocious, and utterly intolerable in a civilized community," *Restatement (Second) of Torts* § 46, Comment d; (3) the actions of the defendant caused the plaintiff's emotional distress; and (4) the emotional distress suffered by the plaintiff was "severe" so that "no reasonable man could be expected to endure it." *Restatement (Second) of Torts* § 46, Comment j. Although "severe" emotional distress is usually manifested by "shock, illness or other bodily harm," such objective symptomatology is not an absolute prerequisite for recovery of damages for intentional, as opposed to negligent, infliction of emotional distress. *Restatement (Second) of Torts* § 46, Comment k. In appropriate cases, "severe" emotional distress may be inferred from the "extreme and outrageous" nature of the defendant's conduct alone. Id.

To summarize, a plaintiff may recover damages for emotional distress resulting from the tortious conduct of a defendant in three distinct situations. First, as traditionally provided, mental distress or "pain and suffering" accompanying physical injury caused by tortious conduct is compensable. Second, as established in Wallace, a plaintiff may recover damages for emotional distress resulting from negligent conduct (even though that conduct caused no direct physical injury) if the distress is "substantial and manifested by objective symptomatology," that is, results in illness or bodily harm. And, third, as recognized in this opinion, a defendant is subject to liability if he engages in extreme or outrageous conduct that intentionally or recklessly inflicts severe emotional distress upon another.

In the instant case, the presiding justice set aside the jury's verdict awarding plaintiff $5,000 in compensatory damages for mental suffering on grounds that "[t]here was no evidence of severe or substantial mental suffering, no evidence of objective symptomatology." A careful review of the record compels agreement with the presiding justice's conclusion. The sole evidence of plaintiff's emotional distress was his own testimony that he felt "kind of down" and "mad" and "nervous for about a month." As a matter of law that evidence could not support a verdict for plaintiff on a theory of negligent infliction of mental distress, since Vicnire suffered no illness or bodily harm (i.e., no objective symptomatology) as a result of his alleged distress. Even were the jury to conclude that defendant by extreme and outrageous conduct intentionally or recklessly inflicted mental distress upon Vicnire, there is no evidence that his alleged mental distress rose to that degree of severity that is required by the law to justify imposing liability upon defendant. This jury heard no evidence from which it could conclude that plaintiff's mental distress was so "severe" that "no reasonable man could be expected to endure it." In short, the presiding justice's order setting aside the jury's verdict of $5,000 in compensatory damages for emotional distress was entirely proper. (Footnote omitted.)

4. Invasion of Privacy

Most if not all states have privacy laws which dictate what information is private and what is considered public. Public figures like elected officials and movie stars have less protection of their privacy than ordinary persons. An individual's right to privacy does not mean a right to total secrecy. A person's privacy may be invaded by four different methods: intentional instruction, appropriation, public disclosure of private facts, and holding another to the public eye in a false light. As noted in the *Candebat v. Flanagan*, 487 So.2d 207 (Miss. 1986) "the four sub-torts differ as to their elements and as to the damages available."

4.1 Invasion of Privacy—Unreasonable Intrusion

This tort creates liability for intentional intrusion in another's private affairs if the intrusion would be highly offensive to a reasonable person.

A. Elements

1. Unreasonable intrusion
2. into the seclusion (private life) of another
3. that is offensive to a reasonable person
4. resulting in mental anguish or suffering to that person.

B. Sample Case

The plaintiffs in *Reid v. Pierce County*, 961 P. 2d 333, 340 (Wash, 1998) that for a period of at least ten years employees of the Pierce County Medical Examiner's office appropriated autopsy photographs of corpses, showing them at cocktail parties and using the photographs to create personal scrapbooks. Some relatives of the deceased individuals aware of the appropriation and use of the autopsy photographs through the press. The plaintiff's complaint alleged the appropriation and use of the autopsy photographs subjected the county to liability for tort of common law invasion of privacy, among other causes of action. The county argued if any right of privacy was violated, it was that of the deceased and not of the relatives of the deceased based on the general rule is that privacy is a personal interest and may not be brought by a relative of a deceased person. The appellate court disagreed and enumerated some of the areas commonly considered to be private:

> It is clear that had the County employees physically mutilated or otherwise physically interfered with the corpses of the Plaintiffs' relatives, liability would certainly exist. See *Wright v. Beardsley*, 46 Wash. 16, 20, 89 P. 172 (1907); *Gadbury v. Bleitz*, 133 Wash. 134, 233 P. 299, 44 A.L.R. 425 (1925). However, the County asserts that because the actions here involved photographs only, no harm was done. That argument is one of degree, not of distinction ...
> We agree with the Plaintiffs' interpretation of the common law right of privacy and recognize that the cases relied upon by Plaintiffs are more consistent with our own jurisprudence on this issue than those relied upon by the County.

In *Cowles Publ'g Co. v. State Patrol*, 109 Wash.2d 712, 748 P.2d 597 (1988), we identified the nature of facts protected by the right of privacy, stating:

> Every individual has some phases of his life and his activities and some facts about himself that he does not expose to the public eye, but keeps entirely to himself or at most reveals only to his family or to close personal friends. Sexual relations, for example, are normally entirely private matters, as are family quarrels, many unpleasant or disgraceful or humiliating illnesses, most intimate personal letters, most details of a man's life in his home, and some of his past history that he would rather forget. When these intimate details of his life are spread before the public gaze in a manner highly offensive to the ordinary reasonable man, there is an

actionable invasion of his privacy, unless the matter is one of legitimate public interest.

We fail to see how autopsy photographs of the Plaintiffs' deceased relatives do not constitute intimate details of the Plaintiffs' lives or are not
facts Plaintiffs do not wish exposed "before the public gaze." (Some
citations omitted.)

4.2 Invasion of Privacy—Appropriation

In order to commit the tort of invasion of privacy through appropriation,
the tortfeasor must use or take over for their own benefit the name or likeness
of another without permission. Simply calling one's self another person's name
does not meet the standards of appropriation. One must use another's social
or commercial standing or reputation to obtain some sort of benefit. Many of
these cases involve the use of photographs, artist's sketches, or quotations associated with names to sell someone else's goods or services.

A. Elements

1. A tortfeasor uses another person's name or likeness
2. without consent of that person and
3. obtains some benefit for using the person's name or likeness.

B. Sample Case

Candebat v. Flanagan, 487 So.2d 207, 209–12 (Miss. 1986) is an example of the
tort of invasion of privacy via appropriation. The primary argument is about the
nature of damages available. In this case, a woman was injured and an insurance
company paid her appropriately through her policy. However, the insurance company used her name and information in their flyer to advertise and receive new
business without the plaintiff's permission. The lower court directed a verdict for
the defendants after stating its opinion that in order to recover for an invasion of
privacy, one must specify his damages, and for punitive damages to be available,
there must be "malice, fraud, insult, [or] wanton and reckless disregard of plaintiff's rights." The plaintiffs argued on appeal that he misunderstood the very nature of the tort of invasion of privacy. The appellate court agreed with plaintiffs:

> Although actions for the invasion of privacy have been rare in Mississippi,
> the tort has received almost universal recognition in the United States.
> Every state except Rhode Island provides either statutory or common
> law relief for it. Prosser & Keeton, The Law of Torts, §118 (5th Ed. 1984).
> Mississippi gave implicit recognition to the tort in 1951. *Martin v.*

Dorton, 210 Miss. 668, 672–73, 50 So.2d 391, 393 (1951). The recognition was made explicit in *Deaton v. Delta Democrat Publishing Co.*, 326 So.2d 471, 473 (Miss. 1976). In this century, the doctrines surrounding the tort and the right to privacy have undergone rapid and extensive development. *In Re Brown*, 478 So.2d 1033, 1039–1040 (Miss. 1985). As Prosser remarks, "What has emerged is no simple matter. As it has appeared in the cases thus far decided, it is not one tort, but a complex of four." Prosser, § 117 at 851. As enumerated by Prosser, and recognized by this Court in *Deaton v. Delta Democrat Publishing Co.*, 326 So.2d 471, 473 (Miss. 1976), the four theories underlying the cause of action are as follows:

1. The intentional intrusion upon the solitude or seclusion of another;
2. The appropriation of another's identity for an unpermitted use;
3. The public disclosure of private facts; and
4. Holding another to the public eye in a false light.

This development is important because, as we shall see, the four sub-torts differ as to their elements and as to the damages available....

[T]he pleadings clearly allege that the defendants "either caused to be or did appropriate the names of Mr. James Candebat, Sr. and Mrs. Irene Candebat for the commercial advantage of the corporate defendant ... to further the mercantile goals of aggrandize and enrich [said] defendant ... without the knowledge or express consent of the Candebats." Thus, the gravamen of this action is clearly the appropriation of the identity of the plaintiffs without their consent.

There is no dispute as to the existence of the cause in Mississippi. Nor is it disputed that in Mississippi damages for mental suffering can be recovered even though there was no physical impact. The appellee admits as much in his brief. The decisive question, then, is whether or not the damages sought in the complaint are of the type available under the sub-tort of appropriation ... here are two principal schools of thought as to the damages available under the appropriation sub-tort. Courts side with one or the other according to their understanding of the nature of the interest protected by the action. Dean Prosser's comments on this issue are uncharacteristically opaque:

Although the element of protection of the plaintiff's personal feelings is not to be ignored in such a case, the effect of the appropriation decisions is to recognize or create an exclusive right in the plaintiff to a species of trade name, his own, and a kind of trademark in his likeness. It seems quite pointless to dispute over whether such a right is to be classified as "property"; it is at least clearly proprietary in its nature. (Prosser & Keeton, §117 at 854).

Despite the many qualifications used by Prosser in this discussion, some courts have seized upon the property oriented language and argued that the damages available must be comparable to those available in other suits for misuse of plaintiff's property. That is, the plaintiff can recover only the value of what is lost....

Another line of decisions, relied upon by the Candebats, has refused to interpret the "property" element of the injury as requiring the wholesale importation of property related limitations on damages into privacy actions. The ancestor of this line of cases is *Hinish v. Meier & Frank Co.*, 166 Or. 482, 506, 113 P.2d 438, 448 (1941), which held that recovery in a privacy action is not barred simply because the injury cannot be measured by pecuniary standard. The leading case on damages for mental suffering in a privacy action is *Fairfield v. American Photocopy Equipment Co.*, 138 Cal. App.2d 82, 291 P.2d 194 (1955). There the court stated:

> The gist of the cause of action in a privacy case is not injury to the character or reputation but a direct wrong of a personal character resulting in an injury to the feelings without regard to any effect which the publication may have on the property, business, pecuniary interest or the standing of the individual in the community.... The injury is mental and subjective. (138 Cal. App.2d at 86, 291 P.2d at 197).

On the whole, the approach of the second Restatement and the Fairfield court seem far preferable to that urged by the appellees, because the mere fact that the use of one's name or likeness shares certain characteristics of property does not prove that the law governing injuries to it must be governed solely by property related considerations. The injury to the plaintiff's feelings may very well be the more serious of the two in many instances; often an intrusion which is of very little commercial consequence can nonetheless cause serious emotional distress. The law should protect both the proprietary and emotional interests; it should not focus with tunnel vision on the property-related characteristics of the tort.

4.3 Invasion of Privacy—Public Disclosure of Private Facts

The public disclosure of private facts occurs when someone publicly exploits another person's private affairs in an unreasonably intrusive manner. Truth is not a defense to this tort because it is the unauthorized and offensive public revelation of private facts that is being protected against. The most common example involves communication by the mass media. It is important to note that public figures generally do not succeed in lawsuits against the media when such disclosures are made without malice. Not all jurisdictions recognize this tort; case law for the state and/or jurisdiction should be researched to see if this tort is available.

A. Elements

1. Public disclosure
2. of private facts or information of another person
3. which
    a. would be highly offensive and objectionable to a reasonable person, and
    b. are not of legitimate concern to the public.

B. Sample Case

In *Star-Telegram, Inc. v. Doe*, 915 SW 2d 471, 472–75 (Tex, 1995) the issue was whether a newspaper may be held liable for disclosing private facts about a victim of sexual assault which made the victim identifiable by her acquaintances. The Supreme Court held that under the specific facts presented, the information disclosed by the newspaper concerned matters of legitimate public concern.

A newspaper report obtained access to an unredacted police report of the incident that disclosed certain information about Doe including her age, her occupation as "owner" of a business, her business address, the make, model and color of her automobile, and a narrative description of the details of the offense, including the address where the offense occurred. Because the narrative makes clear that the offense occurred in Doe's home, the police report literally disclosed Doe's home address. The newspaper published stories disclosing Doe's age, the relative location of her residence, that she owned a home security system, that she took medication and that she owned a 1984 black Jaguar automobile and owned a travel agency. The facts revealed in both articles were true. Although the reports did not reveal Doe's name, Doe contended the details in the articles allowed all those who knew her to readily identify her as the victim. The court stated:

> Doe seeks to recover under the invasion of privacy tort for public disclosure of embarrassing private facts, which has three elements: (1) publicity was given to matters concerning one's personal life, (2) publication would be highly offensive to a reasonable person of ordinary sensibilities, and (3) the matter publicized is not of legitimate public concern. *Industrial Found. of the South v. Texas Indus. Accident Bd.*, 540

is not invaded when unimportant false statements are made, even when they are made deliberately. It is only when there is such a major misrepresentation of one's character, history, activities, or beliefs that serious offense may reasonably be expected to be taken by a reasonable person in his or her position, that there is a cause of action for invasion of privacy.... We now find that the facts of the present case properly present the issue of false light invasion of privacy and we hold that a person who places another before the public in a false light may be liable in Missouri for the resulting damages. In recognizing this cause of action, we note that as a result of the accessibility of the internet, the barriers to generating publicity are quickly and inexpensively surmounted. Moreover, the ethical standards regarding the acceptability of certain discourse have been diminished. Thus, as the ability to do harm grows, we believe so must the law's ability to protect the innocent. (Some citations omitted.)

However, the court recognized a concern that the tort might allow recovery beyond that permitted for libel or slander and thus would tend to exacerbate the tension between the First Amendment and these kind of cases. It therefore included an element requiting actual malice or recklessness. Since the plaintiff's complaint did not allege actual malice or recklessness, the plaintiff's cause of action could not succeed.

5. Trespass

Common law, statutory law, and case law all have protections for property and persons. The tort of trespass is designed to protect property, both real and personal. Typically, one of the rights associated with owning real or personal property is the exclusive right to use the property. When someone interferes with the owner's use of the property, the tort of trespass may be applicable. Ignorance may be bliss, but this does not excuse the tort of trespass; it is not a possible defense. Privilege and the doctrine of estoppel, however, may be used as possible defenses to trespass.

5.1 Trespass to Land

This tort occurs when someone enters upon another's real estate without the landowner's or possessor's consent. The tort occurs when the tortfeasor acts in such a way as to violate the possessor's exclusive right to use the land. It is still trespass if the unauthorized entry caused no damage to the real estate because the injury is the mere interference with the possessor's use of their own property. If a person is an invitee and is later asked to leave and does not, then the invitee status is void and that person is a trespasser. If there are no actual damages, only nominal damages are awarded. Trespass may occur below the surface, such as rights to minerals and above the surface, such as placement of utility lines.

A. Elements

1. Rightful possession of the real property by the plaintiff when the alleged trespass occurs. One does not have to be the owner of the property to be a plaintiff in a trespass case. A leaseholder or someone who is in "legal" possession of the property in question is enough.

2. Unauthorized entry upon the land by the defendant. If one does not have permission or a license to travel upon someone's property, any entry upon it is unauthorized.

3. Intent to enter the land without consent. This is not intent to commit trespass but merely the intent to enter upon the land.

B. Sample Case

The exact intent needed to commit trespass is often hard to grasp. In *Burt v. Beautiful Savior Luth. Church*, 809 P. 2d 1064 (Colo, 1990) the court dealt with the concept of "negligent trespass" and the issue of whether the defense of contributory negligence would apply to a claim of trespass:

> Contrary to defendant's contention, the concept of trespass developed much earlier than the concept of negligence. *Publix Cab Co. v. Colorado National Bank,* 139 Colo. 205, 338 P.2d 702 (1959). See C. Gregory, Trespass to Negligence to Absolute Liability, 37 W.Va.L.Rev. 359 (1951).
>
> In early English law, the writ of "trespass" had a basic criminal character and provided a cause of action for all direct and immediate injuries to person or property. "Trespass on the case," a separate writ which developed later, originally allowed remedies for all indirect injuries. It was from this latter writ that negligence emerged as a separate cause of action. Later, the original writ of "trespass" also evolved into separate torts. W. Prosser & W. Keeton, The Law of Torts §6 (5th ed. 1984).
>
> In defining the modern tort of trespass to property, some jurisdictions still make a distinction between direct and indirect injuries, labeling the former an intentional or "simple" trespass and the latter, negligent trespass. These jurisdictions apply the defense of contributory or comparative negligence to the tort of negligent trespass. See *Smith v. McCullough Dredging Co.,* 152 So.2d 194 (Fla.Dist.Ct.App.1963).

In Colorado, however, the present tort of trespass to property has no reference to the nature or immediacy of the harm, nor do we recognize the tort of "negligent trespass." See *Verzuh v. Rouse*, 660 P.2d 1301 (Colo.App.1982).

Consequently, the fact that, as defendant alleges here, the trespass in this case may have been caused by a negligent act is irrelevant. In Colorado, liability for trespass requires only an intent to do the act that itself constitutes, or inevitably causes, the intrusion. *Miller v. Carnation Co.*, 33 Colo.App. 62, 516 P.2d 661 (1973). Specifically, trespass is the physical intrusion upon property of another without the permission of the person lawfully entitled to the possession of the real estate. *Magliocco v. Olson*, 762 P.2d 681 (Colo.App.1987). "One is subject to liability to another for trespass, irrespective of whether he thereby causes harm to any legally protected interest of the other, if he intentionally ... enters land in the possession of the other, or causes a thing or a third person to do so...." *Miller v. Carnation, supra*; Restatement (Second) of Torts § 158 (1965).

Thus, a landowner who sets in motion a force which, in the usual course of events, will damage property of another, is guilty of trespass on such property. *Cobai v. Young*, 679 P.2d 121 (Colo.App.1984) (snow sliding from a roof into plaintiff's house); *Docheff v. City of Broomfield*, 623 P.2d 69 (Colo.App.1980) (discharge of drainage water onto property of adjoining landowner); *Miller v. Carnation Co.*, 39 Colo. App. 1, 564 P.2d 127 (1977) (failure to remove chicken manure resulting in pests intruding on plaintiff's property). Here, defendant's act of constructing the drainpipe in such a way as to cause water leakage into Burt's property amounted to a trespass.

Comparative negligence, however, is an affirmative defense only to negligence actions, that is, to liability based on fault. Section 13-21-111(1), C.R.S. (1987 Repl.Vol. 6A); see *Carman v. Heber*, 43 Colo.App. 5, 601 P.2d 646 (1979). Hence, it is not a proper issue for consideration in a trespass action.

5.2 Trespass to Chattel

A chattel is personal property, as opposed to real property. When a tortfeasor intentionally possesses or uses someone's chattel without consent, they have committed a trespass to chattel. Any unlawful interference with another's enjoyment of their personal property is a trespass. Trespass to chattel and conversion are very similar. The greatest distinction between these two torts is the extent of interference with the rightful owner's possession, with conversion being actual deprivation of the use of the property as opposed to simple interference with that use. The measure of damages for conversion is the total value of the chattel, while the measure of damages for trespass is the diminished value of the chattel due to the tortfeasor's use of the personal property.

A. Elements

1. Unauthorized possession or interference with the use of another individual's personal property.

2. Intent to deprive or interfere with the owner's possession or exclusive use of their chattel.

B. Sample Case

In today's technology world, trespass to chattel is often argued when it comes to the possession of internet domain names. In *eBay, Inc. v. Bidder's Edge, Inc.*, 100 F. Supp. 2d 1058, 1065 (Dist Ct, ND CA 2000). eBay argued that defendant interfered with their possessory interest of their computer system. Although eBay did not show a substantial interference, this court stated that simply intermeddling with, or use of, another's personal property, is sufficient to establish a cause of action for trespass to chattel. Thus the simple traversing of the site by a software robot constituted trespass:

> A software robot is a computer program which operates across the Internet to perform searching, copying and retrieving functions on the web sites of others. (Maynor Decl. ¶ 3; Johnson-Laird Decl. ¶ 15.) A software robot is capable of executing 1061*1061 thousands of instructions per minute, far in excess of what a human can accomplish. (Maynor Decl. ¶ 3.) Robots consume the processing and storage resources of a system, making that portion of the system's capacity unavailable to the system owner or other users. (Id.) Consumption of sufficient system resources will slow the processing of the overall system and can overload the system such that it will malfunction or "crash." (Id.) A severe malfunction can cause a loss of data and an interruption in services. (Id.)
>
> The eBay site employs "robot exclusion headers." (Id. ¶ 5.) A robot exclusion header is a message, sent to computers programmed to detect and respond to such headers, that eBay does not permit unauthorized robotic activity. (Id.) Programmers who wish to comply with the Robot Exclusion Standard design their robots to read a particular data file, "robots.txt," and to comply with the control directives it con-

tains. (Johnson-Laird Decl. ¶ 20.) ... According to eBay, the load on its servers resulting from BE's web crawlers represents between 1.11% and 1.53% of the total load on eBay's listing servers. eBay alleges both economic loss from BE's current activities and potential harm resulting

5.3 Toxic Trespass

Toxic trespass is devoted to actions involving toxic chemicals, pollutants, hazardous waste, and the like. When toxic substances enter upon another's property a trespass occurs if the other elements are met.

A. Elements

1. Unauthorized entry upon another person's real estate. This entry may be by seepage or drifting of the hazardous material onto the victim's land.

2. Intent to enter without consent. The intent to enter without consent may be implied from the disposal method used. If the tortfeasor failed to take sufficient precautions, then intent to trespass may be implied.

3. Tortfeasor's actions interfering with the land owner's exclusive right to use the land. The residues from these toxic materials are offensive and can make some real estate uninhabitable.

B. Sample Case

In *Martin v. Reynolds Metals Co.*, 221 Or. 86, 342 P. 2d 790 (Or, 1960) the court was called upon to determine whether the facts constituted trespass or only a nuisance. This was important because the statute of limitations on a nuisance was only two years, but that for trespass was three. The plaintiffs alleged that the defendant, in the operation of its aluminum reduction plant caused fluoride compounds in the form of gases and particulates to become airborne and settle upon the plaintiffs' land rendering it unfit for raising livestock during that period. The case discusses several examples of trespass by particles:

> The gist of the defendant's argument is as follows; a trespass arises only when there has been a "breaking and entering upon real property," constituting a direct, as distinguished from a consequential, invasion of the possessor's interest in land; and the settling upon the land of fluoride compounds consisting of gases, fumes and particulates is not sufficient to satisfy these requirements.... Trespass and private nuisance are separate fields of tort liability relating to actionable interference with the possession of land. They may be distinguished by

comparing the interest invaded; an actionable invasion of a possessor's interest in the exclusive possession of land is a trespass; an actionable invasion of a possessor's interest in the use and enjoyment of his land is a nuisance. 4 Restatement, Torts 224, Intro. Note Chapter 40.

The same conduct on the part of a defendant may and often does result in the actionable invasion of both of these interests, in which case the choice between the two remedies is, in most cases, a matter of little consequence. substances constitute a nuisance, but where the court does not discuss the applicability of the law of trespass to the same set of facts ... [I]t has been held that causing shot from a gun to fall upon the possessor's land is a trespass. *Munro v. Williams,* et al., 94 Conn 377, 109 A 129 (pellets from an air gun fell upon land); *Peters v. Ambridge District Sportsmen's Assn.,* 14 Beaver 99 (Penn 1952) (shot from shotguns fell upon land); *DiGirolamo v. Philadelphia Gun Club,* 371 Pa 40, 89 A2d 357 (1952) (same); *Whittaker v. Stangvick* et al., 100 Minn 386, 111 NW 295 (1907) (same); *Herrin v. Sutherland,* 74 Mont 587, 241 P 328 (1925) (shotgun shot passing over surface of land).

The dropping of particles of molten lead upon the plaintiff's land has been held to be a trespass. *Van Alstyne v. Rochester Telephone Corp.,* 163 Misc 258, 296 NY Supp 726. And the defendant was held liable in trespass where spray from a cooling tower on the roof of its theater fell upon the plaintiff's land. *B & R Luncheonette, Inc. v. Fairmont Theatre Corp.,* 278 App Div 133, 103 NY Supp2d 747.

The deposit of soot and carbon from defendant's mill upon plaintiff's land was held to be a trespass in *Young v. Fort Frances Pulp and Paper Co.,* 17 Ont Wkly Notes 6 (Canada 1919).

And liability on the theory of trespass has been recognized where the harm was produced by the vibration of the soil or by the concussion of the air which, of course, is nothing more than the movement of molecules one against the other. *McNeill v. Redington,* 67 Cal App2d 315, 154 P2d 428 (1945).

6. Conversion

A conversion action charges a person with unauthorized exercise of rights of ownership over personal property. Conversion occurs when a tortfeasor, without the consent of the owner, deprives an owner possession of their chattel and puts or converts the property to the tortfeasor's own use. It is a broader version of the tort of trespass to chattel. It is differentiated based upon the scope of the deprivation of the owner's use of their personal property due to the tortfeasor's control of that property. Unlike trespass to chattel, conversion also requires the tortfeasor convert the personal property for the tortfeasor's own use. The deprivation of possession may occur through physical possession, which is the most common, but it may also happen through damage or destruction to the property. Additionally, deprivation may take place simply through using the chattel.

A. Elements

1. The plaintiff was the owner of the property or entitled to its possession.
2. The defendant took possession of the property with the intent to exercise some control over it. The tortfeasor does not have to injure the chattel to convert it.
3. The defendant thereby deprived the plaintiff of the right to possession.
4. The plaintiff does not consent to the defendant's use of the property.

B. Sample Case

The elements of conversion were first stated in Mississippi through the case of *Miss. Motor Finance, Inc. v. Thomas d/b/a Thomas Auto Parts Co.*, 149 So.2d 20, 21–2 (Miss. 1963). The plaintiff had a lien on a car and the defendant had a mechanic's lien on the same vehicle. The defendant did not provide plaintiff with notice of proceedings to enforce the mechanics lien. Plaintiff alleged that defendant's enforcement of the mechanic's lien by sale of the car constituted conversion. The car was sold under a judgment for the enforcement of the mechanic's lien, and was purchased by the defendant at the execution sale. The court held there was no conversion:

> It is well settled that the acts alleged to constitute a conversion must be positive and tortious. 89 C.J.S. 534, Trover and Conversion, Section 4. (Hn 3) The mere purchase of personal property in good faith from a person who has no right to sell it is not a conversion; there is no conversion until the title of the lawful owner is made known and resisted or the purchaser exercises dominion over the property by use, sale, or otherwise. 89 C.J.S. 552, Trover and Conversion, Section 45 b, and cases cited.
>
> In *McJunkin v. Hancock*, 71 Okla. 257, 176 P. 740, the Court said: "To make out a conversion, there must be proof of a wrongful possession, or the exercise of a dominion in exclusion or defiance of the owner's right, or of an unauthorized and injurious use, or of a wrongful de-

tention after demand. *Sivils v. Aldridge*, 162 Pac. 198." In *Spooner v. Holmes*, 102 Mass. 503, 3 Am. Rep. 491, Mr. Justice Gray, speaking for the Court, said: "Action of tort * * * cannot be maintained without proof that the defendant either did some positive wrongful act with the intention to appropriate the property to himself, or to deprive the rightful owner of it, or destroyed the property." In *Lee Tung v. Burkhart*, 59 Or. 195, 116 Pac. 1066, the Court held that in order to maintain an action for conversion, there must have been, on the part of the defendant, some unlawful assumption of dominion over the personal property involved, in defiance or exclusion of the plaintiff's rights, or else a withholding of the possession under a claim of right or title inconsistent with that of plaintiff. In *Coleman v. Francis*, 102 Conn. 612, 129 A. 718, the Court held that to hold a purchaser in good faith in the regular course of business from the apparent owner in possession liable for conversion, it should be shown that he assumed dominion over the property by use or otherwise after the lawful owner's title was made known to him, or refused to return the property after demand.

7. Defamation

Defamation is the transmission of false statements about one person to others that harm the reputation, business or property rights of that person. People may be "defamed" by either the written tort of libel or the oral tort of slander. Different states may have different elements for these torts. However, many jurisdictions follow the Restatement Second, Torts §558 which lists the elements as the following: (1) a false and defamatory statement concerning the plaintiff; (2) an unprivileged publication to a third party; (3) fault amounting to at least negligence on the part of the publisher; and (4) either actionability of the statement irrespective of special harm or the existence of special harm caused by the publication.

7.1 Libel/Slander

Libel is a written false and disparaging statement to a third party. Slander is an oral false and disparaging statement to a third party. The publication of the defamatory information must injure the victim's reputation in the community. The elements of libel and slander vary by court, so it is important to perform research as to the specific elements based on jurisdiction. Public figures have greater access to the media to refute false charges than the ordinary person so not as much protection is given to them. There are certain statements that are slander *per se*, indicating that some words are defamatory in and of themselves, therefore the victim does not have to prove damages to be successful. Truth is an absolute defense in defamation cases. However, what is considered to be true is often a matter of opinion. Even though the element of intent is typically a part of any libel or slander cause of action, the intent need only be the intent to make the statement, not the specific intent to cause damage to a person. Malice may be required, especially when the person about whom the statement is made is a public figure.

A. Elements

1. Written (libel) or oral (slander) statement
2. that is false and defamatory
3. about another person
4. to a third party (also known as publication). Statements made by the tortfeasor directly to the victim are defamatory only if seen or heard by another
5. that causes
6. harm to the victim's reputation in the community. Community is narrowly defined as a significant number of persons acquainted or familiar with the victim. It is commonly held that statements are libelous or slanderous if they ridicule, humiliate or subject the victim to contempt or hatred among their peers.

B. Sample Case

Ferguson v. Watkins, 448 So.2d 271, 273 (Miss. 1984) explains the nature of the statements required for libel or slander. Three physicians operating the emergency room in the publicly funded hospital demanded ouster of the hospital administrator. They were subjected to searing commentary by an editorial columnist in a local newspaper. The court held that such persons are not libeled even though described in caustic if not contemptuous language and even though to a neutral observer the criticism is unfair, so long as clear falsity of fact is not found in the editorial commentary. Alternatively, it held that such persons are vortex or limited purpose public figures who may not recover in a libel action absent proof of actual malice:

> We have repeatedly recognized the common law rule that:
> Any written or printed language which tends to injure one's reputation, and thereby expose him to public hatred, contempt or ridicule, degrade him in society, lessen him in public esteem or lower him in the confidence of the community is actionable per se.

See, e.g., *Gulf Publishing Co., Inc. v. Lee*, 434 So.2d 687, 695 (Miss. 1983); ... See also, Restatement, Torts 2d §559 (1977).

Two restrictions upon the action for defamation are and must be strictly enforced. First, the words employed must have clearly been directed toward the plaintiff. Beyond that, the defamation must be clear and unmistakable from the words themselves and not be the product of innuendo, speculation or conjecture.

There is no such thing as a libelous idea. Still, a defamatory communication 276*276 may consist of a statement in the form of an opinion. Opinion statements are actionable only if they clearly and unmistakably imply the allegation of undisclosed false and defamatory facts as the basis for the opinion. See Restatement, Torts 2d §566 (1977).

On the other hand, nothing in life or our law guarantees a person immunity from occasional sharp criticism, nor should it. Short of becoming a hermit, no person avoids a few linguistic slings and arrows, many demonstrably unfair. It may be true that our law, quite wisely, has moved beyond the child's retort, "Sticks and stones may break my bones but words can never hurt me," Still our sensitivity to the destructive power of words hardly suggests we assess damages for all bruised feelings.

These considerations have shaped a rule of law in our "fair comment" cases. *Edmonds v. Delta Democrat Publishing Co.*, 230 Miss. 583, 93 So.2d 171 (1957); *Reaves v. Foster,* 200 So.2d 453, 455–456 (Miss. 1967). Caustic commentary is simply not actionable libel.

7.2 Slander of Title

Slander of title is an injury to property which occurs when a tortfeasor makes false statements about an individual's ownership of property. The statements are not designed to personally defame the owner but to injure the owner's ability to use or sell the property. Often cases include real estate and the filing of spurious or false liens. Punitive damages for libel and slander have been found to be unconstitutional by the United States Supreme Court, at least when liability is based upon a simple negligence theory as opposed to one involving malice. *Gertz v. Robert Welch, Inc.*, 418 U.S. 323, 94 S.Ct. 2997, 41 L.Ed.2d 789 (1974).

A. Elements

1. False statements regarding a person's ownership of property. This normally occurs when the tortfeasor falsely impugns the title to another's property.

2. Intent to hinder or damage the owner's use of the property. The tortfeasor must intend to hamper or injure the owner's use of the property.

3. Communication (publication) of the falsehoods to third parties. The false statements of the ownership must be communicated to a third party.

B. Sample Case

In *Ezell v. Graves*, 807 SW 2d 700 (Tenn, 1990) the trial court held that an essential element of the claim of libel of title is that the plaintiff must prove that an actual prospective purchaser was deterred by the defendants actions from buying the property. Since the plaintiffs admitted that they had no intention of selling their property, the trial court granted the defendants' motion for summary judgment. The trial judge also concluded that the plaintiffs' litigation expenses incurred in removing the cloud from their title are not recoverable as special damages in the present action. The appellate court disagreed:

> Libel of title has long been recognized as an actionable tort in Tennessee. *Smith v. Gernt*, 2 Tenn.C.C.A. (Higgins) 65 (1911). As with all other defamation cases, a plaintiff is required to plead and prove the existence of actual damages in order to succeed with his claim.... The first question raised on appeal focuses on the extent of the plaintiffs' burden of proving special damages in a libel of title action. While there are no reported Tennessee decisions on point, a majority of the other jurisdictions addressing the issue have concluded that in order to establish special damages for libel of title, the plaintiff must identify a particular prospective purchaser who was prevented by the slander from buying the disparaged property.... See generally, Annotation, Special Damages in Slander of Title Actions, 4 A.L.R. 4th 532 (1981). While the reasoning of these cases varies, they all apparently focus on the precision with which a plaintiff must prove damages. Absent a showing that a particular purchaser was deterred, these decisions imply that there simply can be no actual damages, or at least the measure would prove too speculative....
>
> But the failure to prove out-of-pocket loss is not necessarily determinative. *Handley v. May*, 588 S.W.2d, at 776. The issue is whether there exists evidence of the types of injury outlined in *Gertz*:
>
> > We need not define "actual injury," as trial courts have wide experience in framing appropriate jury instructions in tort actions. Suffice it to say that actual injury is not limited to out-of-pocket loss. Indeed, the more customary types of actual harm inflicted by defamatory falsehood include impairment of reputation and standing in

the community, personal humiliation, and mental anguish and suffering. Of course, juries must be limited by appropriate instructions, and all awards must be supported by competent evidence concerning the injury, *although there need be no evidence which assigns an actual dollar value to the injury. Gertz v. Robert Welch, Inc.,* 418 U.S. at 350–51, 94 S.Ct. at 3012. (Emphasis added.)

Thus, while a showing that a particular purchaser was deterred from purchasing the plaintiff's property due to the defendant's libelous actions would be sufficient proof of a potential loss, such a showing is not a prerequisite to maintenance of the suit. In such a situation, the value of the plaintiff's damages would be no more precise than is true in the case at bar. The plaintiffs here, while admitting that they do not presently intend to place their property on the market, have presented the testimony of a real estate agent that the value of the land has, in his opinion, decreased in value due to the defendants' libel. In a case where a prospective purchaser has been deterred from buying the property, the measure of damages would be the contract price less the value of the land, *Yarbrough v. Stiles,* 717 S.W.2d 886 (Tenn. App. 1986)—a measure that requires an opinion as to the value. In a case where there was no prospective purchaser, the damages could be established by the same person giving an opinion as to the before and after value of the property. So, the fact that these plaintiffs do not presently intend to sell their property does not necessarily make their damages any more speculative than they would be had a particular purchaser been deterred. If the plaintiffs can show with reasonable certainty that the defendants' actions have caused them actual pecuniary loss, they are entitled to recover for their actual damages. They should not be forced to sell property which they desire to retain in order to be made whole again from the defendants' injurious conduct.

7.3 Commercial Disparagement

This tort to property focuses directly upon the chattel itself. The tort consists of false statements published to third parties about a person's goods, services or business enterprise. Disparagement of goods impedes the chattel owner's ability to use or sell their personal property. Disparagement of services interferes with a service provider's ability to engage in provision of services. Disparagement of business occurs when the tortfeasor impugns the integrity of another's business venture.

A. Elements

1. False statements about an individual's goods, services or business.

2. Intent to injure the victim's ability to use goods, furnish services or conduct business. Disparagement of goods requires the tortfeasor intends to injure the victim's capability of using their personal property, provide services or engage in business.

3. Communication (publication) to third parties.

B. Sample Case

The distinction between defamation and commercial disparagement can lead to confusion. The court in *Allcare, Inc. v. Bork*, 176 Ill. App.3d 993, 531 NE 2d (1988) explicates that distinction:

> *Crinkley v. Dow Jones & Co.* (1978), 67 Ill. App.3d 869, 385 N.E.2d 714, held that a statement that the plaintiff had been involved in "payoffs" to agents of foreign governments while a top officer of G.D. Searle & Co. did not disparage the plaintiff's services and entitle him to injunctive relief under the Trade Practices Act or damages under the Consumer Fraud Act. The court noted that section 2(8) of the Trade Practices Act (Ill. Rev. Stat. 1977, ch. 121 1/2, par. 312(8)) substantially codified the common law tort of commercial disparagement, i.e., disparagement of the quality of one's goods or services. The court held that the statement at issue did not give rise to a cause of action therefor because, while it may have imputed to plaintiff want of integrity in his business, it had not disparaged the quality of his services as an executive. That the statement might constitute defamation did not change the result since defamation and commercial disparagement are two distinct causes of action. Defamation lies when a person's integrity in his business or profession is attacked while commercial disparagement lies when the quality of his goods or services is attacked. Finally, while one statement could simultaneously constitute defamation and commercial disparagement, such was not the case with the statement at issue. *Crinkley*, 67 Ill. App.3d at 876–77.
>
> Similarly, *American Pet Motels, Inc. v. Chicago Veterinary Medical Association* (1982), 106 Ill. App.3d 626, 435 N.E.2d 1297, held that a statement accusing the plaintiff, a pet boarding service, of the unlicensed practice of veterinary medicine, a violation of Illinois law, did not constitute commercial disparagement. The court held that the statement did not disparage the quality of the plaintiff's services because

it did not indicate that its business practices were substandard, negligent or harmful. As such, the plaintiff was not entitled to injunctive relief under the Trade Practices Act. *American Pet Motels*, 106 Ill. App.3d at 633.

We find the statements at issue in *American Pet Motels*, and especially in *Crinkley*, and the statement in this case to be substantially similar. As such, plaintiff's reliance on the fact, noted in *Crinkley*, that a statement may constitute both defamation and commercial disparagement is simply unavailing. Plaintiff argues that an allegation of Medicare fraud in the medical supply industry also impugns the services of the person thereby defamed because it will cause third parties not to do business with it. In so arguing, plaintiff ignores the settled test, applied in *Crinkley* and *American Pet Motels*, to determine when a statement constitutes a defamation and/or commercial disparagement.

Moreover, we believe that in almost every case of defamation of a business or businessman it could be alleged that the defamation caused third parties to refrain from dealing with the plaintiff and, thus, under plaintiff's test, constituted commercial disparagement. However, defamation and commercial disparagement protect different interests. Defamation protects interests of personality. Commercial disparagement protects property interests. As such, there is a " 'clear line of demarcation' " between the two causes of action.

8. Nuisance

The tort of nuisance is difficult to define because the controlling facts are rarely alike and different jurisdictions provide varied definitions. A nuisance is an unreasonable or unlawful use of one's real property that injures another person or interferes with another's use of his/her real property. A nuisance may also be defined as conduct that is either unreasonable or unlawful and causes annoyance, inconvenience, discomfort, or damage to others. Nuisances are defined by common law and statute. There are two types: private and public.

8.1 Private Nuisance

The tort of private nuisance is based on the idea that it is the duty of every person to make reasonable use of his or her property and to not unnecessarily damage or annoy his or her neighbors. It is worth noting that the interference does not need to involve a physical or tangible intrusion. The tortfeasor is the land user who uses the land in such a way that it offends the property's neighbors. Some classic examples are ground vibrations, pollution, crop destruction, flooding, excessive clutter, unwanted excavations, noxious odors, smoke/dust, excessive noise/temperatures, toxic tort nuisances and incessant telephone calls. It is a defense to private nuisance is if a person "comes to the nuisance" meaning the activity in which is a nuisance was already occurring. Many jurisdictions follow the rule in the Restatement Second of Torts, on which the elements below are based.

A. Elements

1. The interference or invasion of one's property in a non-trespass manner,
2. must have been caused by another's conduct in acting or failing to act, and
3. must consist of an invasion by something perceptible to the senses.

B. Sample Case

" 'There is perhaps no more impenetrable jungle in the entire law than that which surrounds the word 'nuisance'. It has meant all things to all men' (Prosser, Torts [4th ed], p 571). From a point someplace within this oft-noted thicket envisioned by Professor Prosser, this appeal emerges," starts the opinion in *Copart Inds. v. Con Ed*, 41 NY 2d 564, 568–9 (NY, 1977). This quote is often found in nuisance decisions. The court here goes on to distinguish between public and private nuisance to explain the role of the latter:

> Much of the uncertainty and confusion surrounding the use of the term nuisance, which in itself means no more than harm, injury, inconvenience, or annoyance (see Webster's Third New International Dictionary, p. 571; American Heritage Dictionary, p. 900), arises from a series of historical accidents covering the invasion of different kinds of interests and referring to various kinds of conduct on the part of defendants (Prosser, Torts [4th ed], pp. 571–572). The word surfaced as early as the twelfth century in the assize of nuisance, which provided redress where the injury was not a disseisin but rather an indirect damage to the land or an interference with its use and enjoyment. Three centuries later the remedy was replaced by the common-law action on the case for nuisance, invoked only for damages upon the invasion of interests in the use and enjoyment of land, as well as of easements and profits ...
>
> A private nuisance threatens one person or a relatively few (*McFarlane v. City of Niagara Falls*, 247 N.Y. 340, 344), an essential feature being an interference with the use or enjoyment of land (*Blessington v. McCrory Stores Corp.*, 198 Misc 291, 299, affd 279 App Div 806, affd 305 N.Y. 140). It is actionable by the individual person or persons

whose rights have been disturbed (Restatement, Torts, notes preceding §822, p. 217). A public, or as sometimes termed a common, nuisance is an offense against the State and is subject to abatement or prosecution on application of the proper governmental agency (Restatement, Torts, notes preceding §822, p 217; see Penal Law, §240.45). It consists of conduct or omissions which offend, interfere with or cause damage to the public in the exercise of rights common to all (*New York Trap Rock Corp. v. Town of Clarkston*, 299 N.Y. 77, 80), in a manner such as to offend public morals, interfere with use by the public of a public place or endanger or injure the property, health, safety or comfort of a considerable number of persons (*Melker v. City of New York*, 190 N.Y. 481, 488; Restatement, Torts, notes preceding §822, p. 217).

As observed by Professor Prosser, public and private nuisances "have almost nothing in common, except that each causes inconvenience to someone, and it would have been fortunate if they had been called from the beginning by different names" (Prosser, Torts [4th ed], p. 573). Not only does confusion arise from sameness in denomination and from the lack of it in applicability, but also from the fact that, although an individual cannot institute an action for public nuisance as such, he may maintain an action when he suffers special damage from a public nuisance (Restatement, Torts, notes preceding §822, p. 217; *Wakeman v. Wilbur*, 147 N.Y. 657, 663–664).

This developmental tracing indicates the erroneous concept under which appellant labors. It also points out that nuisance, as a general term, describes the consequences of conduct, the inconvenience to others, rather than the type of conduct involved (2 NY PJI 653). It is a field of tort liability rather than a single type of tortious conduct (Prosser, Torts [4th ed], p. 573).

Despite early private nuisance cases, which apparently assumed that the defendant was strictly liable, today it is recognized that one is subject to liability for a private nuisance if his conduct is a legal cause of the invasion of the interest in the private use and enjoyment of land and such invasion is (1) intentional and unreasonable, (2) negligent or reckless, or (3) actionable under the rules governing liability for abnormally dangerous conditions or activities (Restatement, Torts 2d [Tent Draft No. 16], §822; Prosser, Torts [4th ed], p 574; 2 NY PJI 653–654; see Spano v. Perini Corp., 25 N.Y.2d 11, 15; Kingsland v. Erie Co. Agric. Soc., 298 N.Y. 409, 426–427; Wright v. Masonite Corp., 237 F Supp 129, 138, affd 368 F.2d 661, cert den 386 US 934).

8.2 Public Nuisance

As with other torts, jurisdictions differ slightly on the definition of a public or common nuisance. A public nuisance is an unreasonable interference with the health, safety, peace, comfort, or convenience of the surrounding community or public. More than one person must be affected. Common examples are gambling, prostitution, distribution of sexually explicit materials, sale of alcohol, toxic waste management, weeds/poisonous plants growing on property, failing to comply with health codes and keeping viscous animals on the property. Due to the fact that public nuisances affect the public at large, the very existence or continuance of the activity is harmful therefore "coming to the nuisance" is not a defense as it is with private nuisance cases. In order for a private individual to bring an action on a public nuisance that individual must be able to show they suffered special harm over and above that experienced by the public.

A. Elements

1. The tortfeasor's activity that
2. unreasonably and substantially interferes with
3. the public's use and enjoyment of legal rights common to the public
4. resulting in
5. damage to the plaintiff over and above that experienced by the public.

B. Sample Case

The interplay between statutes and common law is especially difficult to unwind in public nuisance cases as can be seen in *Brown v. Scioto Cty. Bd. of Commrs.*, 87 Ohio App. 3d 704—Ohio: Court of Appeals 1993:

> Restatement of the Law 2d, Torts (1979) 87, Section 821B, defines public nuisance as an unreasonable interference with a right common to the general public. Conduct does not become a public nuisance merely because it interferes with a large number of people. At common law, there must be some interference with a public right which is common to all members of the general public. In addition to common-law public nuisance, Ohio has adopted statutes and administrative regulations which define certain conduct as being a public nuisance. These statutes amount to a legislative declaration that the proscribed conduct is an unreasonable interference with a public right ... A public nuisance as such does not afford a basis for recovery of damages in tort unless there is particular harm to the plaintiff

that is of a different kind than that suffered by the public in general. See Restatement of the Law 2d, Torts (1979) 94, Section 821C(1). When the particular harm involved consists of interference with the use and enjoyment of land, the landowner may recover either on the basis of the particular harm to her resulting from the public nuisance or on the basis of private nuisance. See Restatement of the Law 2d, Torts (1979) 93, Section 821B, Comment h. Here appellant contends that she lost an opportunity to sell her property and was unable to use and enjoy it. This is a sufficiently distinct or particular harm from the public right so as to allow recovery under a statutory public nuisance theory.

However, just as the appellees' sewage disposal plant cannot be a common-law public nuisance because of the governmental authorization to operate, it likewise cannot be an absolute statutory nuisance. In *Schoener,* the First District Court of Appeals held that a regulated solid waste disposal facility could not be subject to liability as an absolute nuisance. In order for a duly licensed and regulated sanitary landfill to be found liable for maintaining a nuisance, negligence must be established, i.e., a qualified nuisance. The *Schoener* court based its holding upon the following rationale:

> "A standard of strict liability is not appropriate under these circumstances, where the public policy of Ohio has clearly chosen to allow operators such as Rumpke to do business in this state subject to the limitations imposed under what can only be termed a comprehensive and vigilant regulatory scheme. Once an operator becomes licensed by the state, we think it fair to say in law that part of the quid pro quo for the submission to such exacting regulatory oversight is the operator's insulation from liability under a theory of strict liability. Therefore, we conclude that the trial court did not err when it declined to instruct the jury concerning absolute nuisance."

As stated above, appellant introduced no evidence that appellees were not licensed to operate the sewage disposal plant. Consequently, pursuant to *Schoener,* she failed to raise a genuine issue of material fact as to the presence of absolute public nuisance, but may proceed on the theory of qualified statutory. (Citations omitted.)

9. False Imprisonment

This intentional tort occurs when a person intentionally confines someone without that person's consent. It is meant to protect a person's right to control their own freedom of movement. There are several ways in which the tortfeasor may confine their captive, including physical barriers and express/implied threats. A common example of false imprisonment is when a suspected shoplifter is wrongfully detained by a store manager until the proper authorities arrive. Many states grant store owners either a common-law or statutory right called the "shopkeeper's privilege" to stop and detain a suspected shoplifter, as long as the holding is reasonable.

A. Elements

1. Confinement without captive's consent. All methods of confinement include a restriction of the victim's freedom of movement, the victim's awareness of the restriction, and the victim's lack of consent to the restriction. Threats of physical or emotional violence can effectively confine a person.

2. Tortfeasor's intent to confine victim. The tortfeasor must intended to confine the victim for false imprisonment to occur. Intent may be expressed or implied by conduct.

3. Confinement for an appreciable amount of time. The time period depends upon the specific facts of the case. Usually it is defined as unreasonable under the circumstances.

4. No reasonable means of escape. This depends on the case but usually includes any route that a reasonable person would use to flee given the circumstances.

5. (In some jurisdictions) awareness on the part of the plaintiff of the confinement.

B. Sample Case

Molko v. Holy Spirit Assn., 46 Cal.3d 1092, 762 P.2d 46, 252 Cal. Rptr. 122 (1988) deals with in unusual claim of false imprisonment brought by a plaintiff claiming she had been held captive by the Unitarian Church:

> False imprisonment is "the unlawful violation of the personal liberty of another." (Pen. Code, § 236; *see Parrott v. Bank of America* (1950) 97 Cal. App.2d 14, 22 [217 P.2d 89, 35 A.L.R.2d 263] [definition of crime and tort the same].) (20) "The tort of false imprisonment is the nonconsensual, intentional confinement of a person, without lawful privilege, for an appreciable length of time, however short." (*City of Newport Beach v. Sasse* (1970) 9 Cal. App.3d 803, 810 [88 Cal. Rptr. 476].) A person is falsely imprisoned "if he is wrongfully deprived of his freedom to leave a particular place by the conduct of another." (*Schanafelt v. Seaboard Finance Co.* (1951) 108 Cal. App.2d 420, 422–423 [239 P.2d 42].)

Leal contends she was falsely imprisoned by the Church at Boonville, at Camp K, at Boulder, at Los Angeles, and at various locations in San Francisco.[16] She admits she was theoretically free to depart at any time; she was not physically restrained, subjected to threats of physical force, or subjectively afraid of physical force. She insists, however, that her "imprisonment arose from the harm she came to believe would result if she left the community." That harm, specifically, was that her family "would be damned in Hell forever and they would forever feel sorry for having blown their one chance to unite with the Messiah and make it to Heaven."

The claim cannot survive constitutional scrutiny. Although Leal correctly asserts that false imprisonment may be "effected by ... fraud or deceit" (Pen. Code, § 237), her theory implicates the Church's beliefs: it plainly seeks to make the Church liable for threatening divine retribution. As we stated earlier, such threats are protected religious speech (see *Fowler v. Rhode Island, supra,* 345 U.S. at p. 70 [97 L.Ed. at p. 831]; *Van Schaick v. Church of Scientology of Cal., Inc., supra,* 535 F. Supp. at p. 1139) and cannot provide the basis for tort liability. Accordingly, we hold the Court of Appeal correctly affirmed the summary judgment for the Church as to Leal's action for false imprisonment.

10. Sexual Harassment

Title VII of the Civil Rights Act of 1964 makes it unlawful for an employer to discriminate against an individual due to race, color, religion, sex or national origin. Sexual harassment claims can be brought under Title VII, but there is also a basis in tort law for the claims. Sexual harassment is the unwelcome sexual advances, requests for sexual favors and other verbal or physical conduct of a sexual nature that affects an individual's employment or work environment.

A. Elements

(Based on Title VII of the Civil Rights Act of 1964)
1. Plaintiff was a member of a protected class;
2. plaintiff was subjected to unwelcome sexual harassment in the form of
   a. sexual advances,
   b. requests for sexual favors or
   c. other verbal or physical conduct of a sexual nature;
3. the harassment complained of was based upon sex;
4. the charged sexual harassment had the effect of

a. unreasonably interfering with the plaintiff's work performance and

b. creating an intimidating, hostile or offensive working environment that affected the psychological well-being of the plaintiff and

5. the existence of *respondeat superior* liability.

B. Sample Case

The line between workplace activity that every employee must tolerate and conduct that crosses the line into sexual harassment can be hard to draw. The court in *Conti v. Spitzer Auto World Amherst, Inc.*, 2008 Ohio 1320 (2008) explains:

> In order to determine whether an environment is sufficiently hostile to warrant a finding of sexual harassment this Court examines the totality of the circumstances including:
>
> "the frequency of the discriminatory conduct; its severity; whether it is physically threatening or humiliating, or a mere offensive utterance; and whether it unreasonably interferes with an employee's work performance. The effect on the employee's psychological well-being is, of course, relevant to determining whether the plaintiff actually found the environment abusive. But while psychological harm, like any other relevant factor, may be taken into account, no single factor is required." *Harris v. Forklift Sys. Inc.* (1993), 510 U.S. 17, 23.
>
> We also note that the standards for judging hostility are demanding such that "the ordinary tribulations of the work place, such as, sporadic use of abusive language, gender-related jokes, and occasional teasing" will not constitute a hostile work environment. (Quotations and citation omitted.) *Faragher v. Boca Raton* (1998), 524 U.S. 775, 788.

11. Fraud and Misrepresentation

The intentional tort of fraud, or deceit, is when a tortfeasor makes false statements to entice the victim to give up something of value to the tortfeasor. Fraud and misrepresentation are not the same. Fraud includes the element of intent to deceive.

Misrepresentation includes negligent misrepresentation, when a person should have known the statement was false, but made it without intending to deceive. In some instances fraud is referred to as intentional misrepresentation.

The false statement must be a statement of fact, not opinion. Thus when a salesperson uses puffery, this is not a misrepresentation or fraud.

11.1 Fraud (Intentional Misrepresentation)

A. Elements

Defendant:

1. makes materially false statements
2. intending to deceive
3. knowing the statements are false
4. for the purpose of obtaining something of value.

Plaintiff:

5. justifiably relies on the statements
6. to his or her detriment.

B. Sample Case

The court in *Channel Master Corp. v. Aluminium Ltd.*, 4 N.Y.2d 403, 176 N.Y.S.2d 259, 151 N.E.2d 833 (1958) was called upon to determine the sufficiency of a complaint in a tort action for damages based on fraud and deceit. The plaintiff, a manufacturer and processor of aluminum, required for its business a dependable supply of aluminum ingot in large quantity. The defendant was engaged in the business of selling that metal. The plaintiff alleged defendant represented that "its available and uncommitted supplies and productive capacity of aluminum ingot, then existing, were such as rendered it then capable of selling to the plaintiff 400,000 pounds per month and that it had entered into no binding commitments with other customers which could in the future reduce such available and uncommitted supplies and productive capacity."

The complaint then recited that such representations were made "with the intention and knowledge that plaintiff should rely thereon and in order to induce the plaintiff to refrain from entering into commitments with other suppliers and to purchase the greater part of its requirements from the defendant," that the plaintiff acted in reliance on the representations and that they were false and known by the defendant to be so. The complaint further asserted the defendant had previously entered into long-term contracts with other customers that committed all of the defendant's supplies and productive capacity for many years to come. By reason of the defendant's fraudulent misrepresentations and the plaintiff's reliance thereon, the complaint continued, the plaintiff refrained from securing commitments for future supplies from others and was thereby injured in its business. The defendant moved to dismiss the complaint, urging the insufficiency of [the] cause of action.

The appellate court found the complaint sufficient:

To maintain an action based on fraudulent representations, whether it be for the rescission of a contract or, as here, in tort for damages, it is sufficient to show that the defendant knowingly uttered a falsehood intending to deprive the plaintiff of a benefit and that the plaintiff was thereby deceived and damaged. The essential constituents of the action are fixed as representation of a material existing fact, falsity, scienter, deception and injury. (Accordingly, one "who fraudulently makes a misrepresentation of * * * intention * * * for the purpose of inducing another to act or refrain from action in reliance thereon in a business transaction" is liable for the harm caused by the other's justifiable reliance upon the misrepresentation. (3 Restatement, Torts, § 525, p. 59.)

As examination of the complaint demonstrates, it contains all the necessary elements of a good cause of action, including statements of existing fact, as opposed to expressions of future expectation. The representations allegedly made, that the defendant had "available and uncommitted supplies and productive capacity of aluminum ingot" sufficient to render it then capable of selling to the plaintiff 400,000 pounds a month and that it had entered into no binding commitments which could in the future reduce such available and uncommitted supplies and productive capacity and that it was its intention to make available and to sell to the plaintiff the number of pounds specified for a period of five years, related to the defendant's present intention. A person's intent, his state of mind, it has long been recognized, is capable of ascertainment and a statement of present intention is deemed a statement of a material existing fact, sufficient to support a fraud action.... [T]he allegations in the complaint describe a case where a defendant has fraudulently and positively as with personal knowledge stated that something was to be done when he knew all the time it was not to be done and that his representations were false. It is not a case of prophecy and prediction of something which it is merely hoped or expected will occur in the future, but a specific affirmation of an arrangement under which something is to occur, when the party making the affirmation knows perfectly well that no such thing is to occur. Such statements and representations when false are actionable. (Citations omitted.)

11.2 Misrepresentation (Negligent Misrepresentation)

A. Elements

Defendant:

1. makes materially false statement
2. not intending to deceive
3. without reasonable grounds to believe the statement is true.

Plaintiff:

4. justifiably relies on the statements
5. to his or her detriment.

B. Sample Case

An auditor may be held liable for negligent misrepresentations in an audit report to those persons who act in reliance upon those misrepresentations in a transaction which the auditor intended to influence, in accordance with the rule of section 552 of the Restatement Second of Torts according to the court in *Bily v. Arthur Young & Co.*, 3 Cal.4th 370, 407–9, 834 P. 2d 745, 11 Cal. Rptr.2d 51 (1992). The court begins by distinguishing between the torts of negligence and negligent misrepresentation:

> One difficulty in considering the problem before us is that neither the courts (ourselves included), the commentators, nor the authors of the Restatement Second of Torts have made clear or careful distinctions between the tort of negligence and the separate tort of negligent misrepresentation. The distinction is important not only because of the different statutory bases of the two torts, but also because it has practical implications for the trial of cases in complex areas such as the one before us.
>
> Negligent misrepresentation is a separate and distinct tort, a species of the tort of deceit. "Where the defendant makes false statements, honestly believing that they are true, but without reasonable ground for such belief, he may be liable for negligent misrepresentation, a form of deceit." (5 Witkin, Summary of Cal. Law (9th ed. 1988) Torts, § 720 at p. 819; see also § 1572, subd. 2 ["[t]he positive assertion, in a manner not warranted by the information of the person making it, of that which is not true, though he believes it to be true"]; § 1710, subd. 2 ["[t]he assertion, as a fact, of that which is not true, by one who has no reasonable ground for believing it to be true"].)

Under certain circumstances, expressions of professional opinion are treated as representations of fact. When a statement, although in the form of an opinion, is "not a casual expression of belief" but "a deliberate affirmation of the matters stated," it may be regarded as a positive assertion of fact. (*Gagne v. Bertran* (1954) 43 Cal.2d 481, 489 [275 P.2d 15].) Moreover, when a party possesses or holds itself out as possessing superior knowledge or special information or expertise regarding the subject matter and a plaintiff is so situated that it may reasonably rely on such supposed knowledge, information, or expertise, the defendant's representation may be treated as one of material fact. (Summary of Cal. Law, supra, Torts, §680 at pp. 781–782; BAJI No. 12.32.) There is no dispute that Arthur Young's statements in audit opinions fall within these principles.

But the person or "class of persons entitled to rely upon the representations is restricted to those to whom or for whom the misrepresentations were made. Even though the defendant should have anticipated that the misinformation might reach others, he is not liable to them."

Of the approaches we have reviewed, Restatement Second of Torts section 552, subdivision (b) is most consistent with the elements and policy foundations of the tort of negligent misrepresentation. The rule expressed there attempts to define a narrow and circumscribed class of persons to whom or for whom representations are made. In this way, it recognizes commercial realities by avoiding both unlimited and uncertain liability for economic losses in cases of professional mistake and exoneration of the auditor in situations where it clearly intended to undertake the responsibility of influencing particular business transactions involving third persons. The Restatement rule thus appears to be a sensible and moderate approach to the potential consequences of imposing unlimited negligence liability which we have identified.

We recognize the rule expressed in the Restatement Second of Torts has been criticized in some quarters as vague and potentially arbitrary....

We respectfully disagree. In seeking to identify a specific class of persons and a transaction that the supplier of information "intends the information to influence," the authors of the Restatement Second of Torts have applied basic factors of tort liability recognized in this state and elsewhere. By confining what might otherwise be unlimited liability to those persons whom the engagement is designed to benefit, the Restatement rule requires that the supplier of information receive notice of potential third party claims, thereby allowing it to ascertain the potential scope of its liability and make rational decisions regarding the undertaking. The receipt of such notice justifies imposition of auditor liability for conduct that is merely negligent. (Citations omitted.)

12. Malicious Prosecution/Abuse of Process

These torts occur when a tortfeasor misuses a legal proceeding against another to achieve an unlawful objective. Even a threat of a legal proceeding may be considered abuse of process. The most important aspect of this tort is the misuse of a legal proceeding to gain an indirect benefit to which they are not entitled.

A. Elements

1. Misuse of a legal proceeding, or threat of such misuse
2. to achieve unlawful objectives
3. resulting
4. in injury to another person.

B. Sample Case

Abuse of process was examined by the Court in *Ayles ex rel. Allen v. Allen*, 907 So. 2d 300, 303 (Miss. 2005). This was an action against an attorney and his client for abuse of process and invasion of privacy in relation to a custody battle between the parties and the use of the subpoena *duces tecum* process. Plaintiff asserted that defendant's attorney committed the tort of abuse of process by intentionally subverting the subpoena process to obtain privileged school records of a minor, specifically by failing to give notice to plaintiff's attorney prior to serving the subpoena. The court had to determine whether plaintiff had shown that a genuine issue of material fact existed as to the attorney's liability for the torts of abuse of process and/or invasion of privacy. It concluded she had not:

> This Court has defined abuse of process as follows:
> The action of abuse of process consists in the misuse or misapplication of a legal process to accomplish some purpose not warranted or commanded by the writ. It is the malicious perversion of a regularly issued civil or criminal process, for a purpose and to obtain

a result not lawfully warranted or properly attainable thereby, and for which perversion an action will lie to recover the pecuniary loss sustained.

Thus, the three elements of abuse of process are: (1) the party made an illegal use of a legal process, (2) the party had an ulterior motive, and (3) damage resulted from the perverted use of process. This Court has stated that the crucial element of this tort is the intent to abuse the privileges of the legal system.

To overcome summary judgment, Ayles must show the existence of each element of abuse of process. This she has failed to do.

The first element of the tort of abuse of process is illegal use of a legal process. Attempting to show that Graves illegally used the subpoena process, Ayles alleges various violations of the Mississippi Rules of Civil Procedure. Thus, it is not so much the "legal process" (subpoena) that Ayles complains of, as the procedure employed to serve it.

… [W]hether Graves's notice constituted "immediate" service under Rule 45 does not determine whether the subpoena process was illegally used, which is what the law requires to satisfy the elements of abuse of process. Rule 45 in its current form allows a party to obtain records prior to any actual notice to the other parties. Since Graves gained no advantage by waiting until Monday to mail the notice, his decision to mail the notice on Monday rather than Friday cannot serve as the basis for a claim of abuse of process…. to overcome the judgment entered in favor of Coleman and Graves, Ayles is required to show the existence of each element of the tort of abuse of process. Because Ayles has failed to show the existence of the first element of the tort, we need not address the remaining elements of the tort, and Ayles's claim regarding abuse of process must fail. (Citations omitted.)

Doctrines and Rules

1. Transferred Intent Doctrine

Under this rule of a person intends to hit one person but hits another, the intent is transferred to the third person, i.e., the law treats the incident as one in which the tortfeasor intended to hit the person actually hit. As the Sample Case indicates the principle applies even when the tortfeasor did not intend to hit any specific person. The doctrine also applies to the tort of assault, but generally will not apply to torts such as intentional infliction of emotional distress.

A. Elements

Defendant:

1. Engages in conduct that would constitute the tort against one person
2. resulting in injury to another person.

B. Sample Case

In an action for battery brought by a minor to recover for injuries he suffered and by his mother, the named plaintiff, to recover for expenses incurred, the complaint alleged that while the minor plaintiff was playing in the backyard of a home at which he was visiting, the defendant threw a rock, stone or other missile into the yard and struck the minor plaintiff in the eye and "[a]s a result of said battery by the defendant, the minor plaintiff suffered severe, painful and permanent injuries." The court in *Alteiri v. Colasso*, 168 Conn. 329, 333–4 (1975) was required to determine whether a jury upon finding that the defendant threw the stone with the intent to scare someone other than the one who was struck by the stone can legally and logically return a verdict for the plaintiffs for a wilful battery. It found that the jury could:

> In *Rogers v. Doody*, 119 Conn. 532, 534, 178 A. 51, in discussing the distinction between reckless disregard and wilfulness the court stated that a "wilful and malicious injury is one inflicted intentionally without just cause or excuse. It does not necessarily involve the ill will or malevolence shown in express malice. Nor is it sufficient to constitute such an injury that the act resulting in the injury was intentional in the sense that it was the voluntary action of the person involved. Not only the action producing the injury but the resulting injury must be intentional." The defendant claims, in reliance upon this principle, that as there was no intention either to injure the minor plaintiff or to put him in apprehension of bodily harm there could be no recovery for a wilful battery. The intention of the defendant was not only to throw the stone — the act resulting in the injury was intentional — but his intention was also to cause a resulting injury, that is, an apprehension of bodily harm. If the stone had struck the one whom the defendant had intended to frighten, the defendant would have been liable for a battery. The statement in Rogers that the "resulting injury must be intentional" would be satisfied as the injury intended was the ap-

prehension of bodily harm and the resulting bodily harm was the direct and natural consequence of the intended act. Restatement (Second), 1 Torts §13;[3]

It is not essential that the precise injury which was done be the one intended. 1 Cooley, Torts (4th Ed.). §98. An act designed to cause bodily injury to a particular person is actionable as a battery not only by the person intended by the actor to be injured but also by another who is in fact so injured.[4] Restatement (Second), 1 Torts §13 ... This principle of "transferred intent" applies as well to the action of assault. And where one intends merely an assault, if bodily injury results to one other than the person whom the actor intended to put in apprehension of bodily harm, it is battery actionable by the injured person. Restatement (Second), 1 Torts §16;[5]. (Citations omitted.)

2. Actual Malice Rule

This Rule requires that a plaintiff alleging defamation show actual malice if the plaintiff is a public official or a public figure. There are no elements as such, although court decisions for individual jurisdictions should be consulted to determine the criteria for classifying a plaintiff as a public official or figure.

Sample Case

In *WFAA-TV, Inc. v. McLemore*, 978 SW 2d 568, 571–3 (Tex, 1998) the court had to determine whether the plaintiff was a public figure for purposes of applying the actual malice rule:

Public officials and public figures must establish a higher degree of fault. They must prove that the defendant published a defamatory falsehood with actual malice, that is, with "knowledge that it was false or with reckless disregard of whether it was false or not." New York Times, 376 U.S. at 279–80, 84 S.Ct. 710 (defining the actual malice standard and applying it to public officials); see also Curtis Pub. Co. v. Butts, 388 U.S. 130, 87 S.Ct. 1975, 18 L.Ed.2d 1094 (1967) (applying the New York Times actual malice standard to public figures).

Because a defamation plaintiff's status dictates the degree of fault he or she must prove to render the defendant liable, the principal issue in this case is whether McLemore is a public figure. The question of public-figure status is one of constitutional law for courts to decide. See Rosenblatt v. Baer, 383 U.S. 75, 88, 86 S.Ct. 669, 15 L.Ed.2d 597 (1966) ... Public figures fall into two categories: (1) all-purpose, or general-purpose, public figures, and (2) limited-purpose public figures. General-purpose public figures are those individuals who have achieved such pervasive fame or notoriety that they become public figures for all purposes and in all contexts. Limited-purpose public figures, on the other hand, are only public figures for a limited range of issues surrounding a particular public controversy.

To determine whether an individual is a limited-purpose public figure, the Fifth Circuit has adopted a three-part test:

(1) the controversy at issue must be public both in the sense that people are discussing it and people other than the immediate participants in the controversy are likely to feel the impact of its resolution;

(2) the plaintiff must have more than a trivial or tangential role in the controversy; and

(3) the alleged defamation must be germane to the plaintiff's participation in the controversy.

Although the *Trotter/Waldbaum* test does not distinguish between plaintiffs who have voluntarily injected themselves into a controversy and those who are involuntarily drawn into a controversy, some courts have held that plaintiffs who are drawn into a controversy cannot be categorized as limited-purpose public figures.[1] Because, as we explain below, McLemore clearly voluntarily injected himself into the controversy at issue, we need not decide in this case whether "voluntariness" is a requirement under the limited-purpose public-figure test we apply. Nevertheless, the *Trotter/Waldbaum* elements provide a "generally accepted test" to determine limited-purpose public-figure status.

Applying the *Trotter/Waldbaum* limited-purpose public-figure elements to this case, we must first determine the controversy at issue. In *Waldbaum*, the D.C. Circuit elaborated on how to determine the existence and scope of a public controversy:

To determine whether a controversy indeed existed and, if so, to define its contours, the judge must examine whether persons actually were discussing some specific question. A general concern or interest will not suffice. The court can see if the press was covering the debate, reporting what people were saying and uncovering facts and theories to help the public formulate some judgment.

In this case, numerous commentators, analysts, journalists, and public officials were discussing the raid and the reasons why the ATF raid failed. As evidenced by Fair's comments during the Nightline broadcast, as well as reports by The Dallas Morning News and the

Fort Worth Star Telegram, the press was actively covering the debate over why the ATF raid failed. Many such discussions focused on the role of the local media in the ATF's failure to capture the Davidian compound. The controversy surrounding the Branch Davidian raid was public, both in the sense that people were discussing it and people other than the immediate participants in the controversy were likely to feel the impact of its resolution. While the court of appeals defined the controversy as limited to "McLemore's personal ethical standards as a journalist," we do not view it so narrowly. Based on the facts outlined above, we conclude that the public controversy at issue is the broader question of why the ATF agents failed to accomplish their mission.

To determine that an individual is a public figure for purposes of the public controversy at issue, the second *Trotter/Waldbaum* element requires the plaintiff to have had more than a trivial or tangential role in the controversy. In considering a libel plaintiff's role in a public controversy, several inquiries are relevant and instructive: (1) whether the plaintiff actually sought publicity surrounding the controversy; (2) whether the plaintiff had access to the media; and (3) whether the plaintiff "voluntarily engag[ed] in activities that necessarily involve[d] the risk of increased exposure and injury to reputation." "By publishing your views you invite public criticism and rebuttal; you enter voluntarily into one of the submarkets of ideas and opinions and consent therefore to the rough competition in the marketplace."

The record reflects that McLemore acted voluntarily to invite public attention and scrutiny on several occasions and in several different ways during the course of the public debate on the failed ATF raid. For example, McLemore was the only journalist to go onto the grounds of the compound, while other reporters assigned to cover the raid did not. By reporting live from the heart of the controversial raid, McLemore assumed a risk that his involvement in the event would be subject to public debate.... Thus, by choosing to engage in activities that necessarily involved increased public exposure and media scrutiny, McLemore played more than a trivial or tangential role in the controversy and, therefore, bore the risk of injury to his reputation.

The third and final element we consider—that the alleged defamation is germane to the plaintiff's participation in the controversy—is also satisfied in this case. See McLemore alleges that WFAA defamed him by displaying footage of his coverage from the scene of the compound during the raid, while reporting that federal officials believed a member of the local media informed the Branch Davidians about the ATF raid. Therefore, the alleged defamation directly relates to McLemore's participation in the controversy. He was on the scene in his role as a journalist, as conveyed by the footage WFAA broadcast, and WFAA's alleged defamatory comments are indeed germane to McLemore's participation in the controversy over the media's role in the failed attack. See Waldbaum, 627 F.2d at 1298–1300 (explaining that a public figure's talents, education, experience, and motives were relevant to the public's decision to listen to him). Accordingly, McLemore reached limited-purpose public-figure status through his employment-related activities when he voluntarily injected himself into the Branch Davidian raid. (Some citations omitted.)

3. Defamation *per se*

At common law, four categories of statements are generally considered actionable *per se* and give rise to a cause of action for defamation without a showing of special damages. They are: (1) words that impute the commission of a criminal offense; (2) words that impute infection with a loathsome communicable disease; (3) words that impute an inability to perform or want of integrity in the discharge of duties of office or employment; or (4) words that prejudice a party, or impute lack of ability, in his or her trade, profession or business. Additions to these categories may be made by statutes.

A. Elements

Statements that are:

1. words that impute the commission of a criminal offense;
2. words that impute infection with a loathsome communicable disease;
3. words that impute an inability to perform or want of integrity in the discharge of duties of office or employment; or
4. words that prejudice a party, or impute lack of ability, in his or her trade, profession or business,

constitute defamation *per se*.

B. Sample Case

The plaintiff alleged that an article is actionable *per se* because it referred to her as a "slut" and implied that she was an "unchaste" individual. The court noted the four common law categories but went on to apply a statute:

These common law categories continue to exist except where changed by statute. The Slander and Libel Act (740 ILCS 145/1 et seq. (West 1992)) has enlarged the classifications enumerated above by providing that false accusations of fornication and adultery are actionable as a matter of law. Specifically, section 1 of that statute provides:

"If any person shall falsely use, utter or publish words, which in their common acceptance, shall amount to charge any person with having been guilty of fornication or adultery, such words so spoken shall be deemed actionable, and he shall be deemed guilty of slander." 740 ILCS 145/1 (West 1992).

The defendants initially claim that this statute has no application here because it applies only to words that are spoken and not in circumstances, such as those here, where the words are written. We reject the defendants' attempt to so limit the statute. We note initially that the defendants' argument relies upon a distinction between spoken and written defamation (slander and libel) that existed at common law, but was abandoned long ago by our courts. At common law, libel and slander were analyzed under different sets of standards, with libel recognized as the more serious wrong. Illinois law evolved, however, and rejected this bifurcated approach in favor of a single set of rules for slander and libel. Libel and slander are now treated alike and the same rules apply to a defamatory statement regardless of whether the statement is written or oral. Given the merger of libel and slander, we reject the defendants' claim that the statute providing for an action where false accusations of fornication are made is not applicable here simply because the alleged defamation was in writing.

Further, after considering the plaintiff's allegations, as stated in the complaint, we find that they fall within this statute's category of statements that are actionable per se. As previously stated, the statute applies when persons use, utter or publish words which amount to a charge of fornication or adultery. Here, the plaintiff's complaint alleges that the defendants, by using the word "slut," implied that she was "unchaste." The complaint thus alleged, in effect, that the defendants published words that falsely accused the plaintiff of fornication. The defendants' statements fall within this statutorily created category of statements that are considered actionable per se. (Citations omitted.)

4. "Coming to Nuisance" Doctrine

The "Coming to Nuisance" Doctrine states the proposition that if people move to an area they know is not suited for their intended use they cannot argue the existing uses are nuisances. The court will hold the new use "came to" the nuisance and therefore is not protected. This doctrine may be asserted as a defense to a cause of action for private nuisance. As indicated by the Sample Case the exact terms and application of the doctrine are not as clear as the statement above might indicate.

A. Elements

1. Plaintiff moves to an area
2. where a previously existing use
3. meets the criteria for a private nuisance.

B. Sample Case

Mahlstadt v. City of Indianola, 100 NW 2d 189 (Iowa, 1959) involved a complaint against a city for operation of a city dump in a manner that most people would consider a nuisance. The city raised the "coming to nuisance" doctrine as a defense. The court noted that whether an activity was a nuisance was based to a large degree on the lawfulness and the reasonableness of using a particular property for a specific use. The doctrine was thus not an absolute defense, but a factor to be considered in determining whether or not the activity was a nuisance at all:

> We have hereinbefore held defendants were not estopped to show the operation of the dump at that place prior to plaintiff's activities there. Courts have frequently stated that the right of a person to pure air may be surrendered in part by his election to live in a location where the atmosphere is impregnated with smoke, soot and other impurities and that an operation which would be considered a nuisance in a residential locality might not be so considered when conducted in a proper place.
>
> The text in 66 C.J.S. Nuisances § 8e, p. 746, points to the very marked distinction in reason and equity between a long-established business, "which has become a nuisance from the growth of population and the erection of dwellings in proximity to it, and that of a new erection or business threatened in such vicinity; and it requires a much clearer case to justify a court of equity in interfering by injunction to compel a person to remove" such long-established business.

66 C.J.S. Nuisances § 8c, p. 744, states: "In general, a fair test as to whether a business lawful in itself, or a particular use of property, constitutes a nuisance is the reasonableness or unreasonableness of conducting the business or making the use of the property complained of in the particular locality and in the manner and under the circumstances of the case; * * *."

39 Am.Jur., Nuisances, section 197, states, the weight of authority holds that one's coming to a nuisance does not prevent his maintaining action thereon. "But while 195*195 priority of occupation is not conclusive as to the existence of a nuisance, it is to be considered with all the evidence, and the inferences drawn from all the facts proved, in determining whether the use of the property is unreasonable."

The operation of a city dump is a public service essential to the health and general welfare of the community, and its location should be reasonably convenient for public use. Moreover, where, as here, its location has been apart from residential, business and industrial districts, its prior operation at that place should be given substantial weight in determining the character of the locality, and the reasonableness or unreasonableness of operating it there, in the manner and under the circumstances shown.

Defenses

Whether and how a particular defense can be raised in response to individual intentional tort causes of action discussed above varies with the cause of action and the jurisdiction. Depending on the tort, the defenses raised to the standard negligence cause of action, i.e., comparative negligence, contributory negligence, assumption of risk, waiver (written assumption of risk), and sovereign immunity may be raised. For discussion of these defenses see "Defenses" in the "Negligence" section. In additional the following defenses may be applicable.

1. Consent

Consent is a potential defense to every intentional tort. It is similar to assumption of risk in the negligence context, but the two are not the same. A hockey player consents to the contact of checking allowed by the rules and assumes the risk that another player will break the rules and engage in extra-rule contact. The consent must be voluntary and "informed."

While often referred to as a defense in the "affirmative defense" sense, i.e., one admits that the tort occurred but asserts there is no liability anyway, non-consent is often considered to be one of the elements of the actual tort.

A. Elements

1. Voluntary acceptance of an intentionally tortious act
2. with full knowledge or understanding of the consequences.

B. Sample Case

In *Lacey v. Laird*, 166 Ohio St. 12 (Ohio, 1956) the court approved jury instructions stating that absent an emergency a minor could not consent to an operation and described the type of information necessary for informed consent:

> The term, "consent," as used herein carries with it the assumption that previous full disclosure of the implications and probable consequences of the proposed conduct to which such consent applies has been given in such terms as may be fully comprehended by the person giving the consent. It necessarily follows that consent requires a reasonable degree of maturity of mind depending upon the intricacies of the subject matter to which the consent is applicable ...
>
> The general rule seems to be that, unless there exists an emergency, which prevents any delay, or other exceptional circumstances, a surgeon who performs an operation upon a minor without the consent of his parents or guardian is guilty of a trespass and battery. This rule is not based upon the capacity of a minor to consent, so far as he is personally concerned, within the field of the law of torts or law of crimes, but is based upon the right of parents whose liability for support and maintenance of their child may be greatly increased by an unfavorable result from the operational procedures upon the part of a surgeon.
>
> In view of the holdings of the courts generally, as exhibited by the foregoing leading cases, the trial court in the instant case did not err in its charge to the jury on the subject of consent. In this respect, the law is consistent in that parental interest in and responsibility for a minor child are subject to corresponding supervision and control. And, since the parents of such a child are responsible for his nurture and training and are liable for his maintenance and support, others will not be permitted to interfere with such relationship or with matters touching the child's personal welfare.

2. Self-Defense

Self-defense is primarily raised as a defense to the torts of assault and battery. The instinct to defend oneself against harm is a natural one recognized by the law provided the elements of the defense are met.

A. Elements

1. Defendant reasonably believed
2. he was in imminent danger of harmful or offensive contact and
3. he used only those means of self-defense necessary to prevent or defend against the harm.

B. Sample Case

In Louisiana the defense of self-defense could begin with the idea that the plaintiff, as aggressor, provoked the circumstances leading to his injuries until *Landry v. Bellanger*, 851 So. 2d 943, 949–51 (La, 2003) when the court concluded that the aggressor doctrine was not compatible with developments in the state's statutory and common law. The court went on to explain the relationship between provocation in determining the fault underlying whether a tort occurred and self-defense as a justification or excuse for committing the tort:

> A battery is "[a] harmful or offensive contact with a person, resulting from an act intended to cause the plaintiff to suffer such a contact ..." Caudle v. Betts, 512 So.2d 389, 391 (La.1987). The defendant's intention need not be malicious nor need it be an intention to inflict actual damage. Id. It is sufficient if the defendant intends to inflict either a harmful or offensive contact without the other's consent. Id.
>
> Under long-standing Louisiana jurisprudence, a plaintiff's recovery for damages resulting from an assault or battery would be precluded if the plaintiff's own actions were sufficient to provoke the physical retaliation. According to this "aggressor doctrine," plaintiff's recovery is precluded if the evidence establishes "he was at fault in provoking the difficulty [sic] in which he was injured, unless the person retaliating has used excessive force to repel the aggression." ... The aggressor doctrine is unique to Louisiana, having evolved through decades of jurisprudence, but lacking any statutory or common law basis....
>
> In a suit for damages resulting from an intentional tort, the claimant must carry the burden of proving all prima facie elements of the tort, including lack of consent to the invasive conduct. In turn, the defen-

dant may seek to prove that he is without fault because his actions were privileged or justified, such as self-defense. Self-defense, unlike the aggressor doctrine, is a true defense in that it operates as a privilege to committing the intentional tort. In such a case, a plaintiff's conduct must have gone beyond mere provocation under the aggressor doctrine. Under Louisiana jurisprudence, in order to succeed on a claim of self-defense (not involving deadly force), there must be an actual or reasonably apparent threat to the claimant's safety and the force employed cannot be excessive in degree or kind. The privilege of self-defense is based on the prevention of harm to the actor, not on the desire for retaliation or revenge, no matter how understandable that desire. Furthermore, the prevailing view in almost every one of our sister states is:

> Threats and insults may give color to an act of aggression, but in themselves, they do not ordinarily justify an apprehension of immediate harm, and the defendant is not privileged to vindicate his outraged personal feelings at the expense of the physical safety of another. Such provocation is considered only in mitigation of the damages. Prosser and Keeton on The Law of Torts, § 19, at 126.

Absent a qualifying privilege, any provocative or aggressive conduct on the part of the plaintiff should be incorporated into the allocation of fault by the trier of fact. However, simply because the trier of fact must consider the fault of both plaintiff and defendant, does not mean that an aggressive plaintiff can avoid responsibility for his conduct. In fact, nothing prevents a trier of fact from determining that the plaintiff's conduct was of such a provocative nature as to render it the sole cause of his injury. (Some citations omitted.)

3. Defense of Others

The defense of others defense extends the self-defense doctrine discussed above to the defense of a third party. In essence the elements and the concept are the same as self-defense except the defendant is placed "in the shoes" of the third-party and uses only that force that the third-party would be justified in using and only under the circumstances that the third-party could use it.

4. Defense of Property

The defense of property defense is similar to the self-defense and defense of others defenses discussed in (2) and (3) above. However, the defense does not allow the use of force that would cause death or serious bodily injury.

A. Elements

1. Plaintiff's
   a. intrusion on defendant's real property or
   b. unauthorized use or taking of defendant's personal property;
2. Defendant's reasonable belief that force is needed to prevent the plaintiff's wrongful acts;
3. Defendant's request to plaintiff to cease the wrongful acts prior to using force; and
4. Defendant's use of only that force necessary to prevent the continuation of the wrongful act, in no case force likely to cause death or serious bodily injury.

B. Sample Case

The issue in *Katko v. Briney*, 183 N.W.2d 657 (Iowa 1971), was whether an owner may protect personal property in an unoccupied boarded-up farm house against trespassers and thieves by a spring gun capable of inflicting death or serious injury. It was purely an issue of defending only property as the defendant's home and family were several miles away. The court ruled that the owner had gone too far:

> Plaintiff's action is for damages resulting from serious injury caused by a shot from a 20-gauge spring shotgun set by defendants in a bedroom of an old farm house which had been uninhabited for several years. Plaintiff and his companion, Marvin McDonough, had broken and entered the house to find and steal old bottles and dated fruit jars which they considered antiques.... The overwhelming weight of authority, both textbook and case law, supports the trial court's statement of the applicable principles of law.

The court reviewed opinions from courts in several jurisdictions, including the U.S. Supreme Court all of which confirm the view stated by Prosser on Torts, Third Edition, pages 116–118:

> "* * * the law has always placed a higher value upon human safety than upon mere rights in property, it is the accepted rule that there is

no privilege to use any force calculated to cause death or serious bodily injury to repel the threat to land or chattels, unless there is also such a threat to the defendant's personal safety as to justify a self-defense. * * * spring guns and other mankilling devices are not justifiable against a mere trespasser, or even a petty thief. They are privileged only against those upon whom the landowner, if he were present in person would be free to inflict injury of the same kind."

5. Privilege

The defense of privilege is a grant of the right to engage in an intentional tort to particular classes individuals for particular purposes, usually to advance some social purpose. For example, there are several types of privilege with regard to defamation including a legislative privilege that bars an action for any statement made by legislatures on the floor of the legislative body and a conditional privilege that would prevent recovery for false statements made in good faith by an individual to warn the public of a perceived danger. Some privileges are quite simple. For example, we each have the privilege to use force to eject a trespasser from our land, but cannot use the same force to eject a trespasser from someone else's land. One of the most commonly used privileges is the shopkeepers' privilege of detaining persons suspected of shoplifting, a privilege often granted by statute and thus dependent on the language of the statute for its elements. Because the elements are so varied depending on the tort, the privilege, and the source of the privilege (common law or statute), no elements are listed here. A sample shopkeepers' privilege case is included.

Sample Case

The issue of the shopkeeper's privilege is discussed in *Wal-Mart v. Resendez*, 962 SW 2d 539, 540–1 (Tex. 1998). In this case, a customer was seen consuming a product and then leaving the store without paying for said product. The court discussed the three types of reasonableness required by the privilege:

> In a false imprisonment case, if the alleged detention was performed with the authority of law, then no false imprisonment occurred. See Sears, Roebuck & Co. v. Castillo, 693 S.W.2d 374, 375 (Tex.1985) (listing the elements of false imprisonment as a willful detention performed without consent and without the authority of law). The "shopkeeper's privilege" expressly grants an employee the authority of law to detain a customer to investigate the ownership of property in a rea-

sonable manner and for a reasonable period of time if the employee has a reasonable belief that the customer has stolen or is attempting to steal store merchandise. TEX. CIV. PRAC. & REM. CODE ANN. § 124.001.

There was no evidence to support the contention that the detention occurred for an unreasonable period of time. Without deciding the outer parameters of a permissible period of time under section 124.001, the ten to fifteen minute detention in this case was not unreasonable as a matter of law. See Dominguez v. Globe Discount City, Inc., 470 S.W.2d 919, 920 (Tex.Civ.App.—El Paso 1971, no writ) (finding a five to six minute detention reasonable even where the plaintiff was ultimately released by the security guard who detained her); Meadows v. F.W. Woolworth Co., 254 F.Supp. 907, 909 (N.D.Fla.1966) (finding a ten minute detention reasonable under a similar statute). Also, no evidence exists that the detention occurred in an unreasonable manner. The only question is whether it was reasonable for Salinas to believe that Resendez had stolen the peanuts. It was.

Once the facts are established, the existence of probable cause is a question of law for the court. Richey v. Brookshire Grocery Co., 952 S.W.2d 515, 518 (Tex.1997). Based upon the undisputed facts—Resendez looked for peanuts immediately upon entering the Wal-Mart store, she was later seen eating from a bag of peanuts marked with a Wal-Mart price sticker, and she did not pay for the peanuts on leaving the store—probable cause existed to believe that the peanuts were stolen property. In fact, in response to the question on Resendez's malicious prosecution claim, the jury found that Salinas had probable cause to commence criminal proceedings against Resendez. If Salinas had probable cause to initiate criminal proceedings, his belief that Resendez stole the peanuts was necessarily reasonable (finding that reasonable belief for an investigative detention is something less than that required to establish probable cause) ... As a matter of law, the undisputed facts of this case establish that Salinas had the authority of law to detain Resendez and therefore she was not falsely imprisoned. (Citations omitted.)

Index

A

abnormally dangerous activities, 170–1
abuse of process, 229–30
Actual Malice Rule, 232–5
Alternative dispute resolution, 48, 59
animal owner liability, 168, 169–70
   domestic, 169–70
   wild, 168
assault, 7, 190–92, 201, 231, 232, 240
assumption of risk, 53, 159–61, 170, 188, 238
attractive nuisance, 178–9

B

battery, 190, 191, 192–3, 231, 232, 239, 240

C

cause of action analysis, xiii, 15, 19, 32, 49, 52, 54, 59, 63, 64, 66, 67, 68, 94
civil proceeding, stages of, 12–13
Civil Rights Act of 1964, 223
client interview, 10, 12, 14, 19, 32, 34, 70, 94
Coming and Going Rule, 184–6

Coming to Nuisance Doctrine, 237–8
commercial disparagement, 215–7
comparative negligence, 156, 157, 158, 188, 205, 206, 238
compensatory damages, 114
consent (as a defense), 238–9
consequential damages, 116, 119, 140
contract elements, 97, 98–107
contract supplemental interview checklist, 23
contributory negligence, 156–8, 159, 160, 170, 188, 205, 238
conversion, 206, 207, 209–11

D

Damages, 114, 115, 116–8, 120–3, 140, 147, 195–6, 198, 213
   compensatory, 114, 115, 120, 195–6
   consequential, 116, 119, 140
   exemplary, 116
   liquidated, 120–3
   punitive, 116–8, 147, 198, 213
Dangerous Instrumentality Doctrine, 186–7
defamation, 203, 211–7, 232–5, 243
defamation per se, 235

defense of others, 241
defense of property, 242–3
depositions, 13, 56, 65, 73
discovery, xiii, 10, 12, 15, 31, 33, 48, 51, 54–8, 59, 63, 64, 65, 67, 70, 75, 80, 82
discovery plan, 10, 33, 54–6, 67, 70, 75, 80, 82
duress, 53, 62, 136–7

E

Emergency Rule, 153
emotional distress 119, 148, 194–6, 200, 231
   intentional infliction of, 194–6, 231
   negligent infliction of, 148
equitable estoppel, 22, 97, 130–32, 135
estoppel, 34, 53, 54, 143, 204
   equitable, 22, 97, 130–32, 135
   promissory, 22, 97, 128–30, 135
evidence, relation to facts and proof, 7–11
evidence tree, 9, 42, 58, 66, 80
exemplary damages, 116
exhibit list, 82, 86, 87, 88, 91
exhibit page, 79, 86–9, 91

F

facts, relation to evidence and proof, 7–11
fact pleading, 49
false imprisonment, 221–3, 243
fitness for particular use, implied warranty of, 22, 27, 28, 29, 30, 35, 66, 75, 80–6, 97, 110–16
foreseeability test, 155
fraud, 38, 106, 116, 125, 126, 129, 137, 198, 216, 217, 223, 224–6

Frolic and Detour Rule, 183–4

G

Good Samaritan immunity, 162–3
Good Samaritan Doctrine, 160–1
Gregory, David D., v
gross negligence, 147, 162, 163

H

holographic will, 37–9
hypothetical, 16, 18, 20, 22, 27, 49

I

implied warranty
   of fitness for particular use, 22, 27, 28, 29, 30, 35, 66, 75, 80–6, 97, 110–16
   of merchantability, 22, 27, 97, 110–12, 114–16, 174
intentional infliction of emotional distress, 194–6, 231
interrogatories, 12, 15, 56, 57, 65
interview checklist, 22, 23, 54
invasion of privacy, 196–8, 198–200, 200–2, 203–4, 221
   appropriation, 198–200
   false light in the public eye, 203–4
   public disclosure of private facts, 200–2
   unreasonable intrusion, 196–8
investigation plan, 10, 33, 34, 39–45, 57

J

jury instructions, 27, 30, 35, 36, 69, 72, 79, 214, 239

L

laches, 53, 124
legal reasoning, 11, 20, 22, 26, 27